# Authentic Achievement

# Authentic Achievement

## Restructuring Schools for Intellectual Quality

Fred M. Newmann and Associates

Jossey-Bass Publishers • San Francisco

Substantial discounts on bulk quantities of Jossey-Bass books are available to corporations, professional associations, and other organizations. For details and discount information, contact the special sales department at Jossey-Bass Inc., Publishers (415) 433–1740; Fax (800) 605–2665.

For sales outside the United States, please contact your local Simon & Schuster International Office.

 Manufactured in the United States of America on Lyons Falls Pathfinder Tradebook. This paper is acid-free and 100 percent totally chlorine-free.

Epigraph to the Introduction is quoted from David T. Kearns and Dennis P. Doyle, *Winning the Brain Race: A Bold Plan to Make Our Schools Competitive.* San Francisco: Institute for Contemporary Studies Press, 1988.

**Library of Congress Cataloging-in-Publication Data**

Authentic achievement: restructuring schools for intellectual quality
 /Fred M. Newmann . . . [et al.].—1st ed.
    p. cm.—(The Jossey-Bass education series)
   Includes bibliographical references and index.
   ISBN 0-7879-0320-5 (cloth: acid-free paper)
   1. School improvement programs—United States. 2. Academic
achievement—United States. 3. School supervision—United States.
I. Newmann, Fred M.  II. Series
LB2822.82.A88   1996
371.2'00973—dc20

96-25324
CIP

FIRST EDITION
*HB Printing*   10 9 8 7 6 5 4 3 2 1

The Jossey-Bass Education Series

# Contents

# List of Tables, Figures, and Exhibits

## Tables

## Figures

## Exhibits

# Preface

As bleak research findings in the early 1980s exposed poor student performance and tragic school failures, especially in big cities, political and corporate leaders, cheered on by the media, began to cast a piercing spotlight on schools in the United States. As its beam swept across the landscape in search of more promising possibilities, it illuminated contrasts between public and private schools and turned a flattering light on other organizations, especially businesses, that seemed to spur high performance. Since prior attempts at school reform seemed to have produced only middling results at best, a new conventional wisdom arose, calling for top-to-bottom restructuring of the whole educational system. This would entail changes in the authority and governance of education agencies, in the organization of students' and teachers' work, and in standards and incentives for student and school performance. In response, states, districts, the federal government, foundations, universities, professional organizations, independent reform groups, parents, and schools began a variety of restructuring initiatives.

In 1990 the Center on Organization and Restructuring of Schools, sponsored by the U.S. Department of Education, began a five-year program of research that conducted eighteen studies and produced dozens of reports on the process and effects of school restructuring, summarized by Newmann and Wehlage (1995). This book reports on the Center's main study, the School Restructuring Study. We searched nationwide for public schools—elementary, middle, and high—that had adopted unconventional organizational features proposed by advocates of restructuring—for example, site-based management, shared decision making, teacher teaming, sustained student advisory groups, coordination of social services, and school choice. Twenty-four schools in sixteen states participated in the study.

Our central task was not simply to determine whether restructuring works but under what conditions school restructuring promotes high-quality student achievement. To construct an answer, we visited each school in the study twice during a school year for a week at a time observing classes and interviewing school staff, parents, and district administrators. Following the visits, we examined student work in detail and analyzed the results of surveys of teachers and students.

We discovered good news, bad news, and complex news. The good news is that school restructuring can elevate the quality of teaching and student achievement, and in ways that benefit all students, regardless of socioeconomic status, gender, race, or ethnicity. The bad news is that high-quality teaching and student achievement are still relatively rare, even in schools that have accomplished substantial restructuring. The complex news is that to make restructuring work for students, schools and the external agencies that influence them (districts, states, and reform organizations) must learn how to use structural innovation to develop certain cultural qualities. We found that a sustained, schoolwide concentration on the intellectual quality of student learning and a schoolwide professional community among the staff were the keys to successful restructuring.

The School Restructuring Study began as an exploratory venture to see where school restructuring occurred, what it looked like, whether it seemed to have any potential for improving instruction, and whether interesting schools would be willing to participate in the research. Over the ensuing six years, sixty-two staff members (listed in Appendix C) worked on various phases of the study, thanks to the cooperation of students, teachers, and administrators in the schools, who shared with us their interesting and difficult work.

The book builds on collaboration among the research staff in all phases of the study: planning, instrument development, data collection, analysis, report writing, critical review of findings, and beginning in 1995, the conceptualization and writing of this book. The study benefited enormously from deliberations with Anthony Bryk (University of Chicago) and Valerie Lee (University of Michigan), the principal investigators of other studies in the Center; from a distinguished National Advisory Panel (listed in Appendix C) chaired by Richard Wallace Jr.; and from Ron Anson in the Office of Educational Research and Improvement at the U.S. Department of Education. Larry Cuban (Stanford University) and Robert McCarthy (Coalition of Essential Schools) provided helpful reviews of the manuscript, as did anonymous reviewers commissioned by Jossey-Bass.

Throughout the study Diane Randall treated us to her rare combination of exceptional administrative, technical, and human support. Norma Maynard, Jean Norman, and Mary Fish handled complex data collection arrangements with keen competence and good cheer. Thanks to friendly, efficient cooperation and technical assistance from Leslie Iura, Christie Hakim, Carolyn Uno, and Ingrid Owen at Jossey-Bass, and to Beverly Miller, the copyeditor, the book came into print.

If this book contains significant contributions to knowledge or educational practice, they are due to my colleagues' willingness to share their talents and time for the collective effort. From the fundamental issues of research priorities and analysis of findings to the details of questionnaire design, data collection, and scoring of student work, they spent countless hours in probing discussions, reviewing drafts, writing, and rewriting. I had the privilege to coordinate the project. I thank all my colleagues for their illuminating substantive contributions, their support in dealing with complex responsibilities, and the joy of participating in the most exciting professional culture I can imagine. I depended especially on Gary Wehlage, the Center's associate director. Gary's daily counsel on both the big picture and its challenging details fortified my understanding of education and deepened my appreciation for critical collaboration among good friends.

*Madison, Wisconsin*                                        Fred M. Newmann
*August 1996*

# Authentic Achievement

# Introduction: The School Restructuring Study

*Fred M. Newmann*

> *Public education in this country is in crisis. America's public schools graduate 700,000 functionally illiterate students every year, and 700,000 more drop out. Four out of five young adults in a recent survey couldn't summarize the main point of a newspaper article, or read a bus schedule, or figure their change from a restaurant bill.*
> DAVID T. KEARNS, CHAIRMAN AND CEO,
> XEROX CORPORATION[1]

## Origins of School Restructuring

The recent wave of school reform known as school restructuring began in the mid-1980s when a blizzard of reports claimed that large proportions of U.S. students and adults, especially those in minority and low-income groups, were unable to perform the cognitive tasks necessary for successful work, citizenship, and personal life. According to critics, a number of previous reforms had failed to educate most U.S. students to meet the complex demands of contemporary life. In an effort to turn this situation around, some reformers argued that alternative structural conditions—such as increased competition, local organizational control, clear standards, and incentives for success—drawn from business, other professions, and other nations held more promise for success than the familiar, persistent structures of school.

1

Since the early 1980s, reports from scholars, professional organizations, corporate and government leaders, and civic groups have pointed to a failure of U.S. schools based on a number of important indicators (Carnegie Task Force on Teaching as a Profession, 1986; Committee for Economic Development, 1985; National Center for Education Statistics, 1990; National Commission on Excellence, 1983; National Education Goals Panel, 1991; Shanker, 1990; Sizer, 1984).

*Illiteracy.* About 23 million adults, about 13 percent of all seventeen-year-olds, and up to 40 percent of minority youth at this age were considered functionally illiterate by simple tests of everyday reading, writing, and comprehension (National Commission on Excellence in Education, 1983).

*Low-level performance.* Among seventeen-year-olds who had stayed in school, nearly 40 percent could not draw inferences from written material, only 20 percent could write a minimally acceptable persuasive essay, and only one-third could solve a mathematics problem requiring several steps (National Commission on Excellence in Education, 1983). Among high school seniors, fewer than half showed the consistent grasp of fractions, decimals, and percentages expected of competent seventh graders (National Center for Education Statistics, 1990). Poor student performance led to an increase in remedial courses in mathematics, reading, and writing in colleges, and to reports from corporate leaders that too many students lacked the basic intellectual skills, attitudes, and behavior required for productive work (Committee for Economic Development, 1985).

*Test score decline.* Declines were reported in high school students' test scores in certain subjects on standardized tests, the Scholastic Aptitude Test (SAT), and the National Assessment of Educational Progress (NAEP) (National Commission on Excellence in Education, 1983).

*International comparisons.* Examinations given to high school students in other countries demanded more rigorous intellectual performance than U.S. examinations (American Federation of Teachers, 1994; Britton and Raizen, 1996). In math and science, U.S. students have consistently scored far below students in other countries (National Education Goals Panel, 1991).

*Equity.* African American and Hispanic students continued to show substantially less success than whites on test scores, high school graduation, and college completion (National Education Goals Panel, 1991). Students in poor communities were denied the most basic educational amenities (Kozol, 1991).

More recent research, however, has challenged this bleak portrait (Berliner and Biddle, 1995; Bracey, 1991, 1996; Grissmer, Kirby, Berends, and Williamson, 1994; Sandia National Laboratories, 1993; Tyack and Cuban, 1995). These newer analyses point out that the past thirty years have witnessed overall increases in the proportions of children attending and graduating from high school, taking advanced academic courses, and the SAT, and there has been a promising ratio of supply to demand of highly trained persons in science and engineering. Moreover, the gap between white students and students of color in high school graduation rates and on standardized tests has decreased, and test scores in certain subjects (for example, verbal-reading and mathematics) have remained stable or even improved over the past twenty years. Critics of the crisis perspective also contend that comparisons with other countries have been misleading. They argue that because the United States attempts to educate a broader spectrum of its youth than most other countries, teachers have to confront far more difficult educational challenges due to poverty, cultural diversity, the breakdown of neighborhood communities, and changes in family life.[2]

National discussion of the educational crisis was stimulated largely through *A Nation at Risk,* the 1983 report issued by the federally sponsored National Commission on Excellence in Education, which warned that a rising tide of mediocrity in the educational system threatened the nation's security. In 1989 a historic meeting of President Bush and state governors called for the establishment of national education goals to be achieved by the turn of the century, and in 1990 President Bush issued *America 2000,* a plan that set out the strategy for achieving them through a federal-state partnership led by the National Education Goals Panel. In 1994 the U.S. Congress, with vigorous support from President Clinton, enacted legislation, known as Goals 2000, to advance the national goals. But even prior to these later federal initiatives, state governments, foundations, professional organizations, and universities, recognizing the educational crisis, had been taking action. They promoted reforms such as new curriculum standards, new forms of assessment of learning, decentralization of school management, more equitable financing of public schools, and restructuring the familiar routines of schooling.

The many reports, new policies, and innovative activities established a climate for educational reform, and there is now wide agreement that schools should do a better job of helping all students to learn basic skills in reading, writing, arithmetic, speaking, listening, use of technology, and knowledge of subject matter necessary for schooling beyond high school (Johnson and Immerwahr, 1994). But focused consensus on the central educational goals for students (ends) and the kinds of changes in schooling required to achieve them (means) has eluded the nation's 16,000 school districts and 180,000 public schools. Some proposals that enjoy less than universal acceptance advocate far more ambitious intellectual goals. These insist that all students should also demonstrate rigorous, complex problem solving, in-depth understanding, and sophisticated communication skills (Resnick, 1987a; Sizer, 1984; Smith and O'Day, 1991).[3]

Disagreement also continues on the issue of the means or the scope of reform strategies. The less far-reaching strategies include such familiar practices as adding new required courses to the curriculum, producing more up-to-date and engaging curriculum materials, training teachers to use new materials and new teaching practices, and developing new programs for students with special needs. More radical strategies emphasize restructuring, that is, changing the basic organizational structures of schooling—for example, by replacing top-down bureaucratic school governance with school-based collaboration among teachers, administrators, and parents; replacing age-graded classes and curriculum tracking with heterogeneous grouping by age and ability; planning and teaching courses by teams of teachers rather than by individual teachers; or assigning students to schools based on choice of school mission and record of success instead of residential address.

This call for educational improvement during the past decade was often expressed as restructuring rather than as simply reform, and it carried an ambiguous message. Proponents were either unclear or disagreed on the extent to which restructuring referred to fundamental changes in educational goals or the means to those goals, or both. Ambiguity can be troubling, but also politically convenient. America's educational history is punctuated with vague slogans whose multiple meanings have mobilized the energy of diverse constituencies to support educational change, for better or worse.[4]

But why did restructuring seem so appealing? The word signaled an appropriate response to reports of widespread educational failure because it suggested that monumental changes were necessary; terms like *improvement, innovation,* or *reform* were not robust enough to describe the challenge. Moreover, the accumulating research showed that prior approaches to school reform had made at best only incremental improvements on a national scale. The research pointed to problems of bureaucracy, politics, culture, and persistent patterns in teaching that resisted numerous reform initiatives.[5]

Disillusionment with prior reform stimulated the search for radically different models of schooling. From the mid-1980s to the present, possible alternatives were proposed through analyses of factors critical to success in productive businesses, other professions, and education in other countries. The comparisons suggested a need to change structures that had been seen as natural features of the U.S. educational landscape (for example, school assignment based on student residence, student promotion based on "credit" instead of performance, and tenure and automatic salary increases for principals and teachers). These analyses pointed out, for example, that businesses, professions, and educational systems in other countries were often guided by consensus on clear standards for high performance in serving customers, clients, or students; they had access to useful information indicating the degree of success achieved; and the organizations were motivated by significant incentives to succeed and sanctions for failure, through either market or regulatory mechanisms. Furthermore, business firms successful in international competition had restructured to devolve decision-making authority on the details of production. They relied less on traditional hierarchical bureaucratic supervision and more on participatory management by teams of workers with collective responsibility and incentives for the quality of products and services they produced.[6] Although some observers cautioned against imitating models that could be inappropriate for U.S. schools, such analogues helped to stimulate consideration of new structures for schooling.[7]

## What Is School Restructuring?

There are no universally accepted criteria for determining what makes a restructured school (Conley, 1993; Elmore and Associates, 1990; Murphy, 1991). Recognizing the many facets of restructuring, the Center on Organization and Restructuring of Schools defined it as a continuum of departures from conventional practice, from a greater to a lesser extent, rather than as simply restructured or conventional. Restructuring can occur when schools make major changes from conventional practice, but new schools established to implement significant departures from familiar patterns can also be considered examples of school restructuring. We searched for schools with significant departures from conventional practice in four aspects of schooling: student experiences; professional life of teachers; leadership, management, and governance; and coordination of community resources.[8] The twenty-four schools in the study shared no single or common set of structural changes, but each had implemented a number of the following changes:

- Schools found ways to personalize their programs so that teachers and students developed strong and trusting relationships. Common vehicles for achieving this were students' staying with the same teacher for two or more years; student advisory groups that met frequently each week, with a teacher functioning as a counselor to a small group of students over several years; and students' studying several subjects at once with a team of teachers who shared responsibility for the academic success of all the students enrolled with the team.
- When schools organized teachers into interdisciplinary or grade-level teams, they frequently extended instructional periods to more than fifty minutes each as well. And to support collaborative work within the teams, many schools arranged for teams to meet during the school day.
- Most schools had nearly eliminated tracking, ability grouping, and general remedial classes. Some classes for special education, honors, or gifted and talented students remained, but the vast majority of students learned in heterogeneous classes.

- Several schools articulated common standards for student learning. Some schools were exploring new forms of assessment (for example, use of portfolios and performance exhibitions) to measure student progress.
- Almost all schools gained increased autonomy from their districts and states to exert more local control over curriculum, staffing, and budgeting. Rather than managing under bureaucratic directives, these schools set up mechanisms for shared decision making among staff, administrators, and occasionally parents.
- Several schools involved students in community-based learning, such as volunteer service, community surveys, and internships.

Chapters Three through Five describe how six of the twenty-four schools developed these kinds of innovations in diverse contexts.

Although restructuring is loosely defined, it implies significant departures from conventional roles, expectations, and authority relations with the assumption that these changes will be accompanied by improvement in the quality of teaching and learning. Accordingly, we searched for schools that had introduced the features just noted to promote more ambitious, higher-quality learning than has typically been found in U.S. schools.

Estimates of significant school restructuring vary considerably, depending on the criteria and the sample of schools. We believe that comprehensive restructuring includes such features as site-based management, with meaningful authority over staffing, school program, and budget; shared decision making; staff teams, with frequent common planning time and shared responsibility for most of students' instruction; multiyear instructional or advisory groups; and heterogeneous grouping of almost all students for instruction in the core subjects. Using this definition, we estimate that less than 10 percent of the more than 180,000 U.S. public schools are comprehensively restructured.[9]

## Research Problem and Study Design

With so much attention given to school restructuring in the hope that it might improve education for children came the need to study its consequences.

## Initial Questions

In 1990 the Office of Educational Research and Improvement of the U.S. Department of Education funded the Center on Organization and Restructuring of Schools to conduct a five-year program of research on school restructuring. To plan this research we began with the straightforward question, "Does school restructuring work?" But we soon discovered that the question could not be answered in this form; it had to be rephrased. Restructuring could have multiple effects, these effects could vary for different groups, and results could also depend on the kind of restructuring undertaken and how it was implemented. Recognizing that advocates of restructuring and we as researchers valued particular outcomes, we decided to address six critical issues for elementary, middle, and high schools:

1. *How can school restructuring nurture authentic forms of student achievement?* Authentic intellectual achievement extends beyond basic skills to complex thinking and in-depth understanding of knowledge, and is used often to solve problems encountered beyond the classroom.
2. *How can school restructuring enhance educational equity?* This means offering high-quality teaching to students of all social backgrounds and minimizing gaps in achievement traditionally associated with race, socioeconomic status, and gender.
3. *How can decentralization and local empowerment be constructively developed?* As authority for the conduct of education flows from districts and state agencies to individual schools, it becomes important to find ways of encouraging meaningful participation by key stakeholders, especially teachers, administrators, and parents.
4. *How can school restructuring transform schools into communities of learning?* Critiques of traditional schooling emphasize how hierarchical authority and formal regulations in bureaucratic organizations inhibit collaboration, caring, and collective responsibility—features of "natural" communities that seem critical to student learning.
5. *How can school change be approached through thoughtful dialogue and support rather than coercion and regulation?* Research shows

that effective implementation depends on teachers' questioning and adapting innovations, rather than simply complying with mandates.

6. *How can the focus on student achievement and school accountability be shaped to serve these principles?* As parents, policymakers, and educators begin to hold schools more accountable for students' intellectual performance, the criteria for performance, the procedures for gathering information and for judging schools' success, and the incentives for success or sanctions for failure should be consistent with the first five principles.

Our challenge was to determine how and why these outcomes were affected by innovation in the organizational features of schools, such as how students were grouped for instruction, how teachers' and students' work was scheduled, or how authority for school governance was allocated. To examine these issues, we considered the roles of students, teachers, administrators, parents, and reformers in school restructuring. We were particularly concerned with the effects of restructuring on students and teachers, and we paid special attention to the influences of student race, socioeconomic class, gender, and prior academic success on their opportunities for high-quality instruction and for successful academic performance. Given the substantial efforts of some districts, states, and independent reform projects to support school restructuring, we also examined the influence of external agents on the schools.

The Center's research program led to a variety of publications related to the six initial questions.[10] All studies relied on four main sources of data:

1. The School Restructuring Study (SRS) of twenty-four significantly restructured public schools, each studied intensively for one year

2. The National Longitudinal Study of 1988, with survey and test data from about ten thousand nationally represented students followed from grade 8 (1988) through grade 12 (1992) in about eight hundred high schools

3. A study of Chicago school reform with survey data from teachers and principals in more than four hundred Chicago schools from 1990 to 1994

4. The Longitudinal Study of Restructuring of professional community in eight schools from 1991 through 1994

This book reports only on the SRS, which contained the most comprehensive combination of observational data, survey data, interview data, and samples of teachers' assessment tasks and student work in restructured elementary, middle, and high schools. In the SRS we gathered data to address each of the six questions but decided that this book should connect findings on the different questions to the basic problem of student achievement. And so our central question became, "Under what conditions can school restructuring promote authentic student achievement?"

## Design Issues

The research agenda posed problematic issues of design and methodology. The first issue was the ambiguity of school restructuring. Since this key variable of the research had multiple meanings and since schools varied considerably in which aspects of restructuring they had adopted, it was not possible to locate a group of identically restructured schools and compare them with a control group of conventional schools. Instead we studied only schools that had implemented several features of restructuring. These schools all achieved unusual levels of organizational innovation, but we assumed there would still be substantial variation in success within the group with respect to the six critical issues. By studying differences between the more and less successful schools, we hoped to draw conclusions about the conditions under which certain aspects of restructuring pay off.

A second issue involved a trade-off between the depth to which each school was studied and the total number of schools in the sample. We were committed to studying each school in enough depth to understand the connections between organizational conditions, instruction, and student achievement. For the results to be most useful to a broad audience, the study had to include elementary, middle, and high schools nationwide, with at least eight schools at each level. Ideally we would have studied schools over three or more years to see how changing conditions affected the course of restructuring and to chart gains in student achievement from year to year. But with limited resources and only five years to plan, conduct, and report on the research, we considered it impossible to pursue this longitudinal strategy. If we were to study twenty-four schools in sufficient depth, we had enough resources and time to study each school for a single year. This design did not allow us to draw firm conclusions about the school change process, but our many interviews gave us a sense of how each school's restructuring came about, and we did discover relationships among structural conditions, instruction, and student outcomes during a year in each school's life.

Our primary concern—and a third issue for the study's design—was to learn whether and how organizational changes in schooling affected the quality of instruction and student achievement. This research goal presented a complex issue: What criteria should be used to evaluate the quality of instruction and student achievement? In the United States, controversy boils on how to evaluate teaching and student achievement. Should teaching be evaluated on the extent to which teachers use techniques such as lecture, discussion, cooperative learning, or portfolios? Should the extent to which teachers cover particular topics, such as the U.S. Constitution in a middle school U.S. history course or probability and statistics in high school mathematics, be considered? Should student achievement be evaluated on standardized tests, teacher-designed tests geared to the school's curriculum, or new approaches to performance assessment? And regardless of the form of assessment, how much emphasis should be given to traditional knowledge of facts, definitions, and algorithms on a vast range of topics versus higher-order thinking or in-depth understanding on limited topics?

Our response to these issues is presented through standards we developed to assess the quality of teaching and student achievement in SRS schools. The teaching standards, described in Chapter One, were grounded in criteria for intellectual quality and took account of teachers' daily lessons and their special assessment activities. We refer to the combination of these two parts of teaching practice as *pedagogy*. To gather evidence on student achievement, we chose not to impose additional testing. Instead we asked teachers to submit assessment tasks that they normally used and considered to be valid measures of student achievement, and to send us students' written work in response to those tasks. We then scored the quality of the assessment tasks and student work according to the standards for intellectual quality described in Chapter One.

## Summary of the Data

We studied twenty-four significantly restructured public schools, evenly divided among elementary, middle, and high schools, and located in sixteen states and twenty-two districts, most of them in urban settings. There was a large range of enrollment, with an average of 777 students, of whom 21 percent were African American, 22 percent Hispanic, and 37 percent received free or reduced-fee lunch. In nine of the schools most or all students attended by choice instead of compulsory assignment based on residence. All of the schools had experienced their organizational innovations for at least three years, and most schools were connected to restructuring initiatives sponsored by their districts, states, or independent reform organizations.[11]

In this book we identify the schools by pseudonyms, chosen from lists of geographical and recreational locations in the United States. Teachers, administrators, parents, students, and others who participated in the study were promised confidentiality.

From 1991 through 1994 we studied each school for one year during two weeks of on-site observations and interviews of teachers, administrators, parents, and policymakers. We also surveyed students and staff. Without resources to study all school subjects intensively, we chose mathematics and social studies, subjects that offer interesting contrasts. Mathematics is universally recognized as necessary for success in further education and in many occupations. Considerable progress has been made in reaching consensus among scholars and practitioners on standards for mathematics curricula. In contrast, although the social studies, including history and other disciplines, are extensively required and recognized as critical for responsible citizenship, these subjects have received less research support and have made less progress in identifying a coherent set of curriculum standards. Our study of mathematics and social studies instruction in about 130 classrooms included observation of four lessons per class, conventional baseline tests of student achievement, and the scoring of student work on two teacher-assigned assessments according to standards of authentic achievement, with complete data on about two thousand students. Some of our responses to the initial research questions are based on quantitative analysis, but most of our findings depend heavily on qualitative analyses of elaborate descriptive reports (ranging from 150 to 200 pages) for each school.[12]

## Contributions of the Study and Overview of Chapters

Our analyses offer a combination of qualitative insights on school restructuring in specific locations but also generalizations across the group of twenty-four diverse schools according to common themes and variables. Some previous studies of school restructuring have used largely qualitative data to focus on individual teachers (Cohen, 1990; Wasley, 1994), single schools or a small number of schools (Elmore, Peterson, and McCarthey, 1996; Lieberman, 1995; Wagner, 1994), or schools connected primarily with a single reform effort (Fine, 1994; Muncey and McQuillan, 1993). This research is useful in offering detailed narratives about how specific schools, teachers, and students experience reform. Other studies have relied more on quantitative analysis of large numbers of schools (Bryk and others, 1993; Kyle, 1993; Lee and Smith, 1995). This research helps to identify trends and relationships among common variables across a more general population of schools.

Compared to previous work, the SRS is unique in its study of all three levels of schooling; in using the same standards to measure the quality of teaching and achievement in two subjects but standards that nevertheless respect schools' diverse teaching techniques and curriculum content; and in using a common analytic framework (the six initial questions) to examine structural and cultural features of schools in diverse settings.

This study offers three main contributions. First, it provides a set of standards for high-quality pedagogy and student achievement that can be applied to diverse teaching techniques and curriculum content. Chapter One presents and explains the rationale for the standards for authentic pedagogy—that is, for instruction and assessment likely to promote authentic student achievement. Similarly, the chapter presents and explains the standards for authentic student achievement.

The second contribution is to document that, in spite of much skepticism and many obstacles, American public schools are capable of sophisticated teaching that produces achievement of high quality for students regardless of social background. These findings are presented in Chapter Two and elaborated in later chapters. We found that when teaching was consistent with the standards, students achieved at higher levels. Not only did authentic pedagogy boost student achievement, but in this diverse sample of restructured schools, authentic pedagogy was delivered equally to students of different race, class, and gender. Furthermore, the effects of authentic pedagogy were equal for students of different social background.

In spite of this positive news, the highly restructured schools we studied varied considerably in their success in delivering authentic pedagogy, with several showing low ratings on the standards. Chapters Three through Five offer in-depth portraits of six schools that illustrate successes and dilemmas and obstacles faced by many of the schools.

The third contribution is to explain why some schools were more successful in using organizational change to support authentic achievement. There are two parts to the explanation. The first is that innovations in school structures will be helpful only to the extent that they aim toward two central ideas: advancing the intellectual quality of student learning (Chapter Six) and the nurturing of professional community (Chapter Seven). The second is that structural conditions interact with certain human resources and cultural qualities of schools. Structural innovation cannot be understood, and should not be undertaken, without considering school culture. Chapters Eight through Twelve explain how cultural and structural features of schools affect four important practical challenges in school restructuring:

1. How to build a climate of support for student achievement
2. How to offer high-quality pedagogy to all students
3. How shared decision making can strengthen pedagogy
4. How external agents can assist schools

The key to authentic student achievement is to create a coherent integration of cultural and structural conditions that keep schools focused in a sustained way on intellectual quality and professional community. These, in turn, support more authentic pedagogy and authentic student achievement. The main points of the argument are summarized in Figure I.1.

Finally, the Conclusion synthesizes insights on the interaction of culture and structure and suggests how teachers, administrators, and policymakers might use the results of this study.

## Notes

1. Epigraph from Kearns and Doyle (1988, p. 1).
2. Berliner and Biddle (1995) argue that the attack on public schools has been manufactured by conservative, more affluent groups to gain support for public funding of private schools that will allow them to withdraw their children from urban, culturally diverse schools into culturally homogeneous, higher-income enclaves.

**Figure I.1.  Connecting Restructuring to Student Achievement.**

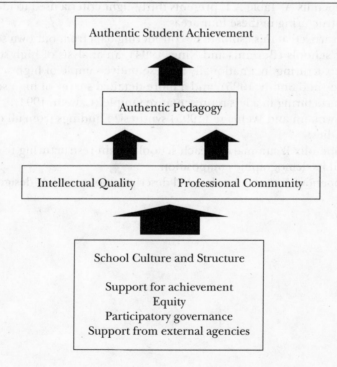

3. Newmann (1993) describes a persistent conflict in educational goals over traditional versus progressive conceptions of knowledge.

4. Recent slogans include "back to basics," "effective schools," "cultural literacy," and "standards without standardization."

5. Diverse accounts of schooling's resistance to change are offered by Berman and McLaughlin (1978); Cuban (1990, 1993); Popkewitz, Tabachnik, and Wehlage (1982); Powell, Farrar, and Cohen (1985); Sarason (1971, 1990); and Tyack and Cuban (1995).

6. Examples of analyses along these lines include Carnegie Task Force on Teaching as a Profession (1986), Kearns and Doyle (1988), Lawler (1991), and Marshall and Tucker (1992). Tyack and Cuban (1995) describe the influence of the business sector in prior reform periods as well.

7. A prominent example was the formation of the New American Schools Development Corporation (NASDC) in 1990 as part of the America 2000 strategy of the Bush administration. Headed primarily by chief executive officers of major corporations and relying largely on private funding, NASDC sponsored a variety of projects to design "break the mold" schools. These schools started well after our research had begun and were not included in our study.

8. Appendix A, Table A.1, presents thirty-eight criteria used to identify restructuring in these four areas.

9. We arrived at this estimate by considering data from our own search for schools (Berends and King, 1994), an analysis of high school restructuring in a nationally representative sample of high schools (Lee and Smith, 1995), and a more-detailed survey of high school restructuring in a less-representative sample (Cawelti, 1994).

10. Newmann and Wehlage (1995) synthesize findings from all of the studies.

11. Appendix B summarizes each school's main restructuring features and its demographic composition.

12. Appendix A contains a detailed description of the study design.

# Part One

# Authentic Achievement

To study the effects of school restructuring, we needed criteria for identifying effective teaching and high-quality student achievement. Choosing such criteria involves persisting controversies over several issues, including the extent to which teachers should control students' learning activities; the extent to which curriculum should connect to students' interests and life experiences; the extent to which all students should learn the same content, in the same way, and at the same pace; and the emphasis given to mastery of discrete, and usually unrelated, facts, definitions, algorithms, and skills versus problem solving and thinking that requires more integration and depth of understanding.

Effective teaching has been the subject of a substantial body of research, but these findings offered neither conclusive results nor sufficient focus to guide our study.[1] Additionally there were at least two other reasons that we had to reach beyond research on teaching techniques to construct criteria for teaching and achievement. First, the effectiveness of any teaching technique or activity, such as lecture, small group discussion, or independent research project, depends in part on the educational goal sought for students. Drill and practice work sheets may be useful for remembering the names of state capitals, for example, but not for understanding the politics that occur within a capital. Conversely some educational goals might be achieved through any of several techniques; students might learn the names of capitals through interesting quiz games, computer simulations, or mnemonic devices. Second, the ultimate effectiveness of teaching depends not simply on whether a technique is used but how well it is used to promote intellectual quality. Two different teachers, for example, may guide student discussion of political conflict in U.S. history; one may stimulate careful explanations of students' ideas, while the other merely elicits superficial opinion.

Since research on teaching does not prescribe unequivocally what educational goals are most worthwhile, we needed to take a position on the kind of student achievement most important to examine. Having chosen to look mainly at the intellectual quality of schooling (in contrast, for example, to other goals such as teaching self-confidence or responsible social behavior), we then needed to specify criteria for teaching that tapped the intellectual quality of teacher and student work—criteria that research on teaching activities often neglects. We realized that studying both mathematics and social studies at three levels of schooling in diverse schools across the United States could lead to an extensive, complex set of criteria and pose problems of reliability, research management, and public understanding of our results. We chose to make the scheme as simple as possible by defining standards common to both subjects and all grade levels and by minimizing the number of standards.

The standards for authentic pedagogy and student achievement presented in Chapter One represent our belief that all students deserve an education that extends beyond transmission of isolated facts and skills to in-depth understanding and complex problem solving and that is useful to students and society outside the classroom. Our standards require—and define—ambitious intellectual work in schools, but they specify neither the curriculum content to study nor the instructional activities to use.

Using the standards to assess the quality of teaching and student achievement in restructuring schools, we set out to answer three important questions. First, how well do teachers and students in restructuring schools perform on these standards? If some schools did well, this evidence would offer an existence proof that more ambitious learning is within reach. Second, do students whose teachers practice according to the standards for authentic instruction and assessment achieve better than other students? Finally, if authentic instruction and assessment, which we call authentic pedagogy, pay off for students, can restructuring schools offer it equitably to students from different socioeconomic and racial and ethnic backgrounds, and do students from different social backgrounds benefit equally? Chapter Two, describing how we studied these issues, presents mixed results on the first question but positive results on the latter two.

**Note**

1. Good and Brophy (1994) provide a comprehensive summary of the research on effective teaching and discuss implications for practice. The standards we articulate in Chapter One are consistent with their summary, but we focus more explicitly on a particular set of educational goals and criteria for intellectual quality, in contrast, for example, to strategies such as teacher questioning or activities that promote active learning.

# Standards for Authentic Achievement and Pedagogy

*Gary G. Wehlage, Fred M. Newmann, Walter G. Secada*

The search to determine whether school restructuring leads to high-quality teaching and learning must begin by identifying standards. Different kinds of standards have been advanced for judging what teachers and students do; some address knowledge and skills, and others focus on the process of teaching. Good teaching has been defined in various ways, such as modeling direct instruction, in which teachers exercise very precise control over student activity and dialogue, or having students engage in active learning, in which students exert more initiative in planning and conducting their studies. Student achievement has been defined as knowing correct answers, using a proper written form, or working cooperatively in a group. For this study, we decided that standards for success should focus on the intellectual quality of teachers' and students' work and developed criteria to measure intellectual quality regardless of the particular form of instruction observed or the specific student outcome produced. We acknowledge persuasive arguments that educational goals should extend beyond intellectual development (for example, to include internalization of moral-social values or the nurturing of specific kinds of socially responsible and economically productive behavior). Recognizing the importance of other goals, we nevertheless chose to focus this study on how the restructuring of schools might enhance the intellectual quality of academic work. Although there is much rhetoric endorsing cognitive development, it is often neglected in schools and in reform programs.

Initially we developed intellectual standards for pedagogy and achievement only as a research tool to study the effects of school restructuring. We did not describe them in any detail to teachers participating in the research or try to influence their instruction and assessment to be consistent with them. But the results and reactions to the standards from a variety of practicing educators after data collection was completed suggest they can also be used to guide school reform to help teachers improve student learning. We therefore explain the standards in some detail.

First, we developed a vision or definition of high-quality intellectual achievement. Called *authentic achievement,* it depends on three main criteria: construction of knowledge, disciplined inquiry, and value of learning beyond school. We examine these below.

Next, we translated these general criteria into more specific standards for evaluating teaching. Teaching consists of two primary functions: daily instruction and assessing student performance. How teachers conduct these functions is critical to student learning. Accordingly we developed four standards for teachers' instruction and seven standards for their assessment tasks. Together these standards for instruction and assessment constitute our definition of authentic pedagogy. At each of the twenty-four schools, we observed a sample of teachers four times and collected at least two assessment tasks from them. The standards were developed into sets of scoring rules, or "rubrics" (scaled from 1 to 5) that researchers used to rate the intellectual quality of the observed pedagogy in mathematics and social studies classes.

Finally, continuing to build on the vision of authentic achievement, we translated the criteria of construction of knowledge and disciplined inquiry into three standards for scoring the quality of student performance. Each of these standards was translated into scoring rubrics (scaled from 1 to 4). Experienced teachers in mathematics and social studies used the standards to score more than four thousand pieces of student written work completed in response to the assessment task teachers submitted.[1]

## Vision: Authentic Achievement

The term *authentic* commonly refers to something that is real, genuine, or true rather than artificial, fake, or misleading. How does this distinction apply to intellectual work in school? The kind of achievement required for students to earn school credits, grades, and high scores on tests is often considered trivial, contrived, and meaningless by both students and adults, and the absence of meaning breeds low student engagement in school work. Meaningless school work is a consequence of a number of factors but especially curriculum that emphasizes superficial exposure to hundreds of isolated pieces of knowledge. Such exposure is reinforced by teacher training institutions, textbook publishers, testing agencies, and universities. Teaching loads and school schedules also make it difficult for teachers to help individual students delve deeply into knowledge to understand its importance. In addition, schools isolate students from adults in the community, making it difficult for young people to understand the ways in which intellectual work can produce significant achievements. Authentic achievement can suggest standards for intellectual accomplishment and goals for schooling that would reduce these misuses of the intellect.

But what qualities are critical to authentic intellectual work? Consider the important adult task of designing a bridge. Typically a bridge requires both new and well-established knowledge in the fields of design and construction. Disciplines of engineering, architecture, science, and mathematics have accumulated bodies of reliable knowledge and procedures for solving the more routine problems of bridge design, but unique problems will require new conceptions of design and construction. New, unique knowledge is produced as special conditions are addressed involving the bridge's particular length, height, and peak points of stress and load but also the impact of possible environmental conditions involving weather extremes of temperature, wind, ice, snow, and floods, as well as the possibility of earthquakes. When completed, the bridge will prove safe and useful to travelers, it may make an aesthetic statement, and it will likely be considered a personally satisfying accomplishment to those who designed it. Successful completion of building the bridge illustrates some essential intellectual qualities of authentic achievement.

The term *authentic achievement* thus stands for intellectual accomplishments that are worthwhile, significant, and meaningful, such as those undertaken by successful adults: scientists, musicians, business entrepreneurs, politicians, crafts people, attorneys, novelists, physicians, designers, and so on. With children we are concerned with a more restricted conception of achievement, one that can be accomplished in schools. For students, we define authentic academic achievement through three criteria critical to significant intellectual accomplishment: construction of knowledge, disciplined inquiry, and the value of achievement beyond school.[2]

## Construction of Knowledge

Adults in diverse fields of endeavor face the primary challenge of constructing or producing, rather than reproducing, meaning or knowledge. They express this knowledge in written and oral discourse (using words and other symbols), by making and repairing things (furniture, bridges, videos, sculpture), and in performances for audiences (musical, dramatic, athletic).

To help children eventually to attain the competence of skilled adults, schools should engage students in the general forms of cognitive work found in the adult world. That is, students should hone their skills and knowledge through guided practice in producing original conversation and writing, repairing and building of physical objects, or performing artistically. In contrast, the conventional curriculum asks students mainly to identify definitions, things, and performances that others have produced (for example, by recognizing the difference between socialism and capitalism, by matching authors with their works, or by correctly labeling rocks or parts of a flower).

For high-quality achievement, student construction of knowledge must be based on a foundation of prior knowledge. That is, students must assimilate a great deal of knowledge that others have produced. But the mere reproduction of that prior knowledge does not constitute authentic achievement, because it does not involve the construction of knowledge found in significant intellectual accomplishment.

## Disciplined Inquiry

The second defining feature of authentic achievement is its reliance on cognitive work that involves disciplined inquiry. Disciplined inquiry consists of three main features: (1) use of a prior knowledge base, (2) striving for in-depth understanding rather than superficial awareness, and (3) expressing one's ideas and findings through elaborated communication. We think all students are capable of engaging in these forms of cognitive work when the work is adapted to students' levels of development.

A broad definition of human achievement might not always illustrate disciplined inquiry as suggested by academic study (Gardner, 1983, 1993). For example, feats of wilderness survival that depend largely on ingenuity and courage, forms of athletic prowess, and selfless acts of caring and personal sacrifice might all be considered authentic, but they may not illustrate much disciplined inquiry. Since schooling, at a minimum, should promote academic study, our conception of human accomplishment is intentionally limited to achievements that depend on the use of formal knowledge.

### Prior Knowledge Base

Human accomplishments build on prior knowledge that has been accumulated in a field. The knowledge base includes facts, vocabularies, concepts, theories, algorithms, and conventions for the conduct and expression of inquiry itself. The ultimate point of disciplined inquiry is to move beyond such knowledge through criticism, testing, and development of new paradigms. Most cognitive work in school, however, consists of transmitting prior knowledge to students and asking them to accept it, reproduce it in fragmented statements, or recognize it on tests. Only rarely are students asked to use what they have learned to construct new knowledge.

### In-Depth Understanding

Disciplined inquiry seeks to develop an in-depth understanding of a problem rather than only a passing familiarity with it or exposure to pieces of knowledge. Prior knowledge is mastered primarily not to become literate about a broad survey of topics but to facilitate complex understanding of discrete problems. In-depth understanding requires more than knowing a lot of details about a topic. It occurs as one looks for, tests, and creates relationships among pieces of knowledge that can illuminate a particular problem or issue. In short, in-depth understanding involves construction of knowledge around a reasonably focused topic. In contrast, many of the cognitive tasks of school ask students to show only superficial awareness of a vast number of topics.

### Elaborated Communication

Scientists, jurists, artists, journalists, designers, engineers, and other accomplished adults working within disciplines rely on complex forms of communication both to conduct their work and to express their conclusions. The language they use—verbal, symbolic, and visual—includes qualifications, nuances, elaborations, details, and analogues woven into extended expositions, narratives, explanations, justifications, and dialogue. In contrast, much of the communication demanded in school asks only for brief responses: choosing true or false, selecting from multiple choices, filling in blanks, or writing short sentences. If students learn to communicate in elaborate forms, they will be better able to construct knowledge, achieve in-depth understanding, and express their intellectual accomplishment more effectively.

## Value Beyond School

The third criterion reflects aesthetic, utilitarian, or personal value evident in significant intellectual accomplishments. In contrast, most conventional school achievement is designed only to document the competence of the learner. When adults write (letters, news articles, poems), speak a foreign language, design a house, create a painting or a piece of music, or build a stereo cabinet, they try to communicate ideas, produce a product, or have an impact on others beyond the simple demonstration that they are competent. Achievements of this sort have a value that is missing in tasks contrived only for the purpose of assessing knowledge (such as spelling quizzes, laboratory exercises, or typical final exams). The call for relevant or student-centered curriculum is, in many cases, a less precise expression of the view that student accomplishments should have value beyond being only indicators of success in school. Some people may want to reserve the term *authentic* for curriculum that is relevant, student centered, or hands-on, but we do not. Value beyond the school is only one criterion for authentic intellectual work.

These three criteria—construction of knowledge, through disciplined inquiry, to produce discourse, products, and performances that have meaning beyond success in school—form the foundation for standards to assess the intellectual quality of teaching and learning. All three criteria are important. For example, students might confront a complex calculus problem demanding much analytical thought (construction of knowledge and disciplined inquiry), but if its solution has no interest or value beyond proving competence to pass a course, its authenticity is diminished. Or a student may write a letter to the editor, saying she opposes a newly proposed welfare plan. This activity may meet the criterion of constructing knowledge to produce discourse with value beyond school, but if the letter shows only shallow understanding of the issues or contains significant errors of fact, it would be less authentic because of shortcomings in disciplined inquiry.

Authentic achievement is demanding in its insistence on all three criteria, but a given achievement in a school could be high on some criteria and lower on others. Similarly we do not expect all classroom activities to meet all three standards all of the time. For example, repetitive practice, retrieving information, and memorization of facts or rules may be necessary to build knowledge and skills as foundations for authentic performance, or to prepare for unauthentic tests required for advancement in the current educational system. The point is not to abandon all forms of unauthentic work in school, but to keep authentic achievement clearly in view as the ideal valued end.

Two points should convince educators to strive for authentic student achievement. First, participation in authentic intellectual activity is more likely to motivate and sustain students in the hard work that learning requires. Evidence from our study supports the connection between authentic pedagogy and student effort and interest in learning (Marks, 1995). Students exposed to authentic pedagogy may have been more engaged because their intellectual work had personal meaning beyond the demonstration of competence to a teacher.

Second, teaching students to master authentic academic challenges should benefit both individuals and the society. The complexities of contemporary society demand that citizens be problem solvers and lifelong learners capable of adapting to changing economic and social conditions. Whether trying to make a living, manage personal affairs, or participate in civic life, citizens are increasingly called on to exercise the kinds of intellectual capacities reflected in authentic achievement. Schools that fail to help students face these challenges deny them opportunities for security, productivity, and fulfillment.

## Authentic Pedagogy: Assessment Tasks

Tests and other assignments used to evaluate performance communicate to students the kind of intellectual work that is valued. We asked teachers to send examples of their assessment tasks—ones that helped them determine how well their students were understanding and mastering the subject taught. We asked for tasks that called on students to respond with written work because, at the very least, we believe that all students should learn to write well in both mathematics and social studies.[3] Teachers provided tasks that asked students to write opinion essays, explain solutions to mathematics problems, synthesize research data, draw maps and mathematical diagrams, and complete short-answer tests.

We developed seven standards for assessment tasks that reflect the three criteria for authentic achievement. They are listed in Exhibit 1.1.

### Applying the Standards for Construction of Knowledge

If students are to succeed in constructing knowledge, the assessment activities they complete must call on them to organize information and consider alternatives. In mathematics, for example, fourth- and fifth-grade students were given the following task involving measurement, fractions, and fraction computation:

> We are making a wooden case to hold our new CD system. We need to have 3 shelves. The top shelf must contain 3 compartments; the second shelf, 2 compartments; and the bottom shelf, 1 compartment. We also have 6 boards that are 60 inches long, 2.5 feet wide, and 1 inch thick. Draw a diagram of what the shelves will look like when finished. Using fractions, show how you will cut the boards to make compartments.

## Exhibit 1.1.  Standards for Authentic Pedagogy: Assessment Tasks.

*Construction of Knowledge*

*Standard 1: Organization of Information.* The task asks students to organize, synthesize, interpret, explain, or evaluate complex information in addressing a concept, problem, or issue.

*Standard 2: Consideration of Alternatives.* The task asks students to consider alternative solutions, strategies, perspectives, or points of view in addressing a concept, problem, or issue.

*Disciplined Inquiry*

*Standard 3: Disciplinary Content.* The task asks students to show understanding and/or to use ideas, theories, or perspectives considered central to an academic or professional discipline.

*Standard 4: Disciplinary Process.* The task asks students to use methods of inquiry, research, or communication characteristic of an academic or professional discipline.

*Standard 5: Elaborated Written Communication.* The task asks students to elaborate on their understanding, explanations, or conclusions through extended writing.

*Value Beyond School*

*Standard 6: Problem Connected to the World Beyond the Classroom.* The task asks students to address a concept, problem, or issue that is similar to one that they have encountered or are likely to encounter in life beyond the classroom.

*Standard 7: Audience Beyond the School.* The task asks students to communicate their knowledge, present a product or performance, or take some action for an audience beyond the teacher, classroom, and school building.

This task was scored high on organization of information (Standard 1) because it could not be completed successfully unless students organized and interpreted information in a new form. They had to use information on the number of shelves and compartments needed and the number of boards with specific dimensions available to create a design that would work mathematically (for example, the dimensions indicated that designs could not exceed the length of the boards that were given). The teacher's grading and comments on student work showed that she expected students not only to label the different parts of the shelves but to show that the measures and fractional parts added correctly. The task also scored high on consideration of alternatives (Standard 2), because it was possible to cut the boards and arrange the shelves, and students had to decide which options were mathematically possible.

## Applying the Standards for Disciplined Inquiry

Students in a combined fourth- and fifth-grade social studies class were involved in a year-long study of their community, the City of the Future, that included a unit on urban geography. Working in small groups, students were given the following task:

First, select one of the neighborhoods marked on the city map. Second, identify its current features by doing an inventory of its buildings, businesses, housing, and public facilities. Also, identify current transportation patterns and traffic flow. From the information made available, identify any special problems this neighborhood has, such as dilapidated housing, traffic congestion, or a high crime rate. Third, as a group consider various plans for changing and improving your neighborhood. If there is a special problem, how will you address it? What kinds of businesses, if any, do you want to attract? What kind of housing do you want? Will there be parks and other recreational facilities? What transportation patterns do you want? Do you want to make the block attractive to different groups of people such as senior citizens and young people? After deciding on a plan, draw and label it on the overlay provided with your map. Based on what you know about urban geography, indicate in your narrative one possible plan that you rejected, and say why it was rejected. Indicate how your plan will promote the neighborhood features you want.

This task required students to use disciplinary content (Standard 3) and disciplinary processes (Standard 4) from geography. Students had to think in some of the same ways as urban planners and geographers do, as demonstrated in previous lessons. They had to collect data and use them to make generalizations about patterns in human behavior. They also had to make choices about preferred uses of resources and space to fulfill different functions within a community. Eventually they had to synthesize all of this information and write an elaborate written narrative (Standard 5) describing their decisions and plans.

## Applying the Standards for Value Beyond School

Since authentic accomplishments have value beyond merely demonstrating competence, tasks need to require students to confront a real-world problem. For example, high school geometry students were given the following task:[4]

> Design packaging that will hold 576 cans of Campbell's tomato soup (net weight, 10¾ ounces) or packaging that will hold 144 boxes of Kellogg's Rice Krispies (net weight, 19 ounces). Use and list the individual package's real measurements; create scale drawings of front, top, and side perspectives; show the unfolded boxes/containers in a scale drawing; build a proportional three-dimensional model.

This task scored high on problem connected to the world (Standard 6) because it required students to apply mathematics to a familiar real-world problem: finding or making packages to hold contents of different volume. On the other hand, since it did not ask students to convey their findings to others beyond the classroom, it scored low on audience beyond school (Standard 7).

In a fourth-grade social studies class students were given the following activity:

> Write a letter to a state assembly representative or state senator expressing your opinion about what should be done about threatened eagles along the Mississippi River. Your letter should be persuasive, and it should also do the following:

Communicate knowledge about the subject

Organize ideas into paragraphs

Begin sentences in different ways

Use dialogue to communicate ideas

Use correct letter format

Use correct punctuation and spelling

Ask a peer to read your letter and offer constructive criticism. When you are
satisfied with your letter, send it.

This task scored high on audience beyond school (Standard 7)
because students used their knowledge to inform or to persuade
others by sending the letter.

## Authentic Pedagogy: Instruction

Student-centered practices such as discussions, small group
work, and hands-on projects are often assumed to provide more
authentic experiences for children. We found, however, that
many activities of this sort do not necessarily support construction of knowledge or disciplined inquiry, nor do they have value
to students beyond completing school assignments. Since no
particular teaching practice, whether teacher centered (for example, teacher-directed discussion) or student centered (for example, cooperative learning), can be assumed to promote the
three qualities central to our conception of authentic intellectual
work, each practice should be examined in context with the three
qualities in mind.

For the SRS study, we used four standards to define the intellectual quality of observed instruction. The first three standards—higher-order thinking, deep knowledge, and substantive
conversation—place special emphasis on cognitive complexity, or
what might be considered teaching for conceptual understanding.
The fourth, connection to the world beyond the classroom, emphasizes teaching that helps students apply such understanding
beyond school.[5] Exhibit 1.2 lists the standards for instruction.

## Exhibit 1.2.  Standards for Authentic Pedagogy: Instruction.

*Construction of Knowledge*

*Standard 1. Higher-Order Thinking.* Instruction involves students in manipulating information and ideas by synthesizing, generalizing, explaining, hypothesizing, or arriving at conclusions that produce new meaning and understandings for them.

*Disciplined Inquiry*

*Standard 2. Deep Knowledge.* Instruction addresses central ideas of a topic or discipline with enough thoroughness to explore connections and relationships and to produce relatively complex understandings.
*Standard 3. Substantive Conversation.* Students engage in extended conversational exchanges with the teacher or their peers about subject matter in a way that builds an improved and shared understanding of ideas or topics.

*Value Beyond School*

*Standard 4. Connections to the World Beyond the Classroom.* Students make connections between substantive knowledge and either public problems or personal experiences.

# Applying the Standards for Construction of Knowledge

Fifth-grade students estimated, without paper and pencil, products of numbers such as 56 × 37, 83 × 52, and 505 × 1,495. The teacher supplied no strategies, procedures, or answers. Students worked alone or in groups. The teacher asked the students to explain their answers and their strategies, often helping them to articulate and elaborate their reasoning by questioning the adequacy of their strategies. She also encouraged students to be aware of multiple solutions. In one situation, students used two different methods to arrive at an estimation; she accepted both and pushed students to explain why each method had worked. This lesson scored high on higher-order thinking (Standard 1) because almost all of the students were involved in both generating strategies of solution and in explaining their ideas about estimation.

## Applying the Standards for Deep Knowledge

A high school social studies class was studying events in South Africa. The teacher had assigned a *New York Times* article about the election of Nelson Mandela as president of South Africa. The following exchanges occurred as part of a longer discussion of the article:

*Student 1:*   Mandela says he will grant amnesty to individuals who supported apartheid in the past. If he does, that should lead to peace after the election. The article makes it sound like everything is positive in the country. It seems to say that democracy can really work.

*Student 2:*   Yes, but I think the media image we get is only half the story. A lot of problems remain. Just because there is an election and democracy doesn't mean that race hatred has disappeared. There are also big problems with the economy.

*Teacher:*   Let's hear from some others on the topic. Should there be amnesty for those who ran apartheid? Should there be reconciliation? Should there be retribution or punishment for those who ran the old system?

*Student 3:*   You can never start out new, like nothing in the past matters. There's a lot of pain that people aren't going to get over. It will take a lot of time, maybe a couple of generations.

*Teacher:*   So are you saying that people who feel the pain should engage in retribution? Should there be punishment like they did to the Nazi war criminals at Nuremberg?

*Student 3:*   No, I don't believe that's a good idea. In the United States the segregationists were not tried or punished. . . . It would just start things up again. . . . So I think amnesty is a good thing. There should be no punishment.

*Student 4:*   What does amnesty really mean? Does it mean you have to forgive the people who made apartheid?

*Teacher:*   Who can define amnesty?

*Student 5:*   It's like a pardon, like when a criminal is pardoned for a crime they committed.

*Student 6:*   Only in this case those who ran apartheid would not be guilty of anything. They would get a pardon in advance. . . .

*Student 7:* I think the article also said that amnesty means people would not be identified. A person who favored apartheid would not be named by the government. . . . No one would actually know them.

*Student 4:* That's a hard one to swallow. It seems like black people have to do all the forgiving. . . . They have to find a way in their hearts to forgive. But maybe that's what he [Mandela] is trying to do. He's trying to break the cycle of hatred that was there under apartheid. It's a problem, because if you are beat down by someone, you want to go after them when you get the chance.

*Teacher:* In addition to amnesty, the article used the word *reconciliation*. What might be Mandela's motive for trying to bring about reconciliation?

*Student 7:* I think he wants to get the support of the whites. If he loses industry, the country will be poor. He has to keep the white people in the country at least for a while. . . . He can't do anything without money.

This dialogue scored high on deep knowledge (Standard 2) because it incorporated important social studies content (amnesty, retribution, apartheid) to advance students' understanding of a critical issue in South Africa. It scored high on substantive conversation (Standard 3) because students and the teacher responded to one another's specific points and developed some of the complex meanings and motivations behind events in South Africa. By making distinctions that helped to clarify their thinking and staying on the topic, students seemed to develop a shared understanding of the amnesty issue.

## Applying the Standards for Value Beyond School

Fourth-grade mathematics students were given an assignment to run a household on no more than $2,000 per month. The teacher gave students a list of typical categories for expenses including rent, groceries, electricity, and telephone. Students were to determine actual costs by looking through a real estate guide for rent, and choosing groceries from a local store's advertisement. By examining these and other materials and discussing the possibilities with one another, students constructed budgets.

Students derived some personal meaning from this lesson. For example, in looking at rental guides, two boys expressed surprise to find that some buildings did not allow pets. "How about the bus line?" one asked. "Bus line? We don't need a bus; we have cars," said the other. In another group, a girl chose a cheaper apartment without a dishwasher. In a third group, two girls, after planning to spend $740 per month for an apartment, changed their minds because they felt it was too expensive given their budget.

This lesson scored high on connections to the world beyond the classroom (Standard 4) because students had to look at real costs and make priority choices in creating their budgets. For instance, they could lower their rent by sharing occupancy or accepting apartments with fewer luxuries. The activities connected mathematical content to decisions that students would need to make in life beyond school.

## Authentic Student Performance

Now we consider how to assess the quality, success, or proficiency of a student's performance. We developed standards of student performance for two of the three general criteria of authenticity: construction of knowledge and disciplined inquiry. Limitations in the SRS made it impossible for us to collect valid information on value beyond the classroom. Making judgments about the meaning or value of each student's performance to the student or to an audience beyond school would have required interviews, surveys, or other ways of assessing the actual impact of the students' work; we did not have the resources to do this. We did, however, make judgments about whether the teachers' assessment tasks posed problems that had significance beyond school and whether they demanded communication with audiences beyond school.

The standards for student performance, set out in Exhibit 1.3, were applied to students' writing, completed in response to the assessment tasks designed by their teachers. These standards— analysis, disciplinary concepts, and elaborated communication— are interpreted slightly differently for mathematics than for social

## Exhibit 1.3.  Standards for Authentic Student Performance.

*Construction of Knowledge*

*Standard 1: Analysis*

*Mathematics.* Student performance demonstrates thinking with mathematical content by organizing, synthesizing, interpreting, hypothesizing, describing patterns, making models or simulations, constructing mathematical arguments, or inventing procedures.
*Social Studies.* Student performance demonstrates higher-order thinking with social studies content by organizing, synthesizing, interpreting, evaluating, and hypothesizing to produce comparisons, contrasts, arguments, application of information to new contexts, and consideration of different ideas or points of view.

*Disciplined Inquiry*

*Standard 2: Disciplinary Concepts*

*Mathematics.* Student performance demonstrates an understanding of important mathematical ideas that goes beyond application of algorithms by elaborating on definitions, making connections to other mathematical concepts, or making connections to other disciplines.
*Social Studies.* Student performance demonstrates an understanding of ideas, concepts, theories, and principles from social disciplines and civic life by using them to interpret and explain specific, concrete information or events.

*Standard 3: Elaborated Written Communication*

*Mathematics.* Student performance demonstrates a concise, logical, and well-articulated explanation or argument that justifies mathematical work.
*Social Studies.* Student performance demonstrates an elaborated account that is clear and coherent and provides richness in details, qualifications and argument. The standard could be met by elaborated consideration of alternative points of view.

*Value Beyond School*

Not applicable in this study as explained in the text.

studies.[6] We define them and provide examples from the classes we observed, first for mathematics and then for social studies.

## Applying the Standards for Construction of Knowledge in Mathematics

High school students in grades 9 and 10 were asked to design rides for an amusement park. They were to conceive the ride's theme, the ride's dimensions, the size of the carriers, the materials that would be used in building the ride, costs of building the ride, and the number of people who could use the ride at the same time.

One student chose to design a water ride: a boat made of balsa wood rounded on either end. The front and back were semicircles with a radius of 75 centimeters; the rectangular portion of the boat measured 250 centimeters by 150 centimeters; and it was 50 centimeters from the floor to the top. The balsa wood seats measured 25 centimeters in width.

The student argued that balsa would be preferred to aluminum or pinewood since it would be cheaper to buy. To make this argument, she computed the mass of each material and multiplied that mass by each material's cost per kilogram. Next she explained how a boat made of balsa wood, given her dimensions, would float carrying one passenger who weighed about 180 pounds, a measurement that entailed determining whether the density of the boat with a passenger is less than the density of water (1 gram per cubic centimeter). In order to find the relevant density, the student first found the total volume of the boat, the total mass of the wood in grams (which equals the total volume of the wood times the average density of balsa wood), and the weight of the person in grams. After determining that the density of her boat carrying one person was 0.09 gram per cubic centimeter, the student concluded that it would float. Since her boat would float in freshwater, the student argued that it would float in saltwater as well.

This performance scored high on mathematical analysis (Standard 1) since the student correctly applied a number of concepts in testing her assumptions. For instance, her choice of balsa wood from among the three possibilities was based on considering three factors simultaneously: the boat's design, the cost to build it, and whether the resulting boat could carry passengers and still float.

She first determined that it could float when empty before calculating that the boat could carry passengers.

## Applying the Standards for Disciplined Inquiry in Mathematics

The Tortoise and the Hare problem was given to eighth graders:

> The hare challenged the tortoise to the best two out of three races. In each case, the race was to be 100 meters.
>
> *Race 1:* The tortoise left the starting line and sprinted at the rate of 4 meters per minute. Twenty-five minutes later, the hare left the starting line. How fast did the hare have to run in order to overtake the tortoise? Who won the race?

One student sketched a distance-time graph showing that at 25 minutes, the tortoise had already gone 100 meters. The hare's graph was a vertical line, and she explained that this meant it was impossible for the hare to win.

> *Race 2:* The hare left 8 minutes after the tortoise. The hare ran at the rate of 20 meters per minute. The tortoise still sprinted at 4 meters per minute. Draw a graph that shows the progress of the race. Use the same grid for both the tortoise and the hare. The horizontal axis should show the time; the vertical axis should show the distance. Who won the second race?

For this version, the same student responded with a graph that plotted two straight lines with appropriate slopes. She labeled each line and highlighted the 100-meter mark on the $y$-axis. She explained that since the tortoise's line crossed through 100 meters before the hare's, the hare won.

> *Race 3:* The hare left 5 minutes after the tortoise. After the hare ran for 3 minutes, it stopped for a 15-minute rest and then resumed the race. The tortoise still sprinted at 4 meters per minute, and the hare ran at 20 meters per minute. Make another graph to show the progress of each. Who won the race?

The student responded with a graph showing how both lines crossed the one-hundred-meter mark at the same time. Her written answer explained that both animals crossed the finish line together.

This student's work demonstrated clear understanding of disciplinary concepts in mathematics (Standard 2); she demonstrated and communicated exemplary mathematical understanding of the relationships of the concepts of distance, time, and rate and of how graphs can be used to represent these problems. In the process she provided elaborated written communication (Standard 3) through her explanations of why the tortoise or hare won, or tied, and her rendering of graphs that represented progress during each race.

## Applying the Standards for Construction of Knowledge in Social Studies

In social studies, eighth graders were asked to write an essay on the underlying causes of the American Revolution. Instructions indicated that students were to provide a chronological account of the major events, but also to explain why an action occurred and to offer an interpretation of its contribution toward the eventual break with England. Excerpts from one student's essay follow:

> The Proclamation of 1763 prevented the colonists from further westward movement, because the British were tired of fighting the Indians over further encroachment by settlers. While this seemed like a reasonable thing from the British point of view, it made the colonists angry. . . . The Stamp Act was passed by the British to raise money to support their army in the colonies, but this produced violence because the colonists believed that taxation without representation was illegal. . . . The Townshend Acts produced the same reaction from the colonists. . . . The need by the colonists to organize their resistance against what they saw as illegal acts by Britain led to the Sons of Liberty. The Committees of Correspondence kept the colonists informed about British actions. The idea of resisting the British spread across the colonies. The Tea Act led to the dumping of tea into Boston Harbor to dramatize colonial opposition. . . . The British became even more oppressive (the colonists called them the Intolerable Acts) by restricting colonial meetings and forcing colonists to quarter soldiers in their homes. These events led to further organizing by the colonists in the form of the Continental Congress and in creating local militia. . . . The Redcoats were on the march to Concord to seize guns that could be used by the colonists to resist British authority when Paul Revere rode through the countryside with his

warning that "the British are coming." This produced the first battle of the American Revolutionary War.

This essay demonstrated analysis in history (Standard 1) because it went beyond a mere chronology of events to include an explanation of how one event led to or was connected to another event in a causal chain that produced the American Revolution.

## Applying the Standards for Disciplined Inquiry in Social Studies

A fifth-grade interdisciplinary unit culminated with students' writing a paper that described and explained an environmental problem and its relationship to the quality of human life. The following excerpts were taken from one student's paper, entitled "Overpopulation":

> Demography is the study of populations. Demographers study the populations of communities and countries. Demographers tells us about population statistics and the social, economic, and health characteristics of people. These studies can help us decide if we are overpopulated.
>
> Most people don't understand how overpopulated we are. Experts say that you can't have five minutes of silence without hearing some kind of man-made machine. . . . If overpopulation keeps happening, we will begin to run out of clean air and water, our natural resources will get used up, and we will lose our food supply. Right now we have to feed almost six billion mouths and we can barely do it. According to Paul Ehrlich, "Overpopulation and rapid population growth are intimately connected with most aspects of the current human predicament, including rapid depletion of nonrenewable resources, deterioration of the environment (including rapid climate change), and increasing international tensions. . . ."
>
> Although most population experts agree that overpopulation is bad, not all agree we are overpopulated. Most experts think that overpopulation occurs when a country, state, or city cannot support itself with food, water, and the necessities for living. While experts agree that overpopulation occurs when people can no longer support themselves, they disagree about when this happens. Garret Hardin estimated that the world could feed 300 billion people. Right now we have a world population of "only" six billion. To feed

300 billion we would all have to eat like the average Ethiopian today (one bowl of rice and one cup of water a day). Other experts say we could feed 60 billion people if everyone ate like the average Chinese (small amounts of meat, a lot of rice, and 3 cups of water daily). . . . While we may not be overpopulated right now, most experts are worried about the rate of population increase. In the graph below [omitted here], we see that the rate of population growth between 1884 and 1984 has been increasing, especially since 1930. . . .

Overpopulation has many fatal effects. It can result in people losing their jobs and to homelessness, hunger, and getting a disease. In some places like Ethiopia and Somalia where there is famine, there is so little food that terrorists steal it for themselves. . . . Overpopulation can also lead to underpopulation. Studies of animals prove this. Wolves hunt hares. If the hare population rises, that means the wolf population rises, because now they have more food . . . , but the wolf doesn't conserve food. He'll just eat away and when the hares die out, the wolf population begins to die out. . . .

There are many possible solutions to overpopulation. If we could have only one baby per mother, then we could stabilize our population. If we send out more birth control devices, we might slow the population growth. If we educate people on overpopulation hazards, then they might have less children. If we ask men and women to be sterilized after two children, we could stop the population growth. . . .

But no solution has had any big impact on the problem. . . . We have fallen so deep into this problem that I am not sure it can be solved.

This paper demonstrated deep understanding and elaboration of a key disciplinary concept (Standard 2)—population density—from demography. The student showed an understanding of the relationship of the concept to a number of social and economic conditions such as hunger and disease. The student also showed an implicit understanding of quality of life, a difficult concept. The paper contained an elaborated discussion (Standard 3), including reference to a theoretical model showing that overpopulation can lead to underpopulation, as demonstrated by wolves and hares.

The discussion recognized ambiguity in the definition of over-population because experts disagree on the threshold beyond which life could not be sustained.

## Responding to Reservations About Authentic Achievement

The standards and examples already presented may convince many people of the value of authentic academic achievement, but some educators, parents, researchers, and policymakers have reservations about it. The ideal, it has been claimed, neglects the teaching of basic skills or important content that will handicap students when taking tests required for college admission. A significant body of evidence contradicts this concern. A recent comprehensive study of alternatives to conventional practice examined the teaching of mathematics, reading, and writing in 140 classrooms in fifteen elementary schools serving disadvantaged students in six school districts (Knapp, Shields, and Turnbull, 1992). Researchers found that when teachers taught for understanding and meaning rather than memorization and when they connected the material to students' experiences, their students consistently outperformed students in more conventional classrooms on advanced skills and did as well as or better on traditional tests.

Studies of mathematics in grades 1, 2, and 8 offer further evidence that instruction consistent with some of these standards benefits students on conventional measures of achievement (Carpenter and others, 1989; Cobb and others, 1991; Silver and Lane, 1995). Similar findings have been reported for the teaching of reading in grades 1, 2, and 3 (Tharp, 1982) and of social studies in high school (Levin, Newmann, and Oliver, 1969).

Finally, students in the SRS schools demonstrating the highest levels of authentic pedagogy performed as well as or better than other comparable students in terms of standardized test scores. Our research suggests that students who think carefully about subjects, study them in depth, and connect them to their personal experiences are more likely to remember the facts and definitions called for on conventional tests. Support for authentic achievement also can be found in the changing content of conventional tests themselves, which increasingly include more items requiring higher-order thinking, depth of understanding, and elaborated written communication.

Some critics believe that focusing on authentic student achievement means that important content will be eliminated from the curriculum in mathematics, history, literature, and science. This assumption is unwarranted because the standards are completely silent on the particular content that ought to be taught. The selection of content is a matter of continuing revision and dispute among educators and the public. From our point of view, whatever the particular content of the curriculum, it should be addressed in ways that stress the qualities essential to authentic intellectual achievement.

Finally, some critics of authentic learning argue that it seems to require a much less structured education, with less emphasis on right answers, more tolerance of ambiguity, and the need for students to take more independent responsibility for learning. They ask whether students who come from cultural backgrounds that emphasize more strict obedience to authority and less independence of action during youth will be at a disadvantage in authentic classrooms.

Authentic achievement does, of course, aim to nurture independent, critical thinking in students, and it intends to help students appreciate, live with, and experience the joy of working with cognitively complex problems. We have found no evidence, though, that students from educationally disadvantaged backgrounds are less capable or less interested than other students in these kinds of challenges, nor that the standards discriminate against any cultural group. Testimony from teachers and other data support our finding that students from all backgrounds are more engaged in cognitively challenging academic work than in conventional low-level work. Supporting evidence includes studies of elementary schools serving low-income students, reports of special projects for students at risk of dropping out of school, and the Center's study of student engagement in twenty-four restructured elementary, middle, and high schools (Knapp, Shields, and Turnbull, 1992; Marks, 1995; Wehlage and others, 1989; Wigginton, 1985).

A careful reading of the standards for authenticity will show that they deliberately refrain from prescribing any particular teaching techniques. Teachers can be highly directive and structured or less prescriptive in the way they organize classroom activities and still meet standards for authentic instruction and assessment presented here. The standards neither dictate nor preclude the stereotypical open classroom implied in this challenge. In fact, the standards rely on teachers to craft their work to respond to the diversity that students bring to school.

Parental objections to new forms of pedagogy are often based more on concerns for proper classroom decorum, discipline, and awarding of grades than on the actual cognitive demands of schoolwork. But our framework, focusing only on intellectual standards, implies no challenge to, or contradiction of, family values, expectations, or cultural norms on these matters. Although we define the central purpose of school as promoting authentic achievement, we recognize that parents and the public also want schools to teach students to cooperate, compete, respect the rights of others, demonstrate personal responsibility, develop self-esteem, and learn other things as well, including specific occupational, musical, and athletic skills. As schools and communities debate the priorities of many worthwhile goals, we hope this book will help focus attention on authentic academic achievement.

## Summary and Implications Within the Standards Movement

Beginning with a vision of significant intellectual accomplishment, we presented specific standards with which to judge the intellectual quality of teachers' pedagogy and student performance. The standards elaborate three central criteria of authentic intellectual achievement: construction of knowledge, disciplined inquiry, and value beyond the classroom. Table 1.1 shows the relationships among the these criteria, the three domains to which they are applied, and the fourteen standards.[7] We believe this framework provides a useful way of addressing the problem of standards for schools.

The usefulness of the standards of intellectual quality lies in their adaptability to the particular context of American public education. In the United States, the absence of common standards for the intellectual quality of student achievement, along

**Table 1.1. Vision for Authentic Achievement, Authentic Pedagogy, and Authentic Student Performance.**

| | Authentic Pedagogy | | |
| Authentic Achievement | Authentic Assessment Tasks | Authentic Instruction | Authentic Student Performance |
| --- | --- | --- | --- |
| Construction of knowledge | Organization of information Consideration of alternatives | Higher-order thinking | Analysis |
| Disciplined inquiry | Content Process Elaborated written communication | Deep knowledge Substantive conversation | Disciplinary concepts Elaborated written communication |
| Value beyond school | Problem Audience | Connections to the world beyond the classroom | |

with autonomy at the district, school, and classroom level, has led to confusion, inconsistency, and in many cases tragically low expectations of students. To address this problem, national organizations, states, districts, individual schools, and teachers within schools have recently begun to articulate separate sets of standards for curriculum, assessment of student performance, and opportunity to learn. Although multiple efforts can produce a rich set of alternatives from which to choose, they can also yield a fragmented profusion of standards that confuse educators and the public. To date, the most serious shortcoming of these diverse efforts has been the lack of integration of standards for different subjects, grade levels, and arenas of practice (assessment, instruction, student performance). For example, when professional organizations representing subject matter disciplines (such as mathematics and history) develop separate standards, it becomes difficult for teachers to discuss schoolwide standards. In the absence of such dialogue, schools are unlikely to develop a unifying, common vision to guide staff. Balkanization of schools by departments and grade levels is a strong possibility.

In contrast, we believe that our standards of intellectual quality, because they cut across disciplines and grade levels, make it possible for schools to embrace a common vision of academic standards. Standards like these can be articulated in a fairly straightforward manner to become a universal currency of public and professional dialogue.[8] They constitute expectations for intellectual quality that teachers, students, and parents can share. If parents have a clear conception of the performance their children should be learning to demonstrate, a conception held in common by teachers across grades and subjects, then parents can interact more meaningfully with teachers about student performance. If students understand the standards, they will be able to talk with teachers and their parents about shared expectations for their performance. Such expectations would provide an avenue out of the game of guessing what the teacher wants. In short, these standards can take much of the mystery out of student evaluation. Attempts by state or federal authorities to establish standards for curriculum and assessment can provoke resistance by teachers, parents, and school officials at the local level who perceive the threat of an imposed oppressive uniformity that stifles the opportunity for local professional judgment and local political determination. Our standards can minimize such problems. They describe in depth the intellectual priority for schools, but they specify neither the specific content to be taught nor the instructional techniques to be used. In this way, they call for and define rigorous intellectual accomplishment, but invite teachers and local school authorities to exercise initiative and discretion in developing specific curriculum and instructional practice.

In the next chapter, we describe the extent to which pedagogy and student performance in the twenty-four schools met the standards of authentic intellectual quality.

## Notes

1. Newmann, Secada, and Wehlage (1995) present the full set of technical scoring rules for the standards, as well as suggestions for how teachers and administrators might use them to make restructuring more effective.

2. The conception of achievement proposed here is based on the work of Archbald and Newmann (1988), Berlak and others (1992), Raven (1992), Resnick (1987b), and Wiggins (1993).

3. We recognize that tasks calling for nonwritten performances or products can also provide impressive evidence of construction of knowledge, disciplined inquiry, and performance that has value beyond success in school (Armstrong, 1994; Herman, Aschbacher, and Winters, 1992). But our resources and expertise permitted scoring only students' written performance.

4. This task was taken from Coalition of Essential Schools (1992).

5. These represent only a limited view of the quality of classroom instruction, a view focused on authentic intellectual quality. A broader, more complete look at instruction would also include features such as orderly classroom atmosphere, student cooperation, and coherence among daily lessons that connect to a larger unit of study. As explained in Chapter Eight, we also recognize that high-quality student performance on authentic tasks demands consistent support for all students to master challenging work. The instructional climate should communicate high expectations for all and should cultivate, through both the teacher and peer behavior, enough trust and respect to reward serious effort. Qualities of social support are necessary to nurture authentic achievement, but since they are not uniquely tied to the concept of authentic intellectual quality, they were not included in our standards.

6. Authorities in mathematics and social studies participated in the development of standards for tasks, instruction, and student performance. Identical standards and scoring criteria for the two subjects were considered appropriate for assessment tasks and instruction, but assessing the quality of student performance required some different scoring criteria between the subjects.

7. The standards for authentic pedagogy are consistent with aspects of constructivist psychology that emphasize students as active constructors of meaning rather than as passive receptors of information. Constructivism itself, however, includes different interpretations (see Bruer, 1993; Brooks and Brooks, 1993; Wells and Chang-Wells, 1992; Marshall, 1992). Newmann, Marks, and Gamoran (1996) explain how our standards for authentic pedagogy reflect but also extend beyond constructivist perspectives by offering more explicit criteria for the intellectual quality of student work.

8. Although we applied the standards only to the subjects of mathematics and social studies, we believe they can be adapted to science, English, and language arts. It may be more difficult to apply them to subjects that depend less on abstract verbal understanding, such as music, art, physical education, or some applied technical fields.

# Chapter Two

# Does Authentic Pedagogy Increase Student Achievement?

*Helen M. Marks, Fred M. Newmann, Adam Gamoran*

Standards for authentic pedagogy pose a daunting challenge for teachers and schools. Meeting them would seem to require major changes in the knowledge, skills, and attitudes of most teachers. Other researchers who have examined efforts to change teaching in similar directions have found enormous difficulties, even among teachers interested in improving their practice.[1] The standards may appeal to reformers who think teaching should be much more challenging and interesting for students. But it is important to gather information about the extent to which this sort of teaching is possible and whether it actually assists student performance on authentic measures before recommending such standards for widespread adoption.

Researchers who have investigated the connection between teaching consistent with these standards and student achievement have found positive results, using both conventional and more authentic measures of achievement, but the studies have been limited, occurring primarily in lower elementary school in mathematics and language arts.[2] The SRS offered a more comprehensive investigation of the effects of authentic pedagogy on student achievement: Using a common set of standards across several elementary, middle, and high schools, SRS researchers assessed teaching and learning in mathematics and social studies.

We used the conception of authentic human achievement and the ensuing standards for the intellectual quality of teachers' practice and student performance to study the extent and effects of authentic pedagogy in restructuring schools. Although authentic pedagogy occurred less than we expected, we found that it contributed substantially to student learning. Since prior research in selected classrooms has indicated great difficulty in teaching toward authentic intellectual standards and since we have heard many people question the connection between authentic pedagogy and student learning, we explain our research on this issue in some detail.

## Central Research Questions and Methods

We concentrated on three central issues: the quality and variability of teaching and learning, the link between authentic pedagogy and student achievement, and equity in the distribution of authentic pedagogy and achievement for students of differing social and academic backgrounds. We addressed these issues through a number of questions.

### Research Questions

Regarding *quality and variability,* we asked: How evident are the standards of intellectual quality in teachers' instruction and assessment tasks and in the work students produce in response to the tasks? The quality of pedagogy depends mainly on individual teachers within schools, but do schools themselves differ in the extent to which they offer high-quality pedagogy in both mathematics and social studies? Is the kind of pedagogy we have described more easily delivered to younger rather than older students? We studied how much variation occurred between teachers, schools, grade levels, and subjects. We hoped to find high levels of pedagogy and student achievement in at least some schools.

To discover the *links to student achievement,* we asked: To what extent does the degree of authentic pedagogy in teachers' classes affect authentic student achievement? Without a strong connection between pedagogy and achievement, it would be difficult to make a case for pursuing the complex challenge of authentic pedagogy. In general, students' academic performance is influenced by their social and academic backgrounds. To deal with this problem, we used statistical controls that allowed us to estimate the link between pedagogy and achievement after taking into account the independent influences of gender, race, ethnicity, socioeconomic status, and prior achievement.

Regarding *equity*, we asked: When authentic pedagogy and achievement occur, how equitable is their distribution among students of differing social and academic backgrounds? In the United States material welfare is strongly related to educational achievement, and educational achievement has persistently depended on students' social background, that is, family income, race or ethnicity, and gender. These conditions contradict the democratic ideal of equal opportunity. Would implementing authentic standards exacerbate the problem of inequity? Or could authentic pedagogy be delivered equally and with equal benefit to students of all social backgrounds?

## Methods

In the twenty-four SRS elementary, middle, and high schools, we examined the relationship of authentic pedagogy to student achievement in about 130 classes, equally divided between mathematics and social studies.[3] Each of these classes received an authentic pedagogy score, ranging from 11 to 43, based on our observations of lessons and our scoring of the quality of the two assessment tasks that the teachers submitted to us. In response to the assessment tasks, over two thousand students in these classes produced written work. We examined the quality of their written performance, scored on a scale of 3 to 12, according to our standards, by experienced teachers in mathematics and social studies. We also gathered information on students' race, gender, socioeconomic status, and prior achievement scores based on tests composed of items from the NAEP in mathematics, reading, and a writing sample.

## Findings

To address each of the main research issues, we analyzed classroom observations, scores on assessment tasks, scores on students' written work, and information on students' background. We concentrated first on the distribution of authentic pedagogy and achievement among the SRS schools.

## Quality and Variability in Authentic Pedagogy and Achievement

At the time of their entry into the study, all the SRS schools had demonstrated clear progress in organizational restructuring and had shown some evidence to Center visitors of authentic practice in mathematics or social studies. Nevertheless, after collecting data systematically during one year in each school, we found that the SRS schools varied substantially in their success on the standards for authentic pedagogy. In some schools, our researchers found many examples of high-quality authentic practice in both mathematics and social studies, but in others very few. Table 2.1 indicates the overall levels we observed of authentic pedagogy and authentic student performance.

Even the most successful teachers and schools scored considerably below the highest levels of authenticity. The means for authentic pedagogy—by subject area, grade level, and overall—are lower than the midpoint of our index (27). These numbers indicate that even in restructured schools, pedagogy scores were far below the highest level of our standards, a finding consistent with the earlier reports that the promotion of authentic teaching is enormously difficult.

Regardless of the overall level of success on our standards, we found tremendous variation on authentic pedagogy within the observed range. As Figure 2.1 shows, both individual teachers and schools as a whole varied substantially relative to one another. Within the possible range of 11 to 43, the most successful teacher scored 33.5 and the least successful 12.5. Because teachers within schools varied considerably on authentic pedagogy, not many schools achieved high average scores. Based on the sum of a school's average mathematics and social studies pedagogy scores, the most successful school scored 54.7 and the least successful scored 33.3, out of a possible range for total authentic pedagogy of 22 to 86.

Overall, about 60 percent of the total variability in classroom scores on authentic pedagogy is due to differences among classrooms within schools, and about 40 percent of the variability

**Table 2.1. Levels of Authentic Pedagogy and Student Authentic Academic Achievement, by Grade and Subject.**

| | Elementary | | Middle | | High | | Total | |
|---|---|---|---|---|---|---|---|---|
| | Pedagogy[a] | Performance[b] | Pedagogy | Performance | Pedagogy | Performance | Pedagogy | Performance |
| **Math** | | | | | | | | |
| $\overline{X}$ | 22.5 | 6.0 | 20.7 | 6.2 | 20.3 | 6.0 | 21.2 | 6.1 |
| S.D. | 5.7 | 1.7 | 4.8 | 1.4 | 5.0 | 1.8 | 5.2 | 1.6 |
| N | 22 | 437 | 21 | 385 | 21 | 294 | 64 | 1116 |
| **Social studies** | | | | | | | | |
| $\overline{X}$ | 22.0 | 6.1 | 22.2 | 7.3 | 22.4 | 6.9 | 22.2 | 6.7 |
| S.D. | 5.1 | 1.9 | 4.1 | 1.9 | 4.0 | 2.1 | 4.4 | 2.0 |
| N | 24 | 531 | 20 | 403 | 23 | 348 | 67 | 1282 |
| **Total** | | | | | | | | |
| $\overline{X}$ | 22.2 | 6.1 | 21.4 | 6.7 | 21.4 | 6.5 | 21.7 | 6.4 |
| S.D. | 5.3 | 1.8 | 4.5 | 1.8 | 4.6 | 2.0 | 4.8 | 1.9 |
| N | 46 | 968 | 41 | 788 | 44 | 642 | 131 | 2398 |

| All Schools | Pedagogy[c] | Performance[d] |
|---|---|---|
| $\overline{X}$ | 21.4 | 6.3 |
| Min, Max | 16.7, 27.3 | 4.5, 8.0 |
| S.D. | 3.0 | .91 |
| N | 23 | 23 |

[a]Class scores.

[b]Student scores.

[c]Class scores averaged for each school, mathematics and social studies combined.

[d]Student scores for each school, mathematics and social studies combined.

### Figure 2.1.  Variability in Authentic Pedagogy Within the SRS Schools.

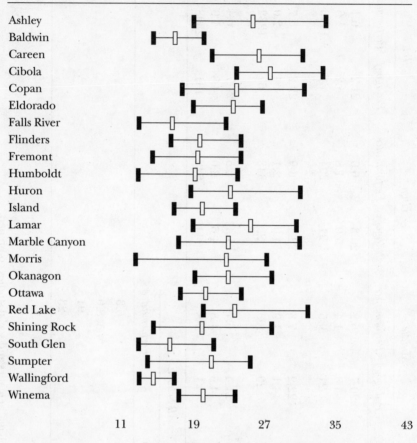

Range of Teachers' Authentic Pedagogy Scores

Key:

▌ Lowest and highest teacher score on authentic pedagogy

▯ School mean authentic pedagogy

reflects differences among school averages.[4] Across the three grade levels in mathematics and social studies, levels of authentic pedagogy were similar.

These averages are useful as indicators, but they also have their limitations. Copan Middle, for example, ranked close to the top on authentic pedagogy due to its exceptionally high scores in social studies, but the mathematics scores at Copan were very low. Ashley Elementary also ranked high on pedagogy but on the strength of mathematics scores alone; the social studies scores were relatively low. Thus although we found no major differences between subjects, on average, in some schools one subject clearly exceeded the other in pedagogical quality.

What are the implications of these numbers? If our standards of intellectual quality are appropriate goals, then there is good news and bad news. The good news is that some teachers and schools have been reasonably successful, signaling hope that authentic pedagogy is achievable. The bad news is that overall levels of authentic pedagogy remain low according to these standards, even in highly restructured schools, and some teachers and schools have barely begun the journey toward authentic pedagogy.

Similarly, we found considerable variation in student performance. In both mathematics and social studies at all three grade levels, student performance was well below the midpoint (7.5) of the range between the lowest (3) and highest (12) possible scores (see Table 2.1). The most successful student in high school mathematics scored 11, for example; the least successful, 3. In middle school social studies, the most successful student scored 9, while the least successful scored 4.[5]

Most of the variability in student achievement occurred within classes (53 percent), but variability among classes accounted for 36 percent, and variability among schools accounted for 11 percent of the total variance in students' authentic academic performance.[6] What causes this variation? To understand why achievement varies within classes, we need to consider student characteristics, such as prior test scores, social background, and gender. (We explore this issue under the equity question later in this chapter and further in Chapter Nine.) To understand achievement differences between classes, we focus on differences in the way classes are taught and ask whether class differences in authentic pedagogy help explain why average authentic achievement is higher in some classes than in others.

## Links Between Authentic Pedagogy and Authentic Student Achievement

Why worry about quality and variability in authentic pedagogy unless it has consequences for student learning? Only if authentic pedagogy actually improves student performance does the variability we found have significant implications. High ratings on these standards would then assure teachers and schools that their efforts are well placed. Less successful teachers and schools could profit by directing their work toward standards like these.

Combining the results for students in mathematics and social studies, our analysis confirmed the positive effect of authentic pedagogy on student performance. After taking into account the effects on academic performance attributable to students' social background (gender, race, ethnicity, socioeconomic status) and academic background (NAEP achievement), authentic pedagogy boosts the academic performance of students at all three grade levels in both mathematics and social studies.[7] Table 2.2 contains the results of the analysis.

Comparisons of the link between pedagogy and performance for each subject across grade levels as well as separately for each subject within each grade level produced virtually identical results.[8] The results of these separate analyses reinforce the strength of the finding. Despite wide disparity in grade level, subject, and school context of these analyses, the consistent results underscore the effectiveness of authentic pedagogy in producing high-quality student achievement.

How consequential are differences in pedagogical quality for the average student (that is, a student of average socioeconomic status who scored at the mean on NAEP achievement)? In a class with average pedagogy, the average white male student would score 6.1 on our scale of 3 to 12. By comparison, that student would score 5.4 in the low-pedagogy class, and the same student would score 6.8 in the class with high pedagogy.[9] Although these increments in the raw test score may seem small relative to the absolute scale of 3 to 12 points,

### Table 2.2. Relationship of Authentic Pedagogy to Authentic Academic Performance, Mathematics and Social Studies Combined.

| Variables | Dependent Variable: Authentic Academic Peformance[a] |
|---|---|
| Intercept[b] | −.07 |
| Female | .10** |
| African American | −.16* |
| Hispanic | −.10 |
| Socioeconomic status | .05 |
| NAEP achievement | .27*** |
| | |
| Class average NAEP achievement | −.01 |
| Class authentic pedagogy | .37*** |
| NAEP Achievement-by-Authentic Pedagogy[c] | .08** |
| | |
| Percentage of between-class variance explained | |
| In average authentic academic performance | 34.7% |
| In effects of NAEP achievement on authentic academic performance | 28.5% |

[a]Estimates from a three-level multilevel model computed with the Hierarchical Linear Modeling program (Bryk and Raudenbush, 1992). Level 3 (school level) has no predictors. Cases with missing values are omitted from the analysis. The final analytic sample contains 2,124 students in 125 classrooms in 23 schools.

[b]All continuous variables are standardized. Female, African American, and Hispanic are indicator variables, coded 1 = yes, 0 = no. The coefficients for the indicator variables represent the increment added to the intercept, that is, average authentic academic performance, for female gender, African American race, and Hispanic ethnicity. The coefficients for the continuous variables represent the increment added to the intercept for a standard deviation increase in the independent variable.

[c]Multilevel interaction of student NAEP achievement by class authentic pedagogy.

*$p \leq .05$

**$p \leq .01$

***$p \leq .001$

they reflect substantial improvements in these students' rankings relative to their peers on authentic academic performance. Regardless of race or gender, an average student would increase from about the thirtieth percentile to about the sixtieth percentile as a result of experiencing high versus low authentic pedagogy.

Figure 2.2 shows the performance consequences of low, medium, and high pedagogy for comparable female and nonwhite students. Authentic pedagogy, as the figure illustrates, makes a major contribution to students' academic performance. Although our focus has been on the effect of pedagogical quality on authentic measures of student achievement, researchers have produced evidence that authentic instructional practice also contributes to student achievement on more conventional tests.[10]

Our statistical findings have shown that the overall achievement benefits of authentic pedagogy are considerable. But what do these findings mean in terms of teachers' classroom practice and the nature of student writing? In the next section we visit four classrooms (two elementary social studies and two high school mathematics) to examine the consequences of specific examples of teachers' pedagogy and student performance. We compare classes in each subject area that received high and low rankings on our standards for pedagogy.

## High and Low Pedagogy: Contrasting Examples

Examples of student work in social studies and mathematics illustrate the importance of authentic pedagogy to student achievement.

### Social Studies

Two students in different SRS elementary schools produced the following examples of student work in response to assessment tasks assigned by their teachers. Despite scoring at identical levels, close to the mean on the NAEP achievement, the two students differed substantially in their scores on the SRS measure of authentic academic performance.

*Example A.* The task for a class of fifth graders required them to copy a set of questions about famous explorers from a work sheet and to add the correct short-answer responses in the appropriate spots. The class spent thirty minutes on this exercise, which was

**Figure 2.2. Authentic Academic Performance for Average Students, by Level of Authentic Pedagogy.**

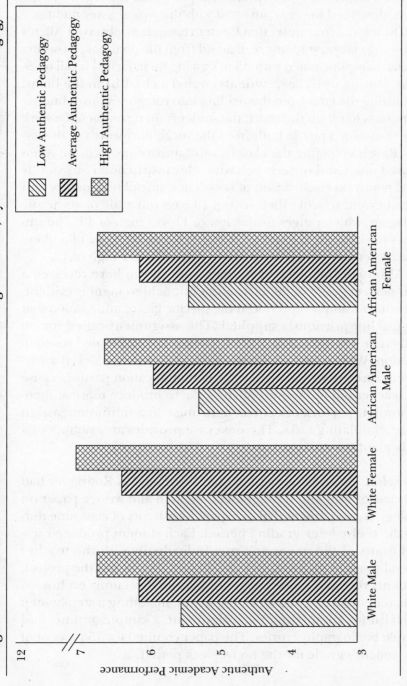

*Note:* An average student is one with mean score on the NAEP Achievement and mean socioeconomic status in the SRS sample. Authentic academic performance scores include students in both mathematics and social studies. Low authentic pedagogy is one standard deviation below mean pedagogy; high is one standard deviation above mean pedagogy in SRS sample classes.

part of a larger unit on exploration and which the teacher, Mrs. Allen, described as very consistent with the typical assessment.

During the four times that Center researchers observed Allen's hour-long classes, students read aloud from the textbook, a routine occasionally punctuated with Allen's asking them factual recall questions. During one class, students copied a chart from the board organizing the facts from the reading into categories. After finding more facts to fill up the chart, the students then completed a work sheet crossword puzzle built from the vocabulary words of the lesson. Rarely engaging the class in substantive conversation, Allen praised quiet and orderly behavior. Her instruction consistently rated poorly on construction of knowledge, disciplined inquiry, and value beyond school. Allen scored 13.5 on our scale of authentic pedagogy, which ranges from a low of 11 to a high of 43. The student's work shown in Exhibit 2.1 scored 3.5 on our scale of authentic achievement, which ranges from a low of 3 to a high of 12.

Although the piece of student work shown here received a near-perfect grade of 99, little authentic achievement is evident. The student simply reproduced the specific bits of information that the teacher previously supplied. The assignment called for no analysis or interpretation of these facts or any elaborated communication. We can assume this student's performance lacked analysis, interpretation, and elaborated communication partly because the teacher did not require such work. To produce more authentic student performance, teachers must, at a minimum, assign more stimulating tasks. The next case provides an example of a high-quality assessment task.

*Example B.*  As an assessment of their learning, Ms. Rodriguez had her class of fifth and sixth graders research and write a paper on ecology, an assignment that occupied forty hours of class time during the twelve-week grading period. Each student produced several drafts of the paper and met individually with the teacher several times to discuss the drafts. Before they began the project, students received eleven pages of written directions on how to research, organize, and write the paper, including a step-by-step checklist for completing the assignment, a sample outline, and sample bibliography entries. The paper counted for 75 percent of the student's grade for the twelve-week period.

**Exhibit 2.1. Student Work from a Low-Authentic-Pedagogy Class in Social Studies.**

---

*Sd p177 (1-10)*

99/A Super!

① Prince Henry encouraged navigation.

② An important instrument for sea captains was a compass.

③ After Columbus there were many Europeans expeditions to exlpore the Americas.

④ The Aztec and Inca civilizations were destroyed by conquistadors

⑤ A legend helped Cortes conquer the Aztecs.

⑥ After Columbus, Europeans started coming to the Americas to live in colonies.

⑦ Europeans who came to the new world included missionaries.

⑧ Several explorers searched for a northwest passage.

The student whose work is excerpted in Exhibit 2.2 submitted seven pages of text, including an introduction to the topic she chose (sea turtles), an overview of issues to be discussed in the paper, detailed information on sea turtle biology drawn from several sources, and information on the hazards that sea turtles face in Costa Rica. The section entitled "What you can do to help" provided a telephone number to call for more information and advice on how to write to the U.S. government to push for more protection of turtles.

At the beginning of Rodriguez's social studies classes (usually ninety minutes in length), students often read silently for ten or

**Exhibit 2.2.  Student Work from a High-Authentic-Pedagogy Class in Social Studies.**

---

The sea turtles are killed for meat and leather, their eggs are taken for food. Their nesting sites are destroyed by man, so they can develop buildings and other places to visit. On some of the beaches they offer boat rides. The boats are located on the sand when they are not being used. The owners are not aware that the boats are resting on top of the sea turtle eggs and killing them.

The sea turtles are classified under two families. The Leatherback and the Regular Sea turtles. The Leatherback Sea Turtles are the largest of the two.

There are alot of unanswered questions today relating to the sea turtles. Despite the explosion of sea turtle research, scientist are frustrated. One of the scientist was quoted saying "I don't know any branch of science where we have applied so much effort and learned so little", "We won't know where each species grows to maturity, or how long it takes them to grow up, or what the survival rates are".

Some of the answers can now be researched because the U.S. and 115 other countries have banned import or export of sea turtle products. By spreading the word and joining support groups, we can also slow down the process.

We can all help by keeping the beaches free of trash and pollution. We can make suggestions to the beach control unit to keep pleasure boating down and only allow it in certain areas where hatching does not take place. Sea turtles have a one percent chance of living to maturity, unlike you or I. We have a greater chance of living a very long life.

fifteen minutes. Later the students typically engage in group discussions based on the reading, and they work on written reports or projects, which Rodriguez displays in the classroom. She tries to keep the students thinking, prodding them, as the Center observer noted, "to be creative, to 'stretch' themselves further."

During a class on the Netsilik people, Rodriguez used a series of questions to orchestrate a discussion: "Why were the Netsilik called the seal people?" "What have you learned about plants in the tundra?" "Why would the Netsilik be so dependent on seals?" "Why did the Netsilik place a higher priority on men than on women?" All the questions involved students in interpretation of and generalization from data; adequate answers could not be gleaned simply from recall of the text.

Rodriguez scored 30.3 on our authentic pedagogy scale of 11 to 43. The student's work scored a 10 on our scale of 3 to 12.

### Mathematics

The mathematics examples are from grade 9 in one high school and grade 10 in another. Similar to the elementary social studies students whose work we have examined, these mathematics students scored at the same level and close to the mean on the NAEP mathematics achievement test. But these students scored at very different levels on the SRS measure of achievement, due largely to the different levels of pedagogy and especially to teachers' differential expectations for what the students should be able to accomplish.

*Example C.* At the end of a unit on angle measures in interconnected figures and geometric polygons, Mr. Hogan assigned students the unit test provided with the textbook. Although the eleventh-grade student whose work is shown in Exhibit 2.3 failed to exhibit mastery of the subject matter, even a perfect paper would represent a limited accomplishment: a demonstration of technical proficiency in calculating angles, apart from any evidence of the ability to apply this skill and to discuss the computations in a substantive manner.

The geometry class (ninety-five minutes in length) typically consisted of students' applying formulas to problems, such as finding the volume of a prism that Hogan drew on the chalkboard. "There are many ways to do this," he told the class—meaning, the

## Exhibit 2.3.  Student Work from a Low-Authentic-Pedagogy Class in Mathematics.

TEST

CHAP. 2
GEOMETRY      .50      50%

LET ∡1 = 50 , ∡12 = 70, ∡5 = 75, ∡19 = 35; FIND THE GIVEN ANGLES. (hint; use what you know about triangles, quadrilaterals, vertical, alternate interior, and corresponding angles)
ASSUME ALL LINES ARE STRAIGHT AND LINE l IS PARALLEL TO LINE m

1) ∡6 = 75-2

2) ∡7 = -2

3) ∡8 = -2

4) ∡9 = 75°

5) ∡15 = 105

6) ∡16 = -2

7) ∡17 = -2

8) ∡18 = -2

9) ∡21 = 35-2

10) ∡22 = 15

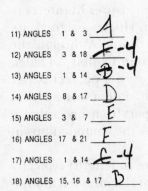

USING THE DRAWING ABOVE, MATCH THE THE GIVEN ANGLES TO THE BEST ANSWER ON THE RIGHT.

11) ANGLES   1 & 3     A

12) ANGLES   3 & 18    E-4

13) ANGLES   1 & 14    B-4

14) ANGLES   8 & 17    D

15) ANGLES   3 & 7     E

16) ANGLES   17 & 21   F

17) ANGLES   1 & 14    E-4

18) ANGLES   15, 16 & 17   B

A) COMPLEMENTARY ANGLES   90°

B) SUPPLEMENTARY ANGLES   180°

C) CORRESPONDING ANGLES

D) ALTERNATE INTERIOR ANGLES

E) VERTICAL ANGLES

F) NONE

Center observer noted, that there are many ways to do the calculation. He immediately said, "You can cancel out or you can multiply the tops and bottoms," and then demonstrated the calculations both ways in great detail. Emphasizing work sheets and drill, Hogan failed to pick up on students' questions as opportunities to dig deeper into the topic or to challenge students to devise and explain different approaches to finding volume.

The teacher scored 19 on our authentic pedagogy scale of 11 to 43. The student's work shown in Exhibit 2.3 scored 4 on a score of 3 to 12.

*Example D.* A ninth-grade student prepared an exhibition to demonstrate her understanding of concepts such as acceleration, velocity, and deceleration and her ability to apply graphing skills to quadratic and linear equations. She and her classmates in an interdisciplinary mathematics and science course spent the school year focusing on three essential questions: How do things move? What makes them move? How can we describe that motion? To provide students with a challenging project on which they could display their grasp of the subject matter, Ms. Enoa built the semester's work around the design of an amusement park ride.

As a field experience related to their class project, Enoa and her students had recently spent a day gathering data at Adventures Unlimited, an amusement park. Equipped with stopwatches and a meter to measure gravity, they traveled there by bus. During a debriefing of the trip, students applied concepts like inertia, centrifugal force, and centripetal force to both the bus and the amusement park rides. Then they critically reviewed their exhibitions to find problems.

When a student asked about the force factor in her exhibition, Enoa asked if anyone had ridden the Scream Machine at Adventures Unlimited and what force they read on their gravity meters when they reached the bottom. A student replied, "4 Gs," that is, four times the force of gravity. The class discussed this unlikely result.

During the class, the students graphed and discussed acceleration and deceleration problems. Drawing on their experiences and demonstrating with the resources at hand, Enoa pushed her students to think and deepen their knowledge with each new problem. According to the observer's report, "Students wrestled with time, distance, velocity, acceleration, deceleration, and the relationships among them for the entire two hour class." In a ten-page paper entitled, "Hold On—Here We Go," a student presented a narrative description of the ride she conceptualized and technical information to show the design was realistic. The paper, excerpted in Exhibit 2.4, explained aspects of acceleration (distance, time, force) and summarized and illustrated Newton's second law. The student briefly described the ride she designed in words (just one paragraph is provided here) and a sketch. In addition to explaining verbally her use of the formulas for acceleration and distance (excerpts provided here), she also supplied annotated diagrams and graphs. She then explained deceleration in comparable depth. The paper concludes with the student's discussion of the design, various choices she made in presenting her work, and some questions her project has not answered, such as the effect of the velocity on the ride's passengers.

The teacher scored 33 on our authentic pedagogy scale of 11 to 43. The student's work scored 11 on a scale of 3 to 12.

## Equitable Distribution of Pedagogy and Student Achievement

Disparity in achievement due to differences in socioeconomic status, race and ethnicity, and gender has long been a problem, and with increasing diversity in schools, the problem is as pressing as ever (Natriello, McDill, and Pallas, 1990). Educators may espouse a commitment to providing an intellectually challenging education to all students, but frequently schools fall short in delivering it. If more schools adopted the standards we have described, would pedagogy and achievement be distributed more equitably? Equitable schools promote authentic academic achievement by providing effective instruction to all students, regardless of their social and academic backgrounds. In such schools, all students, rich and poor, have the same access to authentic pedagogy. Ideally everyone, not just those who already achieve at high levels, should have the opportunity to excel.

Within the SRS schools, we found that students of various social backgrounds had equal access to authentic pedagogy.[11] However, students who started out with higher achievement as measured by NAEP-based tests were slightly more likely to receive authentic pedagogy. Because authentic pedagogy builds on what students know

## Exhibit 2.4. Student Work from a High-Authentic-Pedagogy Class in Mathematics.

I will explain what my ride is like. It is called SkyRide. It runs on a flat track that is elevated about 30 feet over the ground. It runs over a terrain of woods and trees. . . . Riders sit in strong nylon harnesses . . . my ride swings around, goes fast, . . . The ride is also very restful at times. . . .

Now I will provide numbers and characteristics for the ride. There will be two parts of data, one will be for acceleration and the other for deceleration. The following data is just for acceleration, . . . My ride is 2.5 minutes, or 150 seconds long. Now I must decide on a final velocity. 30 m/s. Now I need to get the distance and acceleration. I can get these two things with simple formulas:

Acceleration:

$$\frac{\wedge V}{\wedge T} = \text{Acceleration} \qquad d = Vit + 1\ AT2$$
$$\overline{\phantom{d}}\ 2$$

First I will figure out the acceleration of my ride.

$$\frac{\wedge V}{\wedge T} = \frac{30 \text{ m/s-0 m/s}}{150 \text{ sec.-0 sec.}} = \frac{30 \text{ m/s}}{150 \text{ sec.}} = .2 \text{ m/s/s}$$

Using this formula I figured out that the acceleration was .2 m/s/s.

$$D = Vit + 1\ AT2$$
$$\overline{\phantom{D}}\ 2$$

$$D = 0 \text{ sec. } (150 \text{ sec}) + 1\ (.2 \text{ m/s/s}) (150(20) =$$
$$\overline{\phantom{D}}\ 2$$

d = (.1) (22,500) In this equation the first part is cancelled out because the initial time is zero and anything times zero is zero.
D = 2 250 m The distance of my ride is 2,250 meters long.

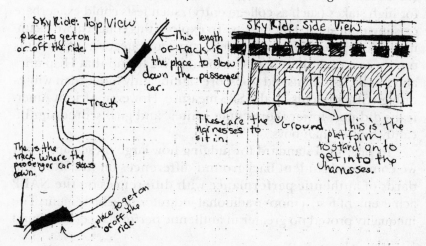

and can do, there may be some tendency for teachers to use it more extensively with higher-performing students. Also, although the restructured schools have substantially reduced their uses of ability grouping, most have not eliminated it, and this fact may have influenced the results.

Although authentic pedagogy is equally distributed among students with differing social backgrounds, it could still promote inequality by boosting the achievement of some students more than others. Critics frequently charge that schooling, traditional or innovative, serves advantaged students better than disadvantaged students (Quality Education for Minorities Project, 1990; Delpit, 1995). Does this charge apply to authentic pedagogy? We found that gender, race and ethnicity, and socioeconomic status (SES) exerted the same effects on performance in all classrooms, regardless of the level of authentic pedagogy. However, the effects of NAEP achievement scores on authentic academic achievement differed across classrooms, with authentic pedagogy adding a boost to students with higher NAEP scores. A low-achieving student who moved from a class that was low in authentic pedagogy to a class that was high would experience a significant gain in performance, but a high-achieving student making the same transfer would gain even more.

Some critics have expressed concern that tests of authentic student performance might highlight previously unrecognized areas of weakness among students from disadvantaged backgrounds (Feinberg, 1990; Wolf, Bixby, Glenn, and Gardner, 1991). If used for high stakes (such as college entry), such tests could exacerbate existing educational inequality. To explore this concern, we examined the degree of inequality among various categories of students on our test of authentic performance. We found that Hispanics and low-SES students did not score significantly lower than whites or high-SES students on the SRS measure. However, African Americans did post lower scores than whites, and girls scored significantly higher than boys.

To provide a standard for judging how large these gaps were, we compared student background differences on the SRS standards of authentic performance with differences on the NAEP achievement test, a more traditional indicator of achievement. The inequality proved no greater in authentic performance, and could quite possibly be less, than inequality on a traditional standardized test. Hence, although the assessment of authentic performance may not have eliminated inequalities, it does not seem to have exacerbated the problem. At least in this sample of restructuring schools, the use of these performance standards did not magnify the differences attributable to social background.

## Conclusions

In this study of about 130 classrooms in twenty-three restructuring public schools, equally divided among elementary, middle, and high schools, three main findings emerged. First, although some classrooms and schools were far more successful than others, the overall levels of authentic pedagogy observed, even in this sample of highly innovative schools, fell well below the highest levels on the proposed standards. This finding is consistent with prior research on the difficulty of strengthening intellectual rigor in American classrooms. In spite of considerable obstacles, however, some teachers and schools have made considerable progress toward such standards of quality. Their success demonstrates that it is possible for U.S. schools to offer teaching focused squarely on high standards of intellectual quality.

Second, authentic pedagogy does pay off in improved authentic academic performance for students at all grade levels and in both mathematics and social studies. Interpreting the cumulative significance of prior research on the link between authentic pedagogy and student achievement is problematic because previous studies have used disparate frameworks, and the most systematic investigations have concentrated largely on mathematics at the elementary level. By using a common, integrated set of standards to examine pedagogy at the three grade levels and in two subjects, this study adds significant empirical knowledge on this question.

Limitations in the design of the study may cast some doubt on the extent to which we have established a clear causal relationship. The teachers and students we studied were not aware of or consciously trying to achieve the specific standards of intellectual quality we used to describe their work. We have not shown that interventions that deliberately set out to use these standards will boost student performance. On the other hand, the robust relationship between authentic pedagogy and student performance suggests reasonable grounds for working toward more deliberate use of the standards.

Finally, we found that it is possible to deliver authentic instruction reasonably equitably and that its effect on students' academic achievement is reasonably equitable. At least in this sample of highly restructured schools, neither gender, race, ethnicity, nor socioeconomic status determined which students received high or low levels of authentic pedagogy. And neither gender, race, ethnicity, nor SES affected the impact of authentic pedagogy on authentic academic achievement, once students' prior NAEP achievement was taken into account. Although females performed better than males and whites better than African Americans on the measure of authentic academic performance, these disparities were no greater (and some were possibly less) than those commonly observed in conventional test performance.

Whether all schools can achieve the levels of equity observed in this special sample remains to be seen, but at least we have shown that authentic pedagogy can be distributed equitably to students from all social backgrounds, with reasonably equitable benefits. Such an "existence proof" is evidence to counteract pessimism and low expectations on the prospects for equity in education. Additional work is necessary to eliminate the disadvantage to African Americans and to males on this particular measure of authentic achievement and on conventional measures as well.

Of course, a low level of inequality is not the same as high-quality pedagogy for all students. Students of diverse backgrounds could be treated equally in classes with either low- or high-quality pedagogy. The routes for minimizing inequality and at the same time ensuring high quality are examined in Chapter Nine.

The main purpose of this analysis was to examine the extent to which pedagogy consistent with our vision for intellectual quality improved authentic student performance. As a whole, the findings support the pursuit of authentic pedagogy to help cultivate authentic academic performance for students. Findings on the generally low levels (and considerable within-school variability) of authentic pedagogy indicate that the task is enormously difficult, even in restructuring schools. Nonetheless, some schools did deliver high-quality pedagogy to their students. Why some restructuring schools were more successful than others and whether their approach to restructuring had any impact on their ability to deliver authentic pedagogy are addressed in succeeding chapters.

## Notes

1. Studies of teaching for understanding and constructivist teaching, while not using the specific standards we propose, found major difficulties in teachers' shifting from emphasis on knowledge transmission to complex thinking and in-depth inquiry (Ball, 1990; Cohen, 1990; Elmore, Peterson, and McCarthey, 1996; McCarthey and Peterson, 1993; Peterson, 1990a, 1990b; Prawat, 1992; Wiemers, 1990; Wilson, 1990).

2. For examples, see Carpenter and others (1989); Cobb and others (1991); Knapp, Shields, and Turnbull (1992); Silver and Lane (1995); and Tharp (1982). Lee, Smith, and Croninger (1995a, 1995b) found positive results for authentic teaching practice in mathematics and science in high schools.

3. Due to incomplete data from one middle school, statistical analyses include only twenty-three schools. Appendix A contains more detailed information on the sampling of schools, subjects, grade levels, classes, assessment tasks, and student performance; descriptions of data collection through observation, collection of teacher assessments, student work, interviews, surveys, and tests of prior academic achievement; and procedures for the scoring of lessons, assessment tasks, and student achievement. Further information dealing with variable construction, interrater reliability, and statistical analysis not reported in this book can be found in Newmann, Marks, and Gamoran (1996), the primary research report of this part of the SRS, and in a technical appendix (Marks, Gamoran, and Newmann, 1995).

4. Estimates of variance were computed using hierarchical linear modeling (Bryk and Raudenbush, 1992; Bryk, Raudenbush, and Congdon, 1994).

5. Social studies performance exceeded mathematics at the middle and high school levels. Across the three grade levels, mathematics performance was similar. In social studies, middle school performance was significantly higher than both elementary and high school performance, and high school performance was higher than elementary school performance.

6. The estimate of the variability in achievement among the SRS schools is comparable to findings in other studies. Jencks (1972), basing his estimate on Project Talent data, reported between-school variability in verbal achievement of about 11 percent. Coleman, Hoffer, and Kilgore

(1982), using the averaged achievement score from twelve separate High School and Beyond tests, estimated the between-school variability for public schools to be about 18 percent (compared with 11 percent for Catholic schools). Unlike the SRS estimate, which pertains to elementary, middle, and high schools, the Jencks and Coleman, Hoffer, and Kilgore estimates are for high school only.

7. Since student performance was scored according to expectations within each grade level, one would not necessarily expect the scores to increase from elementary to high school.

8. The design of the study did not allow the strongest possible test of the link between pedagogy and performance. An ideal test would compare the performance of students on a common, authentic task (or tasks) that asked for extended writing. The students would have been taught a common curriculum, but the authenticity of instruction and teachers' assessment tasks would have varied among the classrooms. In the SRS study, instruction and assessment tasks varied, but so did curriculum, and it was not feasible to administer a common instrument to measure student performance. Instead students' performances were measured using their responses to their teachers' assessment tasks. Students of teachers with low-scoring assessment tasks did not have the same opportunity to demonstrate high performance as students with teachers who assigned high-scoring assessment tasks. As might be expected, assessment tasks of lower quality were associated with lower student performance and also a narrower range of student performance than tasks of high quality. Hierarchical Linear Modeling regression analyses indicated that assessment task quality was the major contributor to the strong correlation between the composite pedagogy variable and student performance. Observed instructional quality alone had almost no effect in social studies; in mathematics, the effect was larger but still relatively small. This finding supports the maxim that what you test is what you get. As teachers' expectations for authentic performance increase, so will the quality of student performance. We examined the relationship of task, instruction, and performance in a way that could reduce the dependence of student performance on the quality of the task. With two samples of student performance (fall and spring), two assessment tasks (fall and spring), and four classroom observations (two fall, two spring), we divided the sample into two patterns that disconnected specific assessment tasks from student performance scores: fall performance, fall instruction, spring task; and spring performance, spring instruction, and fall task. These analyses (Marks, Gamoran, and Newmann, 1995) showed the same general pattern as indicated

in Table 2.2. But if the measure of authentic performance were based on a set of common tasks for all students, we suspect the link between pedagogy and performance would be reduced.

9. We defined an average student as one with a mean score on NAEP achievement and also mean socioeconomic status in the SRS sample. Low-pedagogy classes were defined as those that scored one standard deviation or more below the mean for all classes; high-pedagogy classes were one standard deviation or more above the mean.

10. Based on three waves of data from the National Educational Longitudinal Study of 1988 (NELS:88), mathematics and science achievement gains in both early and late high school were greater in schools where the instructional quality was more authentic (Lee, Smith, and Croninger, 1995a).

11. Levels of authentic pedagogy also were not significantly related to differences in schools' social composition. However, the number of schools was too small to permit a rigorous test of the relation between school social composition and authentic pedagogy.

# Part Two

# Portraits of Restructuring Schools

This part describes restructuring and how it came about in six schools, and it examines issues confronting the schools during the year of our visit. The stories show the variety of restructuring, what it meant to the schools' participants, and how local conditions influenced their approach. The portraits offer scenarios that people in other schools can use to interpret their own experiences. They also provide important background for understanding references to these schools in several later chapters in the book.

In each of the twenty-four schools, we observed dedicated teachers, administrators, and parents working in fascinating and courageous ways to improve learning for students. In Chapters Three through Five we feature two schools at each level (elementary, middle and high), and the introduction to each chapter outlines particular issues salient to that level.[1] The schools portrayed illustrate a variety of features of pedagogy, school structures, school culture, and issues salient in our analysis of all of the schools as a whole.

We refer to these writings as portraits rather than case studies because they represent a discretionary selection of material from far more extensive data. They are documentary but not definitive or exhaustive. As much as possible, we have allowed ideas and concerns of the schools' participants to shape the narratives. Rather than describing the schools according to a common set of headings (such as curriculum, governance, and school climate), we decided that the portraits would be most meaningful if they were organized according to topics unique to the school's context. At the same time, it should be clear that concerns central to the analytic framework of the research (for example, authentic pedagogy, equity, empowerment, community, and so forth as described in the Introduction) are represented in our constructions of each portrait.

The schools are portrayed in the present tense, but by using this style we do not intend to suggest that the conditions we witnessed have persisted. To the contrary, since our one-year periods of data collection from fall 1991 to spring 1994, many schools have experienced important changes, and policies in their districts and states have also changed.[2]

## Notes

1. The design of the study did not permit systematic analysis of restructuring effects due to level, but major differences in students' and teachers' experiences between levels could be expected. Thus individual schools' histories and conditions often seem more meaningful to compare when they are presented within the grade level.
2. Telephone interviews to fifteen of the twenty-four schools indicated that subsequent to our year of research at the school, several schools had experienced important changes in leadership, program, or external support (or more than one of these).

# Chapter Three

# Careen and Lamar Elementary Schools

*Kenneth B. Doane*

For many years, most observers of American education have accepted two related propositions: first, schools work better when stakeholders agree about what the school should do; second, agreement comes easier in elementary schools.[1] Our findings lend strength to the first proposition but raise questions with the second. As expected, we found that most SRS elementary schools fostered a strong sense of purpose within their school communities. In five of the eight schools, staff shared a focused vision of student learning. Six schools recruited and trained parent volunteers to work as tutors, student supervisors, and helpers in other roles that promoted the schools' goals. By contrast, we found learning-focused staff consensus in only three of sixteen middle and high schools, and much less evidence of parents' working to sustain school missions.[2]

The restructuring movement incorporated significant demands on the elementary schools.[3] That these schools generally had less complex structures than the secondary schools did not relieve them of difficulties in reaching agreement on goals and programs. Responsibility to translate higher expectations and new visions into practice fell primarily on teachers and principals, who also had to respond to local interests and traditions. As they worked on these immense tasks, staff in SRS elementary schools challenged many entrenched practices and assumptions; in many schools, staff seemed to find it easier to dismantle traditions than to specify what programs, structures, and practices would replace them. Even in schools where staff were able to agree on ideals, they often struggled to identify practices that all could accept, implement, and explain to parents and others outside the school.

Careen and Lamar elementaries, portrayed in this chapter, adopted somewhat different approaches to these problems, as befitted their unique contexts. Careen, a school of 320 students in the urban Southwest, was created to effect educational aims formulated by educators and business leaders in its school district. Lamar, a school of 385 students in a West Coast city, was conceived and pushed through a reluctant board of education by a group of parents. Careen staff conceived their mission more broadly but strived for greater uniformity of practice than staff at Lamar did. Neither school was immune from the need to translate its ambitious goals into standards for teaching and learning, nor did staff commitment insulate either school from conflict between staff members and among staff, parents, and external authorities. The portraits show how the two schools responded to these challenges.

## Careen Elementary School
### Prologue: "Walls of Poems"

> In February, our class became interested in poems. We began by memorizing poems and keeping a "poem in our pocket." We discussed various ways to share our poems with others—our first grade friends, other people in our school, our families and people in the world. We asked our families to share favorite poems with us and we displayed them on our classroom door. We shared poems on the back of our News of the Day pages. We recited our poems at Tuesday Lunchroom Theater and at the February PTA meeting.

> We had the idea of sharing our poems with the school by copying them and posting them around the school. We surveyed the school and selected poems appropriate for each area. We made a first draft in pencil, rewrote with markers, laminated the paper and then hung the poems. Our Guide To Our Poems book and this brochure were the next projects.

> Also, we noticed that the back of cereal boxes seemed boring to us. So we decided to create our idea of a "Poem On The Back" for the boxes. We have written to the cereal companies and are waiting to

hear their response to our ideas. Please see our Guide To Our Poems in the library for more information.

—From a pamphlet distributed by a first-grade class

## Learning for Living

Students and teachers at Careen Elementary pursue a vision of education that connects the work children do in classrooms to the real demands of adult society. This vision inspired the first-grade class who covered the school walls with the poems they were studying, then reached beyond those walls to propose that manufacturers print poems on the backs of cereal boxes. It moved fourth-grade students to launch a school newspaper and, with the advice of professionals from the city's daily newspaper, assign themselves specific editorial, production, and marketing roles. Seeing that their newsstand price, a quarter, was sufficient only to cover production costs, the children then prepared an itemized budget and applied to their journalist mentors for grant support. When the school needed new playground equipment, students did the research on various models and compared sizes, costs, and safety records. Students surveyed the school courtyard and plotted a garden. They cleared space in the basement and installed a museum of geology. At Careen projects such as these are called Applied Learning, and they form the core of restructuring.

### From Concept to Classroom

Careen is the product of a joint venture initiated in 1989 by its school district and the local chamber of commerce. Together the educators and businesspeople distilled a list of seven universal workplace aptitudes, such as reasoning and problem solving, writing, and computer literacy. Then, through surveys and interviews involving some twenty-five hundred people, they determined in what measures and combinations the aptitudes were required for success in the jobs local workers do. After two years, this research and some existing reform programs coalesced around the idea of Applied Learning.

The district superintendent chose Susan Heywood, a curriculum specialist with expertise in writing, to make Applied Learning a classroom reality. She was a logical choice because writing had been identified as a key workplace competency, but the superintendent may also have been betting that the force of Heywood's personality would expedite the project. In fact, Heywood and her staff soon determined that their charge—to develop model units and train teachers throughout the district to use and replicate them—did not go far enough.

Among the programs the district folded into its new initiative was a project that paired school administrators with business leaders to explore models for site-based management. The coordinator of that project, a skilled advocate well placed in the district hierarchy, helped to advance the idea of a new school in which the district's restructuring goals could be melded and tested. Her entreaties came to fruition in the fall of 1992, when Careen, a quaint ranch-style building some sixty years old and long since converted to office space, reopened as a development school for Applied Learning, to be governed collaboratively by teachers and parents.

### A Concept, Not a Method

Although Applied Learning seems to echo previous curriculum plans that tried to connect school to work through analysis of workplace activities, Careen staff do not conceive it as vocational education for the very young. Rather than focusing exclusively on preparing children for future employment, teachers insist that classroom projects challenge students to achieve something real right now. In this way, Applied Learning draws also on the progressive tradition associated with John Dewey, which holds that tasks of immediate interest and value are prerequisite to learning. Ultimately Applied Learning cannot be understood as any one thing: a scope and sequence chart, a succession of lesson plans, a constellation of techniques. The main artifact of Applied Learning is Careen itself, and the concept acquires different shades of meaning as the Careen staff develop it in various teaching contexts. In writing, for example, Applied Learning privileges exposition and analysis over narrative; nonetheless, Careen hosted a citywide conference of child creative writers because planning and staging it made a meaningful project for students.

Whatever kind of writing they do, students learn to use a process that includes prewriting, response and revision, editing, and publishing, through which teachers hope to instill in them a sense of ownership and responsibility for their work. Commenting on this approach to teaching writing, one teacher said, "The kind of teaching that you do in that environment is a facilitating role. The students are responsible for the work, they are shaping the work, and our responsibility is to guide that and to offer them the support they need when they come to a skill or something that they don't have. It's a challenging role."

How teachers enact their facilitating role depends on the teacher, the class, and the subject at hand. In this sense, Applied Learning can be conceived as a spectrum in which lessons and projects form bands of color that are distinct yet illuminated by a single source. The source in this conception is teachers' commitment to infuse students' work with real-world implications.

At one end of the Applied Learning spectrum, students deal with typical curriculum content, but their teacher encourages them to discover solutions independently. "I let them feel comfortable with letting them divide on the calculator before I even try to give them an algorithm," a fifth-grade teacher explained. "And the only reason I even gave them the algorithm was that they asked for it. I don't try to teach algorithms, for . . . multiplication, until many of them start asking me. A lot of students were adding up these long columns. In other words, I created a need for them to want this other tool."

At the other end of the spectrum, students address issues and problems in public life, as in the following project described by a first-grade teacher:

> This year we are doing a project on the ecology of [our state]. We divided the project into four areas, and each committee decided how it was going to present their area. It ended up with each group contributing to a mural that showed what the area looked like. They also presented facts about each ecological area, like what was special about the hill country, and why wetlands were important to all of us, and what conservation efforts are underway in each area. We did a lot of work with the [state] Nature Conservancy, which is buying land in each of these four areas—the wetlands, hill country,

mountains, and forests. . . . We corresponded with people in the Nature Conservancy and [they] came into the classroom.

The middle bands of the Applied Learning spectrum are the broadest. Here, costumed children deliver speeches and display mock artifacts to create a living museum of state history for an audience of parents and peers, and students search atlases for clues about the geography and climate of the setting in a novel they are reading. In these instances, students bring school knowledge to a real audience and use real-world resources to investigate classroom problems.

### Under the Microscope

Careen was created as a laboratory where Applied Learning practices would be refined for use throughout the district. Therefore district leaders confronted two tasks as they prepared to open the school in 1992: first, to assemble a group of teachers willing and prepared to work under the microscope of public interest; and second, to inform parents and their children about the new school. To some extent, the first task was already accomplished, since Heywood, her staff, and teacher volunteers had been working since 1991 to develop model projects. Many of Careen's original staff of eighteen teachers and two teacher-directors emerged from this preexisting pool. During the inaugural year, staff devoted Saturday and staff development time to Applied Learning workshops.

To publicize the new school, the district distributed flyers in existing elementary schools, produced radio announcements, and conducted more than twenty public meetings throughout the city. A two-stage lottery determines admissions to Careen. First priority goes to families in the surrounding neighborhood, who contribute about one-third of Careen's 320 students. The district then selects applicants from other neighborhoods according to a formula that reflects the racial and ethnic balance of the district as a whole (in all, about 25 percent of students are African American, 20 percent are Hispanic, and 55 percent are non-Hispanic Caucasian; 29 percent receive free or reduced-fee lunch). Over six hundred applicants entered the lottery for the first year's enrollment, and Careen opened at full capacity in fall 1992.

When Center researchers came on the scene a year later, some participants reported unhappily what they perceived as a diminishing African American presence in the school. In fact, African Americans did log a disproportionate share of withdrawals during 1992–93, and their enrollment in the kindergarten class of the following year fell off notably. Staff had expected that some families would have second thoughts about their innovative setting; nonetheless, they were anxious to interrogate the first year's numbers and to prevent them from becoming a trend.

Setting aside family mobility, transportation problems, and similar issues that were beyond their control, some parents and staff identified tensions between home and school cultures as a factor in African American withdrawals. "In the first year, we saw more discipline problems—we call them discipline problems, but I think they were misunderstandings," one teacher said. "I feel a lot of African American kids were not understood [because of] their culture, their dialect, or what they've learned at home. . . . We lost a lot of students who I really feel could have benefited from what we are doing had they stayed."

During the year of the Center's visits, staff elected to channel their concerns about particular groups of students into their ongoing work to develop an environment consistent with Applied Learning and appropriate for all students. Teachers adopted a positive discipline plan, which includes daily class meetings to clarify their expectations and encourage students to speak forthrightly about issues within school and without. They developed weekly music and play therapy groups, and set up mentoring programs through community agencies and a nearby university, the latter being exclusively for African American students. Most teachers attended district-sponsored staff development sessions on multicultural education.

As evidence of their success, staff point to the fact that withdrawals declined by half in the school's second year, both in general and among African American students. In spring 1994, having boosted their recruitment activities in selected neighborhoods, school leaders were pleased to report that African American children accounted for 37 percent of enrollment for the incoming kindergarten class. Staff recognize that to succeed as a development school and survive as a school of choice, Careen must show that its approach can work for a diverse student body.

## Works in Progress

In some ways, Careen's classrooms seem to match its conventional schoolhouse architecture. Teachers generally work alone, all day every day, with twenty-two (grades K–4) to thirty students (grade 5) of about the same age in each class. Aside from one or two computers and personal touches like area rugs and desk lamps, rooms are equipped with the usual shelves, tables, and storage cubbies. But tradition ends with these familiar schoolroom surroundings.

Among Careen's most obvious mold-breaking facets is its year-round schedule of four forty-five-day regular sessions interspersed by three fifteen-day intersessions (plus a traditional winter fortnight and a five-week summer vacation). During intersessions, teachers, parents, and community volunteers offer optional nine-day enrichment workshops in three daily ninety-minute sessions (a full day costs about ten dollars). During the spring 1994 intersession, for example, students chose from workshops including singing and song writing, quilt and puppet making, elementary Spanish, improvisational drama, computer graphics, and "The Great Ocean Rescue," an educational videodisc game. Additionally intersessions enable teachers to do remedial work with small groups of students, free of charge. Careen contracts for child care during the intersessions and charges a modest fee. Scholarships void or reduce intersession fees for some students. In the regular classroom, three of Careen's focal innovations also unfold over a course of time. Portfolio assessment, narrative reports, and classroom placements lasting two consecutive years reflect the Applied Learning vision of students' taking responsibility for their work under the informed guidance of their teachers. All three practices are works in progress, however, and teachers work continually to define and enrich them.

### First Folios

In Careen's first year, 1992–93, students assembled showcase portfolios of their work without explicit directions or criteria from their teachers on what to include. In so doing, teachers hoped, students would begin to reflect on their own learning processes and to develop pride in their work. Although the portfolios were not intended as evaluation instruments, students did present them to their families at an evening program. Many parents construed them as definitive summaries of students' progress, and in that light some were underwhelmed by what they saw. "Families were somewhat dismayed," a teacher recalled. "Rather than the portfolio resulting in a celebration, which was what we had envisioned, in some cases the families were concerned because they did not see any math."

In response to parents' concerns, the staff agreed to take a more active role in constructing the portfolios for 1993–94. If students neglected to include representative work from each of six categories—mathematics, science, social studies, language arts, personal and social development, and class projects—teachers selected work to supplement the children's choices and exchanged written rationales for their choices in conference with each student. In fact, teachers have always believed that specific criteria should be developed to guide students as they construct the portfolios. But Susan Heywood, their mentor, had impressed on teachers the importance of letting children judge their own work, so as to nurture their awareness of their own learning processes. Seeking a middle path, teachers hope to create explicit criteria that they, parents, and students can use to evaluate the portfolios but that also protect students' sense of ownership. Parents, they hope, will more readily accept the innovation when they know that teachers are taking a hand in constructing the portfolios as a record of achievement.

### Early Narratives

Careen eschews report cards with letter or number grades. Instead, twice a year teachers hold a conference with each child and his or her parents, and twice parents receive a written report in which teachers explain what their classes have been doing and what their child has learned and needs to learn.

A fifth-grade teacher, for example, wrote the following about her class as a whole: "Measuring and calculating both area and perimeter using geoboards, graph paper, and a variety of measurement tools was our focus in math. We also measured various parts of our body during our study of human body systems. In constructing models of bones and muscles, we discovered how the skeletal and muscular systems function. We have continued refining and internalizing our problem-solving skills."

Following this and two similar general paragraphs, the teacher reported on each child's progress in three arenas: language arts–social studies, mathematics-science, and "growth as a learner." In the last category, for example, the teacher wrote:

[Kenny] is able to:

- Allocate time and materials in order to meet deadlines

- Monitor and correct performance

- Engage intensely in tasks even when answers or solutions are not immediately apparent

- Act in an increasingly independent, self-directed manner

In order to improve, [Kenny] needs to:

- Work cooperatively with others and negotiate when necessary

- Remain open-minded

- Be accurate and seek accuracy

- Challenge the limits of knowledge and capabilities

As with portfolios, teachers found that their original plans for narrative reports had to be modified. In the first year teachers wrote four original narratives about each student, a task so demanding that it threatened to consume all their time to plan and prepare for teaching. They subsequently replaced two reports with parent-teacher-student conferences, and many teachers streamlined their reports, reducing the purely narrative portion from as much as three pages to three or four paragraphs. Although these reports are less elaborate than before, they still reflect the purposes and methods of Applied Learning. In a context where long-term cooperative projects are the norm, a criterion such as "meet deadlines" connotes an achievement more complex than handing in a work sheet when it is due.

A second problem with the reports is inconsistency between teachers and between grades. Third-grade teachers developed standards around curriculum units they all use, but most teachers wrote their own criteria using guidelines they developed as a whole staff. Teachers are influenced in their thinking about assessment by ideas they have encountered in their Applied Learning workshops—including the work of New Standards, a national performance assessment development project—so their criteria are similar. Nonetheless, parents wonder "exactly what our kids are learning" and if they are "learning all that a student at that level needs to know." It nettles teachers to lack ready answers to these questions; accordingly, in 1994 they began drafting explicit schoolwide standards.

### Extended Roles

Inconsistency among teachers actually is less of a concern at Careen than it might be at other schools, because students are expected to stay with each teacher for at least two years. Teachers see this as a way to deepen their understanding of each child, both developmentally and socially, and to strengthen cooperation among classmates. As of 1994, however, they had not completed a full two-year cycle and so were unable to assess its impact. Teaching groups of students for two consecutive years is one of several ways in which Careen staff extend their roles beyond those of conventional teachers. Another occurs on Friday mornings, when teachers lead student clubs, such as a group of student docents who greet visitors and conduct tours of the school. In some cases, club activities continue during intersessions.

Friday mornings were conceived by Careen's planners as a time for teachers to participate in Applied Learning workshops and for parents and community volunteers to organize clubs as enrichment for the students. In fact, most parents are unable to spare half a day every week, so most teachers spend the time with students, either leading a club or tutoring.

Applied Learning requires that teachers assume new roles to support students, but what supports the teachers? In their former, more traditional schools, they were leaders and innovators, and enjoyed the approbation of colleagues and parents. Now, charged with new roles and responsibilities, they may feel less secure. "One of the hardest things for teachers to do at this school is juggling all the priorities," a teacher explained. "When you are trying to change several things at once, [your] feeling of self-esteem falls dramatically. We were all good teachers before we came here, [but] we don't feel good now because we are struggling with so many difficult issues."

In their struggle teachers need help and they need guidance. For help they rely in part on parents, who are active participants in this school of choice. Guidance comes from the two teacher-directors and through an array of professional development activities. But there is no panacea. Like everything else, these support relationships are new, and participants must define them according to their unfolding experience.

### A Place for Parents

When their children enroll at Careen, parents sign a contract that requires them to do twenty hours of service for the school. (Actually, no clear policy exists about the consequences for parents who do not put in the hours, and about half did not in 1992–93). Parents serve as advisers on governance teams, lead Friday clubs, teach intersession workshops, staff the library, supervise field trips, and assist teachers with classroom activities and projects. In one class, a parent teaches music on Mondays, two others help with science experiments on Wednesdays, and a grandmother comes in on Fridays to teach Spanish. Along more conventional lines, parents raise funds and sponsor special events through a parent-teacher association (PTA).

Many Applied Learning projects rely on the support of adults. For example, some three hundred people, mostly parents, pitched in to build the playground students designed. Nonetheless, teachers sometimes respond cautiously to parents' enthusiasm. For example, parents may see planning, budgeting, and raising money for a class project as a way they can support Applied Learning, but teachers prefer to have students accomplish these tasks. After all, they might say, Applied Learning is about students doing things for themselves.

In a school that forcefully solicits their participation, parents may not know where their input begins to encroach on teachers' professional territory. At Careen, narrative reports seem to mark the border where teachers expect parents to defer. Writing a narrative is more challenging and less expeditious for teachers than calculating a letter grade, and they are frustrated when parents demand an explanation for every phrase and judgment. One teacher recalled the parent who came in to discuss a report she had written. For three hours, she said, "We went line by line and made comparisons with other reports. It would be a lot easier to pull an A out of the air."

### Not a Matter of Principal

Two members of the Careen staff are designated teacher-directors and function as supervisors in lieu of a principal. Both are experienced teachers and veterans of the original Applied Learning development sessions, and they can also be an important support and resource for teachers, as a teacher testified. "The thing that's really different here is the support I have," she said. "I have all the materials that I need, and if I don't have something, [the teacher-directors] will get it for me. . . . If I need help in teaching something and I don't know quite how to do it, I can always go over to the office and get someone in that field, or they will even come in to my room and say, 'OK, do you [want] me to do a lesson for you, to give you an idea of how to do it?'"

The teacher-directors serve also as in-house substitute teachers, helping to maintain some continuity for students when a teacher is ill or attending a professional workshop. Additionally, as the on-site supervisors the teacher-directors oversee Careen's unusual professional evaluation process, in which teachers assess themselves in the same way they assess students: through narratives and portfolios.

### "What We Need to Do"

Every summer most Careen teachers take part in Applied Learning institutes administered by Susan Heywood. Lasting three weeks in 1992 and 1993 and at least one week in later years, these sessions are the core of a staff development program that one teacher characterized as "overwhelming," suggesting both rich opportunities and strenuous demands. In addition to the summer sessions, teachers must participate in at least four Saturday in-service workshops during the year and write a report each spring that describes and evaluates a project they developed during the preceding year. They receive moderate district stipends for completing all three elements of the program. Having done at least one year of this training, four-teen Careen staff are district certified to lead Applied Learning workshops for teachers at other schools.

What occurs in the institute and the workshops is a mixture of reading, curriculum development, and professional dialogue, for which there is no standard agenda. One summer teachers spent a week at a local business studying how mathematics and language skills are used in the workplace. On another occasion they worked on grade-level standards for their narrative reports. Some discussions revolve around subject-specific concepts, such as the writing process, while others are philosophical and might be grounded in an essay by Dewey or Grant Wiggins.

Careen connects its teachers to resources outside Applied Learning too. In 1992–93, for example, the entire staff devoted five district early-dismissal days to training sessions in positive discipline. Through a corporate grant, six teachers attended the National Council of Teachers of Mathematics (NCTM) national and state conventions, and groups of staff have visited other restructuring schools in their home state and beyond. Additionally Careen staff maintain rich relationships with a nearby university: for example, they host some fifteen student-teachers every semester, help to teach university courses in early childhood education, take summer courses in instructional methods, and organize home tutoring classes for parents.

Teachers particularly cherish three voluntary study groups they organized around books and teaching materials the university donated. Groups of five to six staff members use the subject-specific books as the basis for reflective discussions held before and after school. These talks have inspired some teachers to exchange samples of their students' work and to observe lessons in each other's classrooms. "Activities like this are what we need to do," said one teacher. "[They're] what we thought Friday mornings would be."

## Hard Bargains

Staff may feel professionally enhanced by restructuring, but its advantages are offset by longer hours and heavier responsibility. Although they uphold Careen's mission without reservation, many teachers say the school administration has only partially fulfilled its end of the bargain. "Teachers [from other schools] ask us all the time about how hard we have to work," said one, "and we tell the truth: this is a good environment for kids but not for teachers."

Careen teachers are disappointed by what they describe as broken promises: that their daily hours would be similar to those of other teachers in the district, that they would have Friday mornings free for planning and professional enrichment, and that the state standardized tests would be waived. To an outsider, unmet expectations may seem inevitable at the outset of a new and innovative venture, but at Careen these disappointments were felt and expressed as personal misunderstandings. On the issue of work hours, for example, one teacher spoke plainly: "The problem here is a . . . trust problem. We were told that Applied Learning was something they wanted to replicate throughout the district; therefore, we had to make sure that we reduced the number of hours teachers here worked. During the first year we were told that we were spending too much time at our job, [which] wouldn't fly for most teachers at other schools, [so] we were to leave at four-thirty and not take a lot of work home. The juxtaposition of what we were told and the reality has caused me a lot of anxiety."

Although teachers show anguish over their working conditions, they focus mainly on two issues related to the organization and purpose of the school: decision making and mandatory assessment.

### Diffuse Decision Making

Careen employs an elaborate governance system that is meant to maximize participation for parents and staff, but teachers do not perceive it as an unqualified boon. Although teachers make most decisions on curriculum and general affairs, either alone or in various committees, they know their autonomy is bound by a framework set down and maintained by district authorities. At the school, these authorities are represented by the teacher-directors, the first people hired to staff Careen by a committee Susan Heywood chaired. They then shared her responsibility for hiring the remaining staff, and they remain her close associates. Two directors were hired so that each could teach half-time, but their teaching duties were curtailed after the first year, leaving Careen essentially with two building administrators. Although they do not attend every meeting, the directors try to coordinate decision making in the

school. "I don't see my role as a decision maker," said one director. "I have a leadership role, but it is as a facilitator. My role is to
empower other people."

Ensuring that decisions get made while allowing others to
make them is a challenging task for the directors and one that,
in the view of some teachers, easily degenerates from coordination
to control. Observing that the directors often are the originators
of topics for discussion, the main sources of information and
the framers of consensus (this despite the existence of a formal
agenda-setting process that includes teachers), teachers may conclude that decisions are predetermined. As one teacher put it,
"Sometimes the committee decision is not looking like . . . what
was wanted, [so] the teacher-directors kind of manipulate it so it
comes out the way they want it."

What is wanted, it seems to many teachers, are decisions that
conform to the plans Heywood conceived for Careen. Although
she has no official position at the school, Heywood, who ultimately
bears responsibility within the district for Careen's success as a
development site, may be the most influential decision maker of
all. She controls the agenda for teachers' workshops on Applied
Learning, for example, because the training is paid for by a private
grant she obtained. Although teachers praise the workshops, which
they consider a unique opportunity to expand their professional
knowledge, some lament what they perceive as discontinuity
between what they hear and do in training and the specific demands of their practice. For example, in several workshops teachers scored performance assessment items from New Standards.
Teachers saw value in this exercise because they also were working
on alternative assessments, but some said that having scored some
samples, they were eager to begin developing their own performance standards, ones specific to Applied Learning and to the
grade levels they teach. The majority of teachers seem to have
wanted to move on in this way, but their claims did not carry sufficient weight to alter the agenda. The sessions went off as planned,
and grade- and content-specific standards were taken up some
months later. Careen's professional development program is
presumably under the direction of the staff, but in this instance
site-based management did not free teachers' hands to steer their
own ship.

Careen's governance system consists of three teacher groups, referred to as cabinets, in which the members discuss curriculum and plan professional development activities in language arts, social studies, mathematics, and science; six standing teacher committees on topics such as portfolios, discipline, and budget, plus committees on matters such as hiring, all composed of volunteers; six design teams, comprising volunteer teachers and (mainly) parents, that oversee broad domains such as instruction, communications (newsletters, surveys, and bulletin boards), operations (scheduling, attendance, and transportation) and special events; and an advisory council, composed of one teacher and one parent from each design team, in which team actions are discussed and from which they are disseminated to the school community. Given Careen's small pool of participants, memberships on these bodies necessarily overlap. In theory, a hierarchy defines the relationships between these various bodies. The committees and cabinets are at the bottom and deal in the smallest matters, design teams resolve issues affecting the whole school, and the advisory council, atop the hierarchy, coordinates the whole process. In practice, each body seems to occupy its own sphere, and the many components would be described more accurately as communication groups than as decision-making bodies. For example, while the portfolio committee drafted the guidelines for involving teachers in choosing students' work, the instructional design team, which might be assumed to oversee such matters, was working out an unrelated schoolwide instructional theme.

Design teams do serve important purposes, though, as supports for teachers (one project for the instructional team was to develop a database of educational resources in the community) and as forums for parents and teachers to share ideas about Applied Learning and other aspects of school life. In these ways, Careen's governance system helps maintain a spirit of cooperation and shared commitment to the school and its mission.

### Multiple Answers

As a development school, Careen seeks to prove that Applied Learning works. According to the state, what works in education is what prepares children to succeed on its battery of standardized tests. Although these tests do not necessarily reflect the principles of Applied Learning or the workplace aptitudes it is designed to nurture in children, Careen is as accountable to them as any other school in the state.

The state administers tests in reading and mathematics to children in grades 3 through 8 and in writing to fourth graders. Historically these have been multiple-choice tests of basic skills and knowledge, but recent versions include some open-ended questions. Unfortunately for Careen, test scores at eighteen schools in its city in 1992–93 missed the state's minimum mark for competence, creating a public relations calamity for the district leadership. Careen's planners had hoped to win an exemption from the tests and may have passed on their optimism to prospective teachers, but in the end they decided not to venture the political risk. According to a teacher-director, the planners were told that a waiver for the state tests was the one dispensation they could not expect.

Most teachers seem reconciled to the tests, although only one said she expected that Applied Learning would produce high scores "after a few years." In 1994 teachers dedicated meetings of their mathematics and science cabinets to discussions of how Applied Learning could be squared with state objectives in the content areas. Tacking against the prevailing mood, however, several teachers argued that the tests were anathema to Applied Learning and ought to be replaced with more authentic assessments.

"Every national organization I know of has come out against standardized tests, and if we are truly going to be part of restructuring we have to be part of the anti-testing movement," one said. "How can we be part of New Standards and working to raise our [state test] scores? A lot of parents were upset about the aggregate test scores last year, but I can't imagine how you can judge the effectiveness of a new school that has taken kids from sixty schools in the district."

In fact, most of the pressure about test scores at Careen comes from a small number of concerned parents. Although the district will not waive the tests, given Careen's special role and the district's preoccupation with the low-scoring 18, Careen probably could get along with its current rating of "acceptable," which is based on tests administered before the school had been open even a year. But parents, disturbed by news of poor scores in the district and state threats to take over substandard schools, carried their worries to the new school. A special meeting on testing sponsored by the instructional design team in the fall of 1993 drew twenty-seven parents, for whose questions Careen staff had no definitive answers. When a parent asked whether Careen uses the district curriculum, for example, one staff member said yes unambiguously, and another replied that mathematics teachers follow the NCTM standards, which they used to develop the curriculum. And to a parent who worried that traditional content like spelling and mathematics facts is neglected, Susan Heywood could only say, "Applied Learning should be linked to basic skills."

Because parents choose Careen for their children, teachers reasonably assume that they support its innovative mission. But the issue of standardized testing illustrates a degree of uncertainty within the school community about the main standards for student learning. Staff bear a continual responsibility to explicate Careen's vision, but their task is complicated by their own need to question, test, and learn.

## Lamar Elementary School
### A Learning Environment

Within the play yard of a sprawling neighborhood school, a compact herd of small rectangular trailers appears to have found an oasis amid plotted fruit trees, cacti, vegetable gardens, and roses. This surprising blacktop habitat is the creation of Lamar Elementary, and its appearance reflects the structure and intent of the school's program. Each of the six trailers houses two teachers and sixty-four students drawn from two consecutive grades, who mix independent work and group projects in a learning environment known as the open classroom. The school garden facilitates a schoolwide study of human interaction with nature, where ecological concepts such as interdependence are the focus. Teaching pairs try to develop these concepts in lessons that allow students to make choices, manage time, and pursue their curiosities. In this way, staff hope that students will live what they learn.

## Interdependence

Each trailer contains two classrooms, one side with open space for group activities, the other arranged as a maze of cubicles where students do their deskwork. Neither the desks nor the teachers are assigned to individual students; both teachers are equally responsible for all students in their trailer. The teaching pairs set their own schedules, divide or share instructional tasks, and cooperate in every aspect of their professional lives. Teachers compared their partnerships to marriages, and most seemed to share one's belief that "I couldn't imagine teaching without a partner again."

Several teachers identified the key benefit of pairing as the chance to learn from a partner. One teacher said she regularly piloted lessons with her partner as the pupil. Another said of her partner, "Our strong points are not in the same [curriculum] areas, so when she is trying to explain something to me, she gets a lot out of the fact that I say, 'Aha!'"

Students also benefit from the trailer structure, teachers claim. As they progress through the school, most students spend at least one year with each teaching pair and two years with one of them. This weblike pattern sends strands of familiarity throughout the school; for example, a teacher in one of the younger trailers estimated that she maintains relationships close enough to include home visits with twenty students outside her current group.

Staff say the intimacy of their trailer groups enables them to devise activities in which responsibility for learning falls on the child. Lamar stands foursquare on the notion that an unrestrictive classroom stocked with engaging materials–the open model–provides the best medium for converting youthful curiosity into mature comprehension. According to this model, when students choose specific topics or projects, organize time and resources, and cooperate with others on complex tasks, they develop skills of self-regulation that equip them to identify key questions on a given topic, seek ideas and data that address the questions, and express new understandings.

Teachers guide and monitor students' progress, and they pinpoint instruction to suit needs as they arise. Their tasks demand deep knowledge of individual children and of the group as a whole, and Lamar's communal organization is designed to accelerate teachers' learning curves: four eyes on each child are sharper than two, two minds more encompassing than one. By the same logic, however, many teachers said that packing sixty-four students in each cozy trailer strains their capacity to see and act.

## Survival

As they come up through the trailers, Lamar students follow a core curriculum theme, Survival: Humans and Their Interaction with the Environment. The environment for children in the first- and second-grade trailer consists of Myself and My World; the curricular horizon expands as students grow until, in the trailer housing fifth and sixth graders, students encounter Planet Earth.

In the younger group, students trace life cycles by studying how various cultures mark the seasons with holiday rituals, examining the role of different generations in family and society, and looking after small animals—chickens, frogs, insects—that hatch and grow in their classrooms. Their projects require basic research skills of observation, journal keeping, measuring, and classifying.

Students in the older group begin their year with a week-long field trip to a regional outdoor education facility, and throughout the year they focus on human stewardship of nature. Following the outdoor week, students produce and sell an environmental wall calendar, in which each month contains information about a broad environmental topic such as recycling, population, or toxic waste. Proceeds go to support the next year's trip. In the spring, students culminate their studies at Lamar by composing elaborate research papers on specific topics they select, from "Environmental Consequences of the Persian Gulf War" to "Rain Forest Plants That Heal."

Lamar's open classroom structure and Survival theme give teachers specific, common ideals by which to guide their practices. Compare, for example, the credos of two teachers. Asked about her ideal lesson, one teacher said, "I guess it would be one in which I have given lots of background on a subject, [have] given them lots of material to do investigation, posed questions that I would want them to investigate, then I would ask them to report back to me, not necessarily a written report, on what they have learned. I don't want regurgitation of encyclopedia articles."

Another teacher spoke not of a specific lesson but of her over-arching aims. "The three most important things I try to do in teaching are, first, to get students to become independent, strong thinkers," she said. "Second is to become strong writers. Third, I feel the environmental issues in the world are absolutely pressing, and we have a very short time line to deal with these. Everything I do hits one of those goals."

Despite the similarities in their outlooks, teachers have found that the transition from one trailer to the next is not always seamless. In fact, the open classroom, with its emphasis on continuous adjustment to students' unique needs, may make it harder for staff to articulate a consistent strategy across subjects and grades. One teacher called communication between teaching pairs open but said "it's not to a point where we're satisfied."

Another teacher described an ad hoc process, where "when we see that there's a collective gap in [students'] understanding, we can go to [teachers of younger students] and say, 'This is what we're noticing. It would be really great if you could try to do this.' And they're really receptive to that. And we try, if we know something is done a certain way in the classroom before us, if there's a connection to be made, we'll make the connection."

The need to clarify schoolwide goals was pressing when Center researchers visited Lamar in 1993–94. The school had applied for and become a state-recognized charter school, which freed it from all but the most basic state mandates for five years. But the charter legislation required the staff to develop an assessment scheme that would document the effects of their program. In this charter, Lamar staff promised to create performance-oriented instruments and portfolios in consultation with a university-based evaluation center. Before they would be able to define a structure and benchmarks for these assessments, however, staff knew they had to define the curricular territory they wanted the assessments to cover. Toward that end, teachers agreed for the first time in Lamar's seventeen-year history to cover specific concepts within the Survival theme. Previously each teaching team had developed its portion of the theme independently and posted a flowchart of its year plan in the staff workroom for others to consult. The newly made charts document how the chosen ideas—interdependence, transformation, and selfhood—are treated at each level. The curriculum charts of the ideas are a first step, but staff recognize that these charts leave them well short of accountability to coherent, schoolwide achievement standards.

## Evolution

Unlike some other schools that seek charter status as a way to generate a sense of ownership and mission among staff and parents, Lamar is a tight community of long memory. According to its principal of thirteen years, Ronni Rosen, the main advantage of the charter is that it will eliminate her need to chase district waivers with tedious paperwork. Additionally, she said, "it gives us a mandate as a school to be open and attuned to the latest research and literature."

As a small, unique school of choice operating within a large public system, Lamar is well served by Rosen's keen grasp of the prevailing trends in policy and practice. But she does not operate alone. The successful charter application culminates a history of cooperation between staff and parents to realize their educational mission.

### Synergies

The Lamar story begins with a well-turned coincidence. In the mid-1970s a federal court ordered the city board of education to desegregate its schools. The district responded by soliciting proposals for magnet schools, which it hoped would pull diverse families together. Meanwhile a group of parents in one neighborhood school had become concerned about the direction of district policy toward direct instruction in basic skills, away from the inquiry-based curricula of the 1960s. Supported by teachers in their neighborhood school and by Rosen, who was then at a federally funded alternative school, the parents proposed a magnet school based on the open model. To entice district support, they stipulated that their school would structure its admissions lottery to reserve 60 percent of enrollment for students of color and that it would be located for easy access by those students and their families. The proposal succeeded, and Lamar opened in 1977. It has since migrated across the city to its site on the grounds of a neighborhood school, but it remains bound to its original promise of ethnic diversity. In 1992–93, 40 percent of Lamar's 320 students were non-Hispanic Caucasian, 25 percent were African American, 18 percent Hispanic, 14 percent Asian, and 3 percent other ethnic minority; 26 percent qualified for subsidized lunch. Moreover, the trailer curriculum flowcharts show that human diversity is an important branch of the Survival theme.

Parents remain the lifeblood of Lamar. Each trailer has a room parent who draws in classroom help and field trip chaperones, and a parent officer of the school governing council coordinates work on schoolwide projects such as the garden and the library trailer, for which parents volunteer in a yearly fall survey and most turn out at least once a year (Center researchers found that twenty-one of twenty-seven parents randomly selected for a telephone survey had participated in school events). Additionally parents and students evaluate school programs and policies in an annual spring survey.

Parents hold offices and a decisive majority on the governing council, which coordinates school policies, programs, and budgets through a network of subcommittees. The principal sits ex officio but cannot vote. Nonetheless she exerts a guiding influence on the council's monthly meetings by conferring weekly with a cabinet composed of the council president (a parent) and two teacher members, of whom one is the union steward. Within these formal arrangements, decision making is largely an informal—albeit lengthy—process of solving problems among comrades who agree on main principles. Even a decision as significant as the commitment to a charter was seen by most staff and parents as an expedient, not a change of course (to vote for the charter, teachers swallowed bitter concerns about their union affiliation, benefits, and other ties to the district). On matters such as scheduling and curriculum that directly affect their daily work lives, teachers often reach their own consensus before the governing council meets. Nothing is decided, however, until parents have spoken through the council and its subcommittees.

In its early years, Lamar relied heavily on parents to staff and underwrite some of its programs. Shriveling district budgets meant that all but the most central academic services were the school's to fund. Lamar's parents, incorporated as a nonprofit agency called Friends of Lamar, supported field trips and maintained part-time enrichment programs in art, physical education, computers, and the garden.

The school's fortunes blossomed in 1986 when their efforts attracted the attention of a major computer manufacturer (MCM). As MCM's partner in a software development project, Lamar received thirty custom desk-mounted computers in every trailer, and its teachers took home computers, printers, and modems. Lamar staff and MCM designers annually tested new classroom applications during six weeks of staff development supported by MCM. Teachers said these sessions diffused their technophobias, raised the intellectual level of their dialogue about learning, and invigorated their team spirit but did not alter their pedagogy.

According to MCM's liaison to Lamar, the company's intentions were consistent with Lamar's existing philosophy. "We were very interested in what kids could learn using tool-oriented software," he said. "Our goal was to look at some ideas—software ideas and hardware ideas—that would allow kids to create and construct meaning on their own."

On their own initiative, MCM's consultants financed an expansion of Lamar's enrichment programs. Paid employees replaced parent volunteers as part-time aides in the trailers and took art, physical education, and gardening from part to full time. Music, previously offered only to students in state-mandated classes for the gifted, became a schoolwide enrichment. When their partnership ended in 1993, MCM left Lamar with technological riches and a legacy of teacher expertise but also a drastic budget shortfall.

### Sustainability

Staff and parents agree on the value of expanded enrichments, but to keep them, the school now needs to raise as much as $85,000 to $165,000 per year for salaries and supplies, which places unprecedented strains on the community. Many parents cannot afford to contribute much money; others, and some teachers, believe that a public school should not ask parents to pay extra for academic services. Behind these issues stand others. For example, Lamar provides some day care and transportation to parents who otherwise would be unable to attend school functions, and although this broadens participation, it does not ensure that all parents feel that their presence is of equal value. Some participants believe that less affluent parents, feeling beholden to the school, stifle their questions and criticisms. Conversely some wonder whether affluent, educated parents are so active that their leadership lends privilege to their interests, such as the outsized (105 students) gifted program. These thorny issues resist simple solutions, but time and money are short.

In the past, staff and parents have relied on the savvy of Ronni Rosen to guide their deliberations. For example, when the state legislature was drafting its charter schools bill, Rosen asked the governing council to form a watchdog committee. As the law developed, Lamar kept pace with a draft proposal, so that when charters became available, it would be prepared to advance a plan specific enough to earn state approval (but not so specific as to preclude midcourse adjustments). At the decisive moment, Rosen pushed for consensus among the staff, and got it. The governing council finished the charter proposal, off it went, and Lamar became the first charter school in its city.

When Center researchers visited, the governing council had organized a committee to raise money from outside sources. "I want to break the school into marketable pieces and then go for funding for very specific target areas," said the chair of this committee. "For example, taking the garden program and going after environmental groups, commercial seed companies, local gardening companies. We first need a brochure that describes both the program and its success."

The fundraising dilemma was compounded by the need to make another singular decision: hiring a replacement for Rosen, who planned to retire after 1993–94. In February 1994 staff paid their own ways to a weekend retreat to clarify their vision of the leader Lamar needs. "The new person must understand learning and curriculum so thoroughly that when they walk in the classroom they can trust us," one teacher said. "For the most part, we create what we do, so they must be able to see the importance of this for children's learning even though it might not follow some familiar texts or guidelines. As we trust the kids to create, the principal must trust us."

A sign hangs on the play yard fence that encircles Lamar, just where it swings open onto Lamar's trailers, garden, and grounds. During the year of our visit, someone painted the word *Charter* on the sign, in red, between the stenciled black *Lamar* and *School.* The gesture was emblematic of Lamar's culture and history of adaptation, through which staff and parents have put ever-shifting circumstances to the service of their core mission. When Center researchers departed in 1994, Lamar faced three new challenges: to find new sources of support for its enrichment programs, to form an assessment scheme to fulfill its charter goals, and to find a new principal able to preserve and extend its traditions.

## Notes

1. On the importance of consensus and mission, see Bryk, Lee, and Holland (1993). On the relative ease of consensus on elementary education, see Firestone, Herriott, and Wilson (1987).

2. These judgments derive from coding of team reports as described in Appendix A.

3. California Department of Education (1992) cites demographic change, employers' demands for an adaptive workforce, and emergent models of human cognition as indicators of the need to restructure elementary schools in that state.

# Chapter Four

# Red Lake and Okanagon Middle Schools

*Kenneth B. Doane*

Long before school restructuring emerged as a national trend, proponents of the middle school movement had challenged many conventions of school organization. In a typical junior high school, they argued, the curriculum is too fragmented, the structure too rigid, and, most significant, the climate too dispassionate to meet the developmental needs of young adolescents. In short, they contended, junior high is too much like high school. In place of ability groups, single-subject departments, and other commonplace features of secondary schooling, middle school advocates envisioned closely knit learning groups; core curricula for all students; collaboration among educators, families, and civic organizations; and emphasis on connecting knowledge to experience. Since the early 1970s, middle schools have replaced junior highs as the dominant model for educating young adolescents in the United States.[1]

School restructuring offers a new framework in which junior high schools can adopt aspects of the middle school model, and existing middle schools can amend their practices in accordance with the ideals of their movement. Six SRS schools were designated middle schools and two were junior highs, but goals, structures, and programs varied across the entire sample. As a group, the eight schools tended toward the middle school model; in seven schools, for example, teachers worked as interdisciplinary teams, sharing students. But other features that would seem compatible with the middle school model were less evident in SRS middle-level schools; for example, in only two schools did students remain in the same homeroom or advisory for more than one year.[2]

One school portrayed in this chapter, Okanagon, an urban school on the West Coast with 1,400 students, opened in 1990 as a middle school. The other school, Red Lake, located in a small Northwestern city, had converted from a junior high school in the 1970s and in the late 1980s embarked on a new course of innovation through restructuring. Staff at both schools organized themselves in ways they hoped would occasion supportive relationships with their students, but their tactics differed. Okanagon staff assigned themselves in groups of seven to free-standing "families," and took joint responsibility for teaching, counseling, and general oversight of about 150 students. By contrast, staff at Red Lake allowed their eight hundred students to select most of their courses according to their personal interests, but they offered students individual guidance through permanent advisory placements. The portraits show that the two groups of educators, following divergent paths, encountered similar challenges, especially how to create a nurturing school community with respect for individual diversity while maintaining a coherent, rigorous educational program for all students.

## Red Lake Middle School
### Prologue: "Choosing and Producing"

Most of what we know about current events comes to us through the mass media; television, newspapers, and magazines inform us through words and images. It is not easy to make sense of the overwhelming amount of information we receive daily. During our first term, we will learn about mass media techniques and how to apply critical thinking, reading, and viewing skills to issues portrayed in the media. The term will conclude with a student project focusing on the electronic or print media.

For the second term, we will examine specific social movements such as the civil rights movement of the '60s, women's rights movement of the '70s, or the environmental movement of the '80s. We will learn about what motivated people to become involved in these causes and how the portrayal of events by the media influenced our perceptions of these issues. This term will end with students' choosing and producing a research project on a social issue of particular interest to them.

In our last term students will be expected to identify and learn about a local, state, national, or world issue. This choice should be one that will motivate the student to make a difference. Students will be empowered to make changes by influencing leaders, organizing groups to action, or educating the public. Service-learning and mentorship experiences will be tied to the project. The culmination of their social action efforts will be a public presentation of their involvement with this issue.

—From a course description in the Red Lake program guide

## A School of Choice

Choice is the first principle for restructuring at Red Lake Middle. Because its district maintains an open-enrollment policy, choice begins for most of Red Lake's eight hundred students with their decision to attend that school; one of every three students lives outside the neighborhood attendance area. For all students, choice includes the right to select classes and to participate fully in school governance. To teachers, choice brings uncommon liberty to shape curriculum and other programs, freedom that is matched by obligations to form and articulate goals of excellence. And for everyone involved—parents, students, and staff—it means working together to maintain a small society that reflects the best aspirations of its citizens. In short, at Red Lake, choice is the foundation of a democratic community.

### *"Teach to Your Passion"*

Prior to each of three twelve-week terms of their school year, Red Lake staff publish a docket of course descriptions, and students, constrained by very few credit requirements, select eight courses per term. Classes meet for seventy minutes twice weekly and half as long every Monday. Although most courses address one school subject, others are interdisciplinary and carry credit in more than one subject. In keeping with the staff's motto, "Teach to your passion," teachers and teaching teams develop their own courses, but their proposals undergo departmental review. Teachers know the budget will not sustain courses with marginal enrollments, so they shape their offerings to pique students' curiosity.

Staff attribute several benefits to basing the curriculum on choice. First, they believe it invigorates their practices, allowing them to teach what they enjoy, and stimulating them to revise their courses regularly so as to engage students more thoroughly in ever-better curricula. According to one teacher, "Kids come first. This is a student-centered school where we always ask, What do the students get out of it? What's in it for them?"

Second, staff contend that students learn to make responsible decisions only in the presence of real choices that have meaning in their lives, such as what to study and when. In fact, in essays written for this study, forty-one of forty-seven Red Lake students referred to aspects of autonomy among the "best things" about their school.[3] "You get to construct a schedule that fits your interests," wrote one eighth-grader. "You don't have just social studies, you can choose American history, European history, or learn about places like Thailand and Indonesia. . . . It shows our school really trusts us."

The range of courses within subjects varies. For example, social studies offers a broad palette of term-length courses (Youth and the Law, Elements of Geography, Japan) as well as several multi-term sequences (American Roots), whereas mathematics offers three loosely sequential general courses (Explorations, Applications, and Concepts), a prealgebra course (Transitions), Algebra, and Geometry, all a year in length.

Third, most staff believe that allowing students to choose courses according to their interests is more equitable than sorting and placing them by other characteristics, such as prior achievement or test scores, but this point is problematic. Some courses, particularly a small number conducted in French as part of a district language immersion program, consistently draw students with records of high achievement. Other courses seem to appeal mainly to students of one sex, and still others, mainly mathematics and science courses, carry prerequisites. These outcomes confront teachers with complex equity issues (which are treated in Chapter Nine). Where they see problems, some teachers move independently to correct them; for example, two teachers insist that their classes enroll equal numbers of boys and girls. But Red Lake's main effort to ensure that students are able to make informed and responsible choices is an advisory program that is built into the course selection procedure and maintained throughout the school year.

### The Triangle

Students confer at the start of each term with their parents and a staff adviser, and the three must agree to a schedule before the student may register. Every staff member serves as an adviser, responsible for a multiage group, referred to as a house, of about twenty-two students whom they follow through their careers at Red Lake. The school sets out three-year curriculum recommendations in its annual program guide, and the adviser's mission is to hold students' schedules in reasonable proximity to the recommendations. In some situations, courses are not so much chosen as negotiated.

"I take it real seriously, the triangle of adviser, parent, and student," a teacher said. "I explain to my advisees that nothing happens by way of scheduling and classes without us all agreeing. . . . So if a parent and a student say that he can take three PE [physical education courses] and I say no, then we have to go back to the drawing board and look at it. . . . [Likewise] if I want the student to do something, but the parent really is against it."

Advisers serve also as counselors, as conduits between home and school, and, if need be, as disciplinarians. They visit each incoming sixth grader's home as ambassador from the school. Later they may speak to other staff on the child's behalf, particularly for students in crisis whose appearance or behavior might not be understood without some awareness of the circumstances. Houses meet for half an hour three afternoons a week, when they might develop a group project, such as collecting recyclable materials around the school; confer about classwork, grades, or personal concerns; or compete with other houses in intramural athletics.

By cultivating vital relationships with and between their advisees, Red Lake staff hope to keep order by means of mutual concern rather than by top-down authority. Nonetheless, Red Lake does maintain a code of decorum, and staff advisers enforce one firm rule for curriculum: every student must enroll every year in one of the interdisciplinary courses called Connections.

### Connections

Connections courses are team-taught by two or more teachers over the span of a three-term year and are the only courses on Red Lake's schedule that meet daily. All other courses meet on alternate days. Sixth graders take a year-long course, Cultural Connections, that combines instruction in library research, study techniques, and writing, which staff see as necessary for an effective transition from elementary to middle school, with a multicultural social studies curriculum that stresses "an ethos of caring" and mutual respect. Older students choose their own Connections courses, which also tend to follow a full year's sequence.

Connections subjects vary, but every course must include language arts content; for example, the course described in the prologue to this portrait carries one credit per term in language arts and one in social studies. Other courses touch on aspects of science, art, computers, and human health. Overall, Connections courses seem about evenly divided between those organized around experiences, interests, and issues and those explicitly grounded in disciplinary subjects. For example, The Good, the Bad and the Ugly combines a survey of European history with readings in canonical literature and culminates in a class performance of a Shakespearean play. Mathematics teachers have participated in Connections, but according to one, although "you can make math relevant to the real world . . . I don't believe we've figured out how to teach math skills *and* challenge kids *and* integrate with other things."

In order to develop some consistency among Connections courses, teachers refer to a common learning skills document that contains sections on reading, writing, listening and speaking, thinking, research, and study. The descriptors in this document are general ("classes will spend time working on . . . giving and receiving feedback through reflection, paraphrasing and clarification"), and teachers admitted to being less than unanimous on their meanings. They negotiated constantly between the need to connect lessons to students' interests, styles, and prior understandings and the responsibility to ensure that all students acquire essential skills and knowledge. Red Lake staff do not claim to have resolved this perennial dilemma, but they are committed to addressing it through Connections.

Seventh- and eighth-grade Connections include community-based learning, in which students earn class credit for volunteer service. Seventh graders work at a local institution such as a community center or a museum. Eighth-graders meet with adult mentors who share their expertise in an area of each student's interest, regularly if possible, or as one-time events. One day, for example, a group of students visited four health service agencies to see what professionals were doing to prevent the further spread of AIDS. Students are supposed to develop a project related to the mentorship and present it in some way to an audience of peers, staff, and parents. The form and content of students' community-based learning varies from class to class. In the absence of a full-time coordinator (lost to budget cuts), some teachers find themselves relying on parents to make arrangements for their own children, and they worry that less affluent families are thereby at a disadvantage.

Even as they cope with its limitations, most Red Lake staff consider Connections an essential aspect of restructuring, mainly for its integrative role in students' learning, but also for what it adds to their professional lives. Most Connections teams share a daily seventy-minute planning period, an opportunity they relish to collaborate and trade expertise (they also meet in subject area departments). Red Lake does not offer teachers many extra resources or luxuries. More than thirty students pack most classes elbow to elbow, and teachers often must search for space to work during their planning hours. Including their house advisees, many teachers contact nearly two hundred students a week. Teams, they say, supply the confidence and intellectual energy that enables them to persist in challenging their students despite these hectic working conditions.

On the other hand, some teachers worry that teams may mitigate staff unity. In a system where teachers compete for enrollments, schoolwide goals and standards could suffer under a tyranny of self-interests. Red Lake tries to avoid this pitfall by distributing civil responsibility to all its participants. Teachers, students, parents, and administrators share power in a governance process that they hope will fulfill their collective purposes and mutual obligations.

### Decisions

Information and deliberative input seem to flow freely among the four main components of Red Lake's governance structure. The main body is the steering committee, consisting of eight teachers, two parents, two students, a classified staffer (such as a secretary or other member of the nonteaching staff), and the principal, who establish policies, allocate the general budget, hire new employees, and set the school calendar. Steering committee representatives form subcommittees with volunteer members from throughout the school, including committees on planning and counseling, curriculum, multicultural education, computer education, registration (on which parents are especially active), and special events. In their own meetings, the representatives seek consensus but in its absence will vote, a two-thirds majority being necessary to carry a proposition.

The same procedure applies in meetings of the staff (including classified personnel), who act as an executive committee of the whole, developing schoolwide programs, proposing new classes and generating most of the issues the steering committee confronts. The full staff can also veto steering committee decisions on school policy (although no one could recall an instance when the staff exercised this power), but the committee's word on budget and staffing is final. Meetings of the steering committee and of the staff are moderated on a rotating basis by a member of the steering committee chosen by lot; at times this is a student. Staff choose delegates to the steering committee by open election, though they try to select one member of every department and will assign a member to represent a department that lacks one. Together the staff and steering committee form the central decision-making apparatus for Red Lake.

Two ancillary bodies flank the steering committee and the full staff. The all-volunteer Parent Executive Council serves as a forum for discussion and as the school's chief fundraising unit. The council elects representatives to the steering committee, usually to an annual term, from a persistent membership of about fifteen volunteers. Other parents pitch in during special events but do not attend meetings regularly. Events include an annual magazine subscription sale and a dinner auction, which in 1992–93 combined to generate about $18,000 for the student government, $2,000 for house projects, and about $7,000 the council dispersed to teachers, teams, and the school at large.

Student Government is a credit-bearing class, open to any student, where lesson and meetings proceed according to parliamentary procedure, following a written agenda, with a member representing each house. Students consider policy issues such as how to control traffic in and out of the building during lunch and how to manage differences of political opinion between teachers and students. They also decide which of many project proposals they receive from teachers and houses to support with their portion of the magazine sale proceeds. Red Lake's principal, Jack Singer, delighted in describing how this works: "People who request funds from [the students] have to come and formally present their requests. It's real interesting to watch teachers go before kids to beg for money. It breaks down all barriers real fast!"

Participants in Student Government apply to serve on the steering committee for a term by submitting an essay to the teacher of the government course. Like parents, students bring issues to the steering committee through their house representatives. But in some ways students are even more thoroughly involved in running their school than their parents; for example, teachers may choose to be evaluated by students rather than administrators.

### Relationships

A model of Red Lake's governance structure would show arrows of information and consent moving in all directions among the various constituent bodies, but no chart could reveal the dynamic web of relationships that bind and support the community. Informal loyalties could subvert the democratic ideals represented by the governance model's arrows. Nonetheless, according to participants, decision making at Red Lake is genuinely shared, sometimes more widely than the model requires.

"In terms of influencing programs and policies, this school is exceptionally known for the fact that everybody gets involved in making decisions . . . [and] when you voice an opinion people really listen," a teacher reported. "I've seen staff meetings completely turned around by one person's plea if it's something that really makes sense. . . . So I think that all of us really have a lot of influence. . . . There really is a connection between parents, students, and teachers and other staff in making decisions."

Other evidence confirms that informal relationships complement the formal governance system and suggests that participants strive to ensure that everyone voices an opinion before decisions are made. For example, having come into possession of about $40,000 through a district payout to schools that exceeded their projected enrollments, the steering committee asked staff, students, and parents for ideas on how to use the money. The committee developed a budget based on these possibilities and gave top priority to the purchase of multiple telephone lines for every classroom, at a cost of about $15,000. But parent representatives predicted that their executive council might object to spending so much on noninstructional equipment, and they suggested that a staff member present the council with a rationale for the allocation. Technically the steering committee does not need the executive council's approval in order to act, but they willingly sought parents' advice and consent. Ultimately parents agreed that by saving teachers' time and improving communication between home and school, telephones and voice mail would support instruction, and they endorsed the steering committee's proposed budget. By restraining their authority to allow consultation by an important constituency, the steering committee affirmed Red Lake's commitment to participatory decision making. One indication of the strength of this commitment is what happened in another situation, when it appeared to be violated.

### Limits

In fall 1991 Jack Singer, entering the fourth year of his tenure as principal, suggested to the steering committee that the time was right to examine the implications of restructuring for curriculum and instruction. Two teachers and two parents volunteered to serve on a committee, and Singer recruited an additional four teachers and two students. So constituted, the committee set to work on evenings, Saturdays, and grant-supported retreat days to study key curriculum issues and develop recommendations for change. Members read widely, focusing their attention on four areas: authentic assessment, thinking skills, interdisciplinary curriculum, and multicultural education. After thirteen months, however, the committee found itself unable to distill practical suggestions from its ever-widening discussions. Members decided to present summaries of the literature and of their discussions, and let the staff decide what to make of them.

The matter was not so simple, however. Unknown to the committee, questions about its goals and authority had been festering, unanswered, during the year. Was it a legitimate subsidiary of the steering committee, or the principal's handpicked team? Would its recommendations carry the force of mandate? And what were the members doing all that time, and why weren't other faculty kept informed of their activities? Although it is not unusual for ad hoc committees to take up issues and projects on behalf of the steering committee, a group whose charge appeared so broad, so fundamental, and yet undefined, whose membership had been mainly determined by one person—the principal—and whose proceedings seemed to go on and on, out of view of the majority, seemed to violate Red Lake's unwritten code of democratic conduct, which calls for open, inclusive deliberation, in the manner of a town hall meeting.

Teachers, knowing little of the committee's intentions, had developed dark premonitions that it would demand more change and broader responsibilities, for which they felt unprepared. Thus even before the curriculum committee came before the staff to present its findings in November 1992, its standing had been severely compromised. At the meeting, a single veteran teacher, in whose voice the community's sentiments found authoritative expression, effectively tabled the notion that Red Lake needed a critical review of curriculum. "I basically raised the question . . . as part of the process of looking at curriculum, of whether we were also going to look at the identification and celebration of what was working here, before we say, 'Let's have some new stuff'?" he recalled, adding in a bittersweet tone that "raising that question at the beginning of their presentation robbed a lot of energy from the group, [who were] simply trying to share what they had found out." Following this meeting, the curriculum committee disbanded.

The saga of the curriculum committee reveals the importance of timing and process in restructuring at Red Lake. Reflecting on their experiences, not one participant maintained that the curriculum could not have benefited from comprehensive review. But by working outside Red Lake's democratic tradition, the committee squandered an opportunity to guide others in reflection. Committee members bitterly lamented their lost effort, but to the staff as a whole, the episode represented a misstep in the right direction.

## New Assumptions, New Challenges

Change has taken a long arc at Red Lake; not everything that is unusual about the school results from its current restructuring.

Although they have been modified recently, the house advisory, open enrollment policy, and steering committee are rooted in reforms of the early 1970s. A few veterans of that first wave of change remain on the staff, and they remember "fighting the state" to free themselves from curricular and administrative requirements. The new wave of restructuring, in contrast, has proceeded with the blessing and fiscal support of both district and state authorities, although, now as then, the impulse to change came from within the Red Lake staff.

The second wave began quietly in December 1987, when, anticipating the arrival of a new principal for 1988–89, a small group of staff began meeting to discuss school improvement. Hopeful that new leadership would provide an impetus for new ideas, they wanted to greet the incoming principal with plans in hand. As it turned out, the principal chosen by the district in January 1988, Jack Singer, was just the kind of leader they wanted: a facilitator.

"I have some core beliefs on how you work with kids, but I'm not going to lay that on people," Singer said. "My job is to facilitate the group's figuring it out. I'll have a voice in that and share my thoughts. But I just don't believe you change by telling people what to do. You have to learn to work together. I'm a process person and pretty good at the process. That's how I keep the change going. I just work on the process: identify issues and try to look at the reasonableness, timeliness [of solutions]."

Although he was not scheduled to assume his office at Red Lake until April 1988, Singer immediately joined the informal school improvement group, which soon evolved into a caucus for restructuring. Over the course of the next year, membership swelled to about twenty-five teachers. As it does now, a steering committee then governed the school, but it lacked student and parent representation and its members did not perceive a vital need for fundamental change. After January 1989, when the improvement group presented its vision to the assembled staff as well as some parents and students, the old steering committee was a lame duck.

### Vision

Red Lake's vision statement of January 1989 opens as follows:

> With the approach of the 21st century, we at [Red Lake] recognize the need to depart from what has been tradition. By recognizing

emerging global and social issues, we choose to challenge ourselves to design a school based upon a new set of assumptions. These assumptions must include a new definition of "school," in which learning is lifelong and encompasses the whole community.

The concerns prompting these assumptions include: the doubling of information every nine months, the changing family structure, the emphasis on new skills needed to empower us in an informational world, and finally, the need to instill a sense of purpose, direction, and humanity to the future.

To address these concerns, the improvement group proposed that Red Lake pursue sixteen ideals. The newly defined school, they suggested in five of the sixteen, should be "a place . . . where people relate to each other in a cooperative and caring manner . . . where our program dictates time and time does not dictate program . . . where everyone shares in teaching and learning . . . where we recognize parents as partners in the educational process . . . [and] where curriculum and program are boundless and continue to evolve."

Having adopted the sixteen ideals, the assembly resolved that no aspect of the existing program would continue beyond fall 1990 unless it was expressly reenacted. Staff formed committees on curriculum and instruction, time and organization, community involvement, and so forth and set a spring 1990 deadline for the development of a comprehensive restructuring plan. Their work during 1989–90, including summer and winter staff retreats, was supported by the first of four $40,000 state grants Red Lake received for site-based staff and program development. Matters came to a head at the summer 1990 retreat, as one participant recalled: "We agonized over this restructuring plan. We had decided that we wanted a two-thirds vote to accept anything, and proposals kept coming up, and every one was going down, some by one vote short of two-thirds. Our feeder schools were waiting on information, and we didn't even have a program in place."

### Details

A particular sticking point was the schedule. Finally Singer made a desperate and uncharacteristic threat: if the staff could not agree on a plan, he would choose a special cabinet, sequester them for a day in his home, and enact by executive fiat whatever plan they constructed. His gambit forced the committee on time and organization to adopt as a compromise the alternate-day schedule of seventy-minute classes.

"This every-other-day schedule was not ever one of the bids, [but] the group basically said that looks like the best of our alternatives," a teacher remembered. "So we came back with it. . . . At the end, what it came down to was everyone believing that, whatever we did, we were just going to take this leap, and if it didn't work we were smart enough to change it; that we were going to make whatever we did work, even if we were leery about the details."

Staff resolved, in addition, to disassemble ability tracks, to extend membership on the steering committee to students and parents, and to develop the Connections program for seventh and eighth graders, including service learning and mentorships. When first adopted in 1990–91, these commitments required painful adjustments, and again anxiety centered on the schedule.

One teacher remembered that many colleagues at first were "very dissatisfied. One teacher left largely on that basis. Math, foreign language, performance classes—people were very unhappy, because they wanted to see their kids every day. . . . It was a hard sell from the start, and it was not something that was popular. [But] within the first month of school, after we started the Connections classes, community service learning, mentorships, all these amazing new things that we had done, it was pretty obvious that the most influential thing we had done was the schedule."

By the time Center researchers visited Red Lake in 1992–93, staff had fully accommodated to the blocked schedule and said it allowed them to teach responsively and in depth. Their main lingering reservations about the programs enacted in 1990 were that the demands of team planning allowed little time for personal lesson preparation and that the eight-period Mondays were so hectic that they had become known to students and staff as "the day we don't learn anything."

Since restructuring began, Red Lake has been able to modify and enhance some programs with the support of district and especially state authorities, but it struggles now to shield them from the budget cutter's blade.

### Retreats and Retrenchment

The story of its restructuring suggests that Red Lake operates independently, apparently neither encumbered by regulations nor motivated by extrinsic incentives. According to the local school district's curriculum coordinator, that is just how district administration wants it. "As central office people, what we did not want to do was to say 'No' to schools, because our belief is that schools know best what will allow them to increase student achievement. And that's what all the school restructuring is about in our opinion," he said. "At the heart of the culture of the district is bringing everything to bear to allow that to happen, instead of being an oppressive, top-down central office organization. We try to be service oriented and to say 'Yes' as much as possible. Because of that, we are a district that is a confederation of schools."

Although its approach is not highly prescriptive, the district does actively support restructuring. In addition to putting its imprimatur on Red Lake's innovations, it provides modest financial support through $1,000 grants to teachers who team to develop interdisciplinary projects and up to two days' bonus pay for staff development during extracontractual hours. And when Red Lake's new classroom telephone system overran its budget by some $9,000, the district picked up the difference. "If we're willing to make some interesting moves, then they'll tend to provide support for that," Jack Singer explained.

Red Lake's most active partner in restructuring is its state. Red Lake was among the first cadre of schools (1989–90) to win state grants for site-based innovation and staff development, and it was the only school whose reapplications the state approved every year through 1993 (the total of state outlays to Red Lake was about $160,000). These grants supported biannual staff retreats, including the pivotal 1990 session where staff conceived the main features of restructuring. Subsequent retreats afforded staff time and space to revisit their vision statement, check their progress and renew their commitments, as well as to consider additional emphases such as instructional technology and networking with community resources.

The state grants have also released teachers, paid consultants, and purchased supplies for an array of activities and programs that continue to undergird restructuring. In 1992–93, for example, a portion of the grant enabled Red Lake to hire a coordinator for its new computer lab (the school took a bank loan to pay for the hardware), another gave teachers release time to experiment with the computers and plan their use in lessons, and a third delivered three teachers to a conference, Technology and Inquiry in the Middle School. The largest share of the year's grant paid for clerical time to coordinate social services and counseling. About $6,000 directly supported classroom projects.

Although it discontinued development grants after 1993, the state remains active in education. Its 1991 comprehensive reform act mandates local school councils, extended school calendars, and periodic public reports of student achievement on both standard and performance measures, aggregated to the school and district, and it offers waivers and grants to schools that "substantially modify traditional methods of delivering educational services." Red Lake is not likely to feel strong effects of this legislation, since its programs are largely consistent with the state's new direction.

Staff have not entirely accepted the state's aims for assessment reform. The state's intended measures of student achievement include portfolios and exhibitions, methods Red Lake teachers have yet to incorporate systematically in their classroom practice. In fact they have no consistent approach or standards for assessment, and teachers employ everything from textbook quizzes to group exhibitions. Both teachers and parents recognize this inconsistency as a problem.

"My daughter doesn't know the times tables," one parent reported. "I don't mind that she doesn't know it, that's not a critical problem. What bothers me is that nobody here knows that she doesn't know it. There's no standard that gives the content knowledge and the intellectual processes that children need to know."

Although they can refer to the outline of learning skills for Connections classes, this fails to drive assessment. Instead teachers tend to check their practices against their shared ideal that students build new knowledge and abilities by following their interests into "an informational world." They find this ecumenical ideal difficult to translate into specific standards. Perhaps the state's new outcome statements and performance standards will provide models Red Lake staff can use to develop more explicit norms. In 1994, a year after we visited Red Lake, its assistant principal reported that staff were piloting for the state test items, scoring rubrics, and portfolios and that departments, supported by a new $27,000 state grant, were meeting to review their programs in the light of state outcomes.

Not all the news from state government has been good for Red Lake. Since 1992, when state voters approved a measure to equalize school financing that reduced allocations to its district, Red Lake has felt the pressure of contracting resources. Leaner budgets mean rising class sizes and diminished chances for collaboration and professional development. Staff fear that the weight of their responsibilities soon may exceed the strength of the support structures they have worked so hard to build. When houses swell from twenty-two students to thirty or thirty-five, will their social bonds remain close? Will Connections classes be feasible if teachers cannot find the time to meet and plan? A shrinking budget is not unique to Red Lake, of course, but it presents special problems for a school where choice is the engine of common effort and a vehicle for restructuring. Scarcity for all could result in choice for none. Against this danger, Red Lake sets the strength of its democratic ideals.

## Okanagon Middle School
### All for One

A half-vacant building in a modest city neighborhood, the Okanagon School of 1988 seemed an unlikely beacon, yet it attracted a variety of sponsors. At the offices of local school authorities, it captured the attention of restructuring advocates who proposed to reopen it as a magnet school. From the surrounding area it drew parents and social service providers anxious to revitalize their community. From the state government it attracted nearly $2 million in grants to support innovative uses of time and personnel and to fortify the well-being of students and their families. Private foundations and educational reform organizations also offered their resources, supporting school planning and staff development, and helping teachers create assessment tools.

Reborn as a magnet middle school, Okanagon enticed a group of itinerant resource staff from the district's department of human relations. These six teachers and a principal pledged themselves to create a learning environment in which traditionally disadvantaged students would rise to high standards of achievement and conduct.

### Family Matters

Okanagon enrolls nearly fourteen hundred students in grades 6 to 8. Generous numbers of African American (34 percent), Filipino (32 percent), and Hispanic (18 percent) students make it a hub of cultural diversity. More than half of all students receive a federal lunch subsidy. To organize this vast, eclectic population for instruction, Okanagon's eighty-four teachers form semiautonomous teaching groups known as families. Seventh and eighth graders are mixed and distributed in groups of about 150 across six families. Each family comprises a teacher for each of the four core academic subjects and for computers and PE, plus a permanent substitute. The six regular teachers serve as homeroom mentors to about twenty-five students, and one teacher, designated the family leader, acts as administrator for each unit. Despite its size, Okanagon employs just one building administrator: Roy Stack, known as the chief educational officer.

The district tapped Stack in January 1989 to lead a commission of sixty educators, parents, and civic representatives to plan the new school, which reopened in September 1990. According to Stack, one of the commission's main goals was to "create a school . . . where all of the people have a sense of responsibility and commitment and power."

The family structure that emerged from this ideal places Stack, as school leader, in what he described as a "godfather-like" position, with teachers cast as surrogate parents for their large broods. Stack helps staff resolve issues within their teams, and he acts as liaison between the school and outside authorities, but his main function is as avatar of Okanagon's cultural norms. In that capacity, his duties include reminding teachers of their vital and unguarded position within the family structure. "Everybody has power," Stack said. He explained that most people in schools tend to feel powerless, with someone else making all the decisions. But "here we're totally responsible for everything, so if we don't get the system to cooperate with us, we failed."

Virtually everything that schools do, Okanagon does through its families. Teachers divide their students into class groups and set their own schedules for instruction. They have a daily common planning hour while their students attend enrichment classes such as art, foreign language, and woodshop. Some families divide their students into six classes, which yields a minimal class size (about twenty-five students) but confines teachers' planning time to the standard hour, while others opt for four or five larger classes and additional preparation time. Roy Stack described family autonomy as a sacred tenet, and in fact each family organizes its planning time uniquely. "My family meets three to five times per week for forty-five minutes to talk about our curriculum, our outcomes, [and] about our interdisciplinary projects," one teacher explained. "We had been meeting five days, but then we decided that we needed to set aside one day a week to schedule parent conferences during the daytime."

Families plan their curricula with an interdisciplinary commitment that demands collaboration. For example, social studies, mathematics, computer, and PE teachers in one family jointly developed a civil war simulation, in which students projected battle casualty statistics, then tested their computer models by staging an uphill charge against classmates armed with water balloons.

One teacher described how the combination of flexible scheduling, time for dialogue, and cooperation allowed her family to redirect a language arts project in midcourse:

> [Students] had to write a letter to somebody in LA why they should not riot but instead follow the teachings of Dr. King, Gandhi and Thoreau, and respond in a nonviolent way. In social studies we had taught all about the civil rights movement, [and] our kids did very well on that. [But] we were sitting there talking when all of a sudden it dawned on us that the kids needed to hear *us* talking about these ideas. So we went back to my room and all of the teachers sat in the middle and had a dialogue right in the middle of the kids. What they finally ended up writing was really powerful, because they saw us struggling with the ideas.

Teachers said the plans they devise often require more preparation time than they can find during the day. "We don't wing it, we want to go in there with the lesson prepared 100 percent," said one family leader. "But it takes two or three months of preparation where you sit down and brainstorm [to] devise it all. Last summer we met three times, about six hours each time, to get our first week together. That's what we need to do all the time, [but] the interruptions and other things we have to deal with are constant, just constant."

Not all families plan or adjust to circumstances in solidarity. Some are, in one teacher's words, "not philosophically in sync"; one has formally split into two triads, each with custody of half the students. Additionally many staff lament the schoolwide bonds they say are sacrificed in the interest of family autonomy. One teacher described families as "nine little schools," and another saw "a big, big wall" separating teachers from colleagues in other families.

Despite their concerns about fragmentation, staff strive for diversity within families as well as between them. Variety is critical to Okanagon's instructional philosophy. "We don't accept a model of teaching, except in the broadest sense that all kids ought to be in there and be active in their learning," said one teacher, a member of the original staff. "You may hear some value statements about pedagogy, but you won't see people speak the language of [one] model. I would fight real hard to keep [us] from speaking about such things."

One value Okanagon staff consistently emphasized was that learning cannot be separated from other human needs such as health, dignity, and social membership. "One of [our] ideas is that everyone ought to get everything," a veteran teacher explained. "There is concern about treating the whole child, an understanding that we are teaching more than the content."

Teachers' concern for students' welfare is reinforced outside the classroom in Okanagon's comprehensive social services unit.

### The Whole Child

The unit is both a service provider and a gateway through which students and their families can connect to some two dozen affiliated agencies. Unit "case workers" counsel Okanagon students referred to them by homeroom teachers, train student mediators, lead group cultural activities during and after school, and oversee the service learning programs to which Okanagon requires all students to commit twelve hours per year. A full-time nurse screens students for basic health problems, administers vaccines, and refers students to partner clinics in the community, while a second, part-time nurse practitioner delivers some treatments on site.

The county government, from which a social services administrator sat on the Okanagon planning committee, underwrites about half of the unit's personnel. By administering the unit through an intermediate community agency, the county and district are able to join funding streams and form a bridge between public and private service providers. Third-party funders support the unit's affiliated agencies, whose focus issues include cultural awareness, mental health, parenting, drugs, gangs, domestic violence, grieving, and youth advocacy.

At the nexus of this network of providers, homeroom teachers act as Okanagon's primary case managers. To sustain the vital connection between classrooms and counselors, the unit director meets weekly with family leaders, and during the year of Center visit (1993–94), unit staff led eight clinical workshops for teachers. The unit is set up to provide services to individual parents or entire families, but its capacity to reach adult clients depends on the central link between teachers and their students.

### Family to Family

A small group of parent volunteers, up to six, also finds its way to Okanagon through a collaborative council that is the formal authority on schoolwide policies and programs. The council includes representatives of the nine families, the classified staff, the unit, and the student body, as well as Roy Stack. As we have seen, however, the key domains of programming and instruction are mainly the purview of families. Faculty are also the main movers on budget and staffing, and especially on curriculum. Nonetheless, significant issues such as criteria for graduation do land on the council's agenda.

Staff say they get better parent turnout at quarterly family open houses than at schoolwide events and council meetings. Although Okanagon draws most of its population from its own area, few parents live at a convenient distance, and fewer still have the means to travel across town regularly for school events. One parent who was a steady council participant suggested that most "parents don't come unless it's something about their kids."

Mindful of the difficulty parents may have in getting to the school, some teachers said they were reluctant to call home about everyday issues. "Parents are stressed out . . . and it's hard to get them involved," one teacher explained. "I try to solve as many problems as I can without talking to the parents, just to get it done. That's why they send their kids to this school, so we will get it done."

While Okanagon reaches out to parents and the community through the social services unit, the collaborative governance council, and family events, staff concentrate mainly on building community within the school, among themselves and with students. "We try to operate as . . . a unit that cares for one another," one teacher said. "We try to make sure that the students take hold of that, that they realize everybody has a stake in this school."

## One for All?

A 1990 vision document requires sixteen statements to express Okanagon's schoolwide goals, but most teachers seem to follow personal creeds similar to one colleague's abridgment: "All students can learn, and all decisions should be based on what is good for the child."

To operationalize these fundamental beliefs, Okanagon staff have created norms of conduct and of performance. The five norms of conduct begin with "focus on learning" and "respect the rights of others to learn." Staff say these norms apply everywhere and to everyone. "It's not just for students, but we say that teachers also have to follow it," one teacher stressed.

The staff's commitment to ideals of thoughtfulness and mutual respect is reinforced by their use of the protocol process, a dialogue format in which discussants successively present ideas, silently absorb comments, respond to questions, put questions back to the audience, then exchange roles. A group of teachers encountered the protocol at a state-sponsored restructuring symposium, and it subsequently became a schoolwide practice. Some families use it in their planning sessions. By adopting the protocol in their monthly meetings, biannual retreats (funded through a private grant), and summer workshops (supported mainly by the state restructuring grant), staff have tried to develop their own focus on learning through dialogue and consensus.

The norms of conduct compose just one of six challenges posed to students by Okanagon's norms of performance. To earn their school's official certification of merit (diplomas are issued by the district), students must also complete the service learning requirement; present an annual summary exhibition to a panel of peers, staff, and other adults; complete a major research project; demonstrate competence in reading, writing, research, and mathematical reasoning, as judged by teachers in their families; and prove their understanding of the school program by conducting an introductory tour of the building.

The challenges set a high standard as Okanagon began its restructuring, and in its first years only about one-third of eighth graders earned merit certificates to go with their diplomas. In fall 1994, however, Okanagon adopted a charter in which staff promise a steady climb in the proportion of graduates who meet all six challenges, toward a goal of 80 percent in 1998. Staff said they talk about requiring students to complete the challenges in order to graduate, but the proposition founders on their belief that the meaning of success is different for each student. When we visited Okanagon in 1993–94, staff faced a corresponding challenge: to devise an assessment system that would provide credible schoolwide measures of students' academic progress without imposing excessive standardization on teachers and families.

## Reality Checks: Assessment, Equity, and Identity

Staff hope to construct their assessment system around schoolwide performance events and portfolios. A curriculum committee composed of a volunteer from every family leads their efforts. The committee is responsible for maintaining an instructional framework across grades and subjects. It established a sequence of four quarterly schoolwide emphases ("social commitment, personal challenge, making connections, applying learning"), wrote outcomes statements for the six achievement challenges, and set guidelines for teachers to use as they prepare their quarterly progress reports on individual students, which also include traditional grades. To address assessment in detail, seven committee members work as a task group on portfolios.

Portfolios hold students' work related to the six challenges. Additionally some families call for something from each academic subject, while others expect to see several drafts of some pieces, along with self-reflection sheets (designed by the portfolio group) and peer reviews. Portfolios provide the resources for students to meet the annual exhibition challenge.

Each student's portfolio includes evidence from schoolwide assessment events in mathematics and in language arts, one each per semester. The letter to someone in Los Angeles, for example, culminated a language arts event that focused on civil rights and incorporated text, video, group activities, and preliminary writing tasks, as well as time for peer review and revision of the final letter. A mathematics event required students to compose an essay about a coin-flipping game, from which they were to induce rules of probability and to suggest revisions to make the game fair.

These events, and holistic scoring rubrics for them, are designed by members of the portfolio group with other faculty in the appropriate subjects. The group's leaders are active in two national performance assessment development projects, and by combining these contacts with resources from the district and state, Okanagon is able to train all teachers as scorers and to develop tasks that resemble validated models. Still, not all teachers are convinced that a schoolwide assessment scheme is necessary, or desirable. "Because of the family structure, we are able to talk about what is best for children [and] plan together about our common ground," one teacher said. "When I first came here that was really open, but there is a movement now to standardize more and more across the school."

A colleague elaborated, saying, "One group of people think that portfolio is the way to go, [but] others feel that the power belongs much more in the educational family, that the family needs to look at the kid . . . and say, 'Okay, in our professional opinion this student meets the requirements.' It's my fear that kid[s] will take the [portfolios] to high school, and they will say, 'What are we supposed to do with this?'"

A member of the portfolio group offered this perspective: "The whole issue is, how can we draw more out of the students . . . how to take a learning experience and grow from it."

Along those lines, some staff have suggested that students with extraordinary needs, including those qualified for special education services, require academic support other than what they receive. Currently students who are referred by their homeroom teachers take a support class during their enrichment hour. Here, they work with resource staff on skills such as note taking and on regular classwork. This arrangement allows students to remain with their families for instruction in the core subjects, where, according to one teacher, close supervision and cooperative learning allow most to "survive and succeed." "But," she continued, "in every family there are three to five kids who will never have the ability. You can just see—they look at you with a blank stare."

A support room staff member said, "I have a sort of sketchy curriculum for [the lowest-achieving students]. We have a lot of things on the computer that they can do, and they're safe here. That's really what they want, to get out of a situation that's embarrassing for them. It would be much better if they had . . . separate classes."

But most staff steadfastly oppose pull-out classes and echoed the sentiments of a colleague who said, "[They are] against our vision, which says all children deserve the best of everything."

Many teachers believe that Okanagon will not have realized its vision until all its graduates are able to succeed in the most advanced classes their high schools have to offer. Toward that end, the district is following Okanagon graduates in two high schools and comparing their grades for academics and citizenship to those of students from other middle schools. Preliminary data on ninth graders suggest that Okanagon graduates are faring relatively well, but staff keep a self-critical attitude.

"The term *advanced academic study* is used to describe what's going on here, but I would not consider my class advanced," one teacher said. "It sounds good, [and] it looks good. . . . But there [still] are some things that we feel are wrong."

Amid the diversity of the student body and their concerns about equity, Okanagon staff confront questions about race, social status, and educational opportunity. "Some problems we have are because teachers don't know how to deal with certain cultures," one teacher said. In particular, "there are too many African Americans in [the support class] who were wrongly placed." A parent agreed, saying that although the staff show real commitment to educational equity, some students are marked by their ethnicity as behaviorally suspect. To the extent that this occurs, some staff said a partial solution may come through the charter, which empowers Okanagon to hire only teachers who demonstrate a commitment to the multicultural perspective embedded in its mission.

Struggles over equity issues force Okanagon staff to clarify their mission. The social services unit encourages various ethnic clubs, but many staff see this as undercutting a shared identity for the school as a whole.

"You can't have folks come and tell me they are speaking for the community," said Roy Stack. "This is a multiracial, multicultural, multilingual school community. And it has to be the moral, social, and pedagogical commitment of this school to represent all of the children, all of the parents, and all of the teachers, everybody."

## Notes

1. A concise introduction to the middle school model is presented by George, Stevenson, Thomason, and Beane (1992). Brough (1995) offers a capsule summary of the middle school movement and its antecedents. Alexander and McEwin (1989) document the shift from junior highs to middle schools. Ames and Miller (1994) give close attention to efforts to personalize middle-level schools.
2. These findings are based on coding of school reports described in Appendix A.
3. Center analysis of student essays is described in note 5 in Chapter Eight.

# Chapter Five

# Cibola and Island High Schools

*Kenneth B. Doane*

Critics have put forests to the blade to depict the need for change in American high schools, which they have described as sprawling, impersonal institutions whose mechanistic culture and diffuse organization seem to defy reform.[1] Recent evidence suggests that fundamental restructuring is rare in high schools, even where staff consider themselves committed to it.[2] In the preceding chapters, we watched middle school staff working to create supportive learning environments for all their students and elementary school staff laboring to clarify and hold course toward unique visions of teaching and learning. Did SRS high schools evidence similar progress? Yes and no.

We found only one high school in which staff shared a focused vision for student learning. Cibola High, a school of 450 students located in a major Eastern city, was the smallest of the SRS high schools, which may have made it simpler for staff there to communicate and pull together.[3] Moreover, as an alternative school Cibola attracted staff who embraced its unique goals and demands. But Cibola's success in forging a schoolwide mission cannot be attributed entirely to these organizational advantages. As the portrait in this chapter shows, Cibola staff worked hard to preserve their focus by collaborating to assess the performance of one another's students, by negotiating decisions, and by exposing their practices to the scrutiny of outside observers. Several later chapters also consider Cibola's structures, programs, and accomplishments.

In counterpoint to Cibola, Island High, an urban school in the upper South, began restructuring with few organizational resources. Whereas Cibola was created whole in 1985, Island began restructuring in 1991 when school district leaders determined that it could no longer serve its 1,200 students as a traditional, comprehensive school. Despite strong efforts by staff and other stakeholders, Island remains big, diffuse, and bureaucratic. These features remained in many other SRS high schools as well. We found only one high school where restructuring had resulted in a coherent organization of programs. Nonetheless, we found evidence that high school staff can change some organizational features to encourage collegiality and to create more humane environments for themselves and for students. Five of eight SRS high schools had moved teachers into interdisciplinary teams with common students. Five had divided students and staff into divisions or houses to offer students support and identity with a familiar group. In four high schools, teachers advised or hosted a homeroom with the same students for more than one year.

Many teachers in SRS high schools had begun to reflect on their classroom practices and, in some cases, to retarget them toward goals consistent with authentic pedagogy and achievement. In sum, we found that the challenge of reshaping American high schools persists, but also that, rather than retreating from the challenge, high school educators are actively scouting for new ways to meet it.

## Cibola High School

### Prologue: "Never Stop Struggling"

> We struggle over two things. One is how to translate the "habits of mind" into our classrooms, because it's both a matter of accepting what's written down, understanding what's written down, and of translating it into practice on a day-to-day level. And that's very, very hard. Then the second thing to struggle over [is] . . . every year we should get better. What we accepted as minimum one year should be unsatisfactory the next year. It has to be that way. We have to ask for more every year. That's an ongoing thing, we'll never stop struggling over that . . . [because] when you get down to it, it's all a matter of what's going on in the classroom.
>
> —A Cibola teacher

## Ends in View

Students at Cibola High follow many paths over common ground. The curriculum they pursue encompasses intellectual habits as well as fields of knowledge, and because their teachers organize themselves in a way that nurtures close, comprehensive relationships between staff and students, the way is open for students to develop their unique faculties and aspirations within a focused curriculum. Cibola staff expect every student to reach high standards for intellectual performance, so they struggle along the way to reconcile their expectations with the unique needs and sensibilities of each one.

### *"Everybody Has That"*

Cibola staff define their primary responsibility as teaching students to "use their minds well," which they define as developing, applying, and sustaining five habits of mind. One way to express the habits is as clusters of questions, along the following lines:

*Viewpoint.* From whose perspective is something being presented?

*Evidence.* How do we know what we know? Is our information reliable?

*Connections.* How are these things, these events, connected with other like events?

*Relevance.* Why is it important? Why are we studying this?

*Supposition.* What if . . . ? Suppose things had been different.

By learning to apply these kinds of questions to various problems and situations, staff believe, students will prepare themselves for productive, responsible, and satisfying lives, beginning with success in college. Staff regard access to higher education as a promise they make to each student, and because Cibola draws many of its students from historically marginalized and underserved social quarters—85 percent are of color, more than half are eligible for free or reduced-fee lunch, and about a quarter are eligible for special education services—the deal is neither made nor accepted lightly.

"Because, traditionally, a lot of the kids who go to school here would not have had a chance to go to a college of their choice, that means we have to do certain things, and it may mean giving up certain things," a teacher explained. "[Our] position is that [college] is a very important opportunity to have in America going into the next century. Therefore, the school needs to do certain things to make sure that everybody has that potential option open to them."

To fulfill its promises, Cibola requires students to succeed in specific performances. For those nineteen of every twenty students who eventually earn a diploma, graduation practice begins at the start of the eleventh grade, when they enter Cibola's Senior Institute and begin working on specific activities required for graduation. There they collaborate with their families and a staff adviser to develop a personal academic plan based on their college plans and long-term goals. The plan includes at least one seminar taught by faculty from local colleges, and a sequence of courses with institute staff, who unlike their colleagues in the lower divisions teach traditional, daily classes on discrete subjects. Options in literature for 1992–93 included Good and Evil, Greek Drama, Novels of Toni Morrison, and Literature of the Spanish-Speaking World. Drawing on assignments from these courses as well as previous work, students must also develop portfolios in fourteen content areas ranging from mathematics, history, and geography to ethics and social issues, fine arts, and a second language. To complete the portfolio in science and technology, for example, students must:

- Write a summary of their high school studies in science and technology
- Pass an examination on basic science terminology, procedures, and issues. The exam may be a standardized test or one developed by Cibola faculty.
- Demonstrate knowledge of the experimental method by writing a report, conducting an original experiment, or providing documents from a previous experimental exhibition.
- Demonstrate an understanding of the role science plays in society, including its social costs and benefits, by writing a report, participating in a public debate, or creating an appropriate exhibition.

The ultimate requirement for prospective Cibola graduates is a demonstration of mastery based on the portfolios. Sometime during their tenure in the institute, students must present and defend seven of their portfolios to a committee consisting of their staff adviser; another teacher; a third adult, who may be a parent; and a fellow student. In evaluating these portfolios, committee members look for evidence of three capacities: mastery of skills and knowledge in specific subjects; competence in a variety of communication media such as writing and graphic arts, and in computer applications such as spreadsheets and on-line databases; and integration of the five habits, as demonstrated both by the content of each portfolio and in the quality of their preparation, presentation, and defense.

### Standards Without Standardization

Committee members apply a four-point scale across five criteria, of which three—"viewpoint," "connections," and "evidence"—correspond directly to habits of mind. The remaining criteria are "voice," meaning clarity and vitality of expression, and "conventions" of writing and speaking. Although every committee uses this rubric, each one applies it according to the unique knowledge and concerns of its members. One of Cibola's codirectors, Donna Melrose, explained:

> The issue [when] looking at the individual student's work is how to avoid these standards becoming abstracted and separate from the particulars of that kid, and being able to see that every single kid in our school is going to meet these standards in a unique way [as] an expression of their own interests and engagements. . . . And that's continuously a tension in the school, to insist that we look at the work with a standard in mind but [also] with that particular child or young person in mind, in terms both of where they've been and in what way they express their interests. . . . I think it's an approach that allows us to remember that [although] standards and standardization have a similar root, they're enemies of each other.

In addition to their coursework and portfolios, Cibola graduates must intern or apprentice in a workplace for a semester, pass a battery of state competency exams, and complete a senior project—usually an elaborated portfolio in an area of particular interest to the student.

At the moment students enter Cibola, in the seventh grade for all but a handful, the school makes its expectations clear. Students must master the skills, knowledge, and intellectual habits they will need to demonstrate to their graduation committees (and ultimately to the staff as a whole, who approve all graduations). Though it stands at the end of a long, steep road, the goal is visible. In the intervening years, all students need to find their footing in the core subjects, develop long-term goals, and learn to demonstrate what they know in ways that are accessible and meaningful to others. Therefore Cibola's programs for seventh through tenth graders combine broad-fields curricula with instruction that aims to be personal, collaborative, and focused on performance.

## Getting There

Seventh and eighth grade at Cibola compose one division, and ninth and tenth grades a second. Each division comprises two multigrade houses of about eighty students, and each house comprises two teams, the basic instructional unit. Each team is composed of a mathematics-science teacher, an English–social studies humanities teacher, and about forty students. Teachers meet two groups of twenty students for two hours every day. Students remain with their teaching team for two years.

These simple structures carry profound consequences. By organizing themselves in this way, Cibola staff take up unusual challenges in three domains: in the personal domain they must accept near-constant charge of their students for long and successive blocks of time; intellectually they have to construct curricula that span multiple subjects and sustain extended lessons; and as professionals they must negotiate their practices with peers who share their responsibility for particular students and subjects as well as schoolwide norms. The three domains intersect, of course, creating tensions that teachers have learned to manage.

"This is a place where we can disagree without worrying about the wrath of God, or falling apart," said one. "We're constantly at it, constantly discussing issues. We haven't solved problems, but we have addressed them and taken them out of the closet, out of the dark, and looked at them."

### Taking It Personally

In stark contrast to staff at conventional high schools, who typically teach two or three different courses to some 150 students whose schedules are otherwise unrelated, a Cibola teaching team inter-acts with only 40 students for whose progress in the core subjects, and social well-being, they share total responsibility. (Cibola employs no counselors, deans, or department chairs.) Moreover, while teachers at conventional high schools often acquire a new roster of students every semester, Cibola teachers work with students for two years, long enough to observe and, ideally, to guide their development. The school structure gives them a chance to know their students well as learners and as people. A staff member put it this way: "If a kid sneezes on the fourth floor, we say gesundheit on the third. They resent it, but they love it. They [say], 'Ahh, you're always in my face, and you know my business,' but what kid would-n't like that kind of attention?"

In fact, in essays about their school written for this study, Cibola students were unusually expressive of positive feelings about their relationships with teachers and staff. A tenth grader, for example, wrote, "I recognized from the first day the student-teacher relationships. The unusually small classes make sure you know everyone's name and their little habits. . . . I transferred from a 5,000-student school and I really see a humongous differ-ence. In [Cibola] you are a name and a face, in other words, a person. In some other schools you are just an ID number."

Each teacher serves as adviser to about thirteen students within his or her team; a resource teacher or administrator advises the remaining students in a given house. Advisories meet daily as a group or in adult-to-student conferences. Like the teaching teams, adviser-advisee pairs continue over the two years a student remains in the division, and during those years the adviser oversees every aspect of the student's life in school. Advisers are the face of Cibola to each student and family, a conduit between families and social service agencies, and a liaison for students with other adults.

## The Essentials

Instruction in the lower divisions is mainly interdisciplinary and focused on essential questions. Content-area departments within the divisions develop the questions and curricula. When we visited Cibola in 1993–94, second division mathematics-science classes were studying motion. Their questions were, "What causes something to move, what keeps it moving, what stops its motion, and how can motion be described mathematically?" Throughout the division, students addressed these questions in a series of four projects, called exhibitions, in which they conducted research on amusement park rides. For the summary exhibition, each student presented a scale model or diagram of an original free-fall ride accompanied by writing, graphs, and sample calculations proving its safety and efficacy. Lower-division teachers employ exhibitions as their main assessment tool and as points of departure for their long-term lesson planning.

Teachers base the essential questions on four-year core curriculum themes set out in a schoolwide curriculum plan. In addition to the two main academic blocks, humanities and mathematics–science, the plan includes themes in geography and library and computer literacy, which are integrated with the block courses; foreign languages and health education, which are stand-alone courses; the arts, which are taught both within the main curricula and separately; and physical education, which is mainly an extended day program (3 P.M. to 5 P.M.).

The themes are most highly elaborated for the academic blocks. In humanities, for example, one of four main concerns is the pattern of settlement and cultural development in American history, a theme that supports essential questions about individual and group identity within a plural society. Another theme, justice, supports questions about the sources of authority and about the competing ideals of fairness and equity under law, among others. Each division treats two themes on a rotating schedule, so students focus on one theme a year and eventually study all four.

Students share one other important experience in the lower divisions: community service. Beginning in the eighth grade, students devote a weekly three-hour morning block to volunteer work in service institutions such as hospitals, child care centers, museums or libraries, an elementary school, or an office at Cibola. Students apply for their placements by writing an essay on their interests and goals, and they submit quarterly self-evaluations to their advisers. Their on-site supervisors also evaluate their performance each semester. Eventually students' experiences in community service and in the internship required by the Senior Institute form the basis of a graduation portfolio in which they develop a resumé, collect letters of reference, and so forth.

Although teachers plan collectively—they have 150 minutes in divisional departments (for example, first-division humanities) per week—each class traverses the common themes and exhibitions at its own pace and in ways that suit the students, teacher, and team. Teachers described this process variously; one said staff focus on "things they're most interested in" and "that excite students," while another said, "I do things when I feel they're ready for it."

From the habits of mind, the core curriculum themes, and principles such as "student as worker" that Cibola shares with the Coalition of Essential Schools, of which it is a charter member, Cibola teachers construct what one called "a structure that allows a process" of continual program development.[4] In a sense, the habits, themes, and other norms function as Cibola's equivalent of a scope and sequence chart, with one crucial difference: Cibola's norms do not give teachers pat answers. Rather, they prompt questions: Will organizing a lesson in such-and-such a way help students perceive causes and effects? Will this reading force them to weigh evidence or examine multiple perspectives? Does this exhibition go to the essence of a subject? Working together, teachers test their responses to questions such as these against those of their students and colleagues.

### Open Doors

The network of professional relationships at Cibola is complex and mutable, but its organizing principles are simple: individuals are accountable for their part in a collective enterprise. As codirector Donna Melrose said, "[Teachers] have a lot of freedom but it's always collective—it's always in a context of a group, whom they are responsible to and accountable to."

As staff see it, the primary group is the whole group—all thirty-four teachers, four aides, and seven other staff. One teacher pointed out, "The highest ruling body in this school is the staff. As [Donna] used to say, if we wanted to, we could fire her with a vote."

Along a similar line, codirector Perry Stein proudly described how his own power is circumscribed. "My vote is no more than anybody else's, nor is [Donna]'s nor anyone's," he said. "There are no decisions that I am empowered to make by our governance structure or our informal understandings based on my being designated principal of the school. There's a cabinet that we meet with, but the highest decision-making group in the school is the staff as a whole, and we hold that as a sort of sacred thing."

Even so, in practice the whole staff is not the primary decision-making body. It does not meet regularly, and most decisions are made by smaller groups that bear immediate responsibility to carry them out. Divisions, for example, set their own policy on student attendance and manage their own modest discretionary budgets. Lower-division staffs meet monthly, houses meet weekly, and a weekly 150-minute planning block (while students are out at their community service placements) is reserved for departments within the divisions. Occasionally teachers meet as vertical departments to articulate programs between divisions and review the core curriculum plan.

In the lower divisions, shared decision making finds its fullest expression in the teams, where teachers share their most basic tasks and concerns. Team meetings are not scheduled, but teachers said they confer and counsel one another nearly every day. "I'd say every other afternoon we talk to each other," one teacher reported. "We are constantly coming to each other's room. When I get frustrated with a kid [and] I don't know what to do—it could be academic, it could be behavioral—I go to [my teammate], 'What do you do that works with this kid?' We sit down and brainstorm. Even talking about the frustrations is helpful to both of us."

Senior Institute teachers are more independent than their lower-division counterparts, but staff divide some general responsibilities; for example, one teacher serves as liaison to the local colleges that offer courses to Cibola students. Yet there too teachers expose their practices to the scrutiny of peers, as an institute staff member explained: "This year, we decided our theme would be exhibitions. So every week at meetings different people volunteer to present their exhibitions to the group and we critique them—to help them, but also in the light of what we all could learn about it."

An executive cabinet, composed of two representatives from each division, two at-large members, and the codirectors, meets biweekly to handle long-range scheduling, special programming, and other managerial tasks that do not bear directly on everyday instruction. The cabinet also hires new staff, although teachers who will work closely with the newcomer and, in some cases students, participate in observations and interviews with top candidates.

Important and necessary as they are, decision-making arrangements do not define relationships among Cibola staff. Their ethos of collective responsibility is not primarily about how decisions get made or who makes them. Teachers seem quite willing to let others make many decisions with consequence for themselves. The crucial point, rather, is that no one acts in isolation.

"We have a public system of accountability," a teacher explained. "I mean, I don't close my door to visitors, to interns, to teaching fellows [from other schools]. It's very hard for me to do the same old thing when I have somebody always asking why you're doing what you're doing. . . . I'm accountable, both because people come in my room and because the work my students will produce goes to a graduation committee. . . . Those people see the work that is being produced in my class, [so] I am responsible for the kind of work my students do."

To augment their interactions in teams, divisions, and committees, Cibola staff have experimented with formal methods of observing one another in the classroom, but their efforts have not resulted in a standard system of peer review. Ironically some teachers suggested that such a system would develop only through the leadership of the directors. In fact, one teacher reported that codirector Melrose instigated one of Cibola's experiments with peer review, but after a time "it was just dropped." Lacking Melrose's imprimatur, subsequent efforts have been slow to develop. By contrast, when teachers in the Senior Institute expressed concern that students were entering their program lacking adequate experience with portfolio assessment, teachers in the lower divisions did not hesitate to adopt portfolios and move them to the top of their agendas in divisional meetings and in their professional development activities. For example, four teachers undertook an intensive study of portfolios over a summer break, exchanging items by their own students and reviewing relevant literature, and presented their findings at a staff retreat (an annual late summer event). The difference may be that although portfolios jibe easily with teachers' notions of "using one's mind well," formal peer review strikes them as a potential retreat to mindless bureaucracy. Therefore teachers look to their leader for a vision of staff evaluation that makes sense for Cibola.

## "The Power of the Work"

More than three-quarters of Cibola's students come up from three elementary schools that Donna Melrose developed in the 1970s, and all four schools are part of an alternative division of the city school district. To many observers, including the division administrator who helped Melrose organize Cibola, the four are "Donna's schools." Cibola opened in 1985 with a class of seventh graders and added a new class each year until its first graduates completed the Senior Institute in 1991. As an alternative school, Cibola has been free to develop according to its own vision such features as an interdisciplinary curriculum and graduation based on demonstrations rather than course credits. Cibola can also hire its own teachers and deploy them in subjects outside their state certification.

Cibola received from the district some $160,000 in supplemental funding over its first three years of operation. In explaining his support for Cibola, the alternative division administrator said, "The norms for our schools are not like norms for other superintendencies. We don't need waivers. We expect these schools to do things differently."

### The Vision and the Visionary

From the start, Cibola's vision—a small school offering personalized instruction based on explicit intellectual standards—was a challenge to convention and to the capacities of its own staff and students. Ten years down the road, its leaders continue to act as *principals provocateurs,* goading and guiding staff in equal measure. In some instances, as in the case of peer review, some staff regret the loss of take-charge leadership such as they might have known at traditional schools. Conversely teachers sometimes may feel that their contributions are overshadowed by those of their resident visionary, Donna Melrose.

"[Donna] can be very inspiring oftentimes when she speaks, and that is very, very helpful," said one teacher. "She's also good at really putting things in their place and realizing that, as you are doing something new and moving along, you're changing things as you go, and things aren't always going to be perfect all of the time, and that's okay. I think it's part of what sets up the environment that you can take risks. [But] she's a strong person, a strong personality, and when she wants something and she's committed to it, it tends to go down that way. . . . Even though this is a staff-run school and we do have final say about how things get done . . . it doesn't always play out that way."

Despite their occasional reservations, staff generally agree with another teacher's belief that, at Cibola as nowhere else in their experience, "we're treated as professionals, [and] all the education and experience we've had isn't going to waste." Indeed if the habits of mind and other ideals are to be more than slogans, teachers must deliberately apply them to shape and evaluate their practices. In a teacher's words, "Since there is no magic answer, and even though we are fortunate to work in a place with someone with as much of a vision as [Donna] has . . . we still need to grapple with and talk about these things all the time."

During our visits, staff talked most pointedly about the need to incorporate basic skills in their instruction and about redressing social inequities across lines of race, class, and gender.

### "Try to Go On"

Committed though they are to a pedagogy that values intellectual depth, Cibola teachers recognize that students cannot very well demonstrate what they know if they lack basic literacy and numeracy. On this point a teacher in the second division spoke with evident anguish. "I shouldn't have to be teaching fractions," he said. "If I have to teach fractions, then all my high aspirations of what I can do with the course are shot to hell. What do I do? I feel guilty no matter what I do. . . . It's a lose-lose situation. I try to go on. I've told kids, if you need work on your basic math skills, I don't slow down for you. You're supposed to be putting in extra time. We have somebody here on Saturdays [for tutoring]. You can stay after school. . . . We're willing to help you, but you also have to put in extra work."

Teachers balance depth and basic skills over a fulcrum of common expectations; that is, if all students are to master the habits of mind, succeed before their graduation committees, and have a chance to go to college, their teachers can neither ignore basic skills nor allow some students to get by with basic skills alone. The best balance for each student varies depending on the subject, and it changes over time as students develop and clarify their goals. Moreover, teachers take different approaches to the challenge. "Students can use their minds well, that's our premise," a veteran teacher said. "All students can learn; therefore we need to create a school where all students can learn to use their minds well. [But personal] values . . . come in [when we ask] 'For what?' or 'To do what?' I think there's a wide range of answers among the staff as to what the 'for what' is. That, I think, gives us a very complex—in some ways common and some ways different—way of seeing the school, [its] purpose, the role of teachers, the role of students in class."

### "Deal with the Kid"

Although they may note disparities in performance among groups of their students, in the light of their emphasis on students' individuality, Cibola teachers hesitate to consider students as groups defined by social categories. They seem to fear that delineating groups within the student body could be a first slippery step away from their commitment to common standards for all students, toward a cycle of diminished expectations and arrested achievement for certain groups.

Asked to compare the involvement of different parents as a factor in their children's success, for example, one teacher said: "It's a variety who aren't involved enough, and it differs from year to year. In some ways, [to discuss inequities] would force me to say that I'd have to characterize my families according to certain like concepts, you know, they're lower socioeconomic such and such.

And I just don't do that. I deal with the kid as an individual; what explains some of their behavior and how to deal with negative patterns that kids have created for himself or herself."

Teachers may be reluctant to look at students and their families through a lens of social identity, but they cannot blind themselves to patterns of behavior, interaction, and achievement among their students. In some cases, staff have adjusted academic programs to alleviate conditions that were seen to undermine the learning environment for some students. For example, in order to signal the school's respect for the cultural heritage of its Hispanic students, the staff added a requirement that all students study Spanish for two years and complete a graduation portfolio in Spanish language and Hispanic culture. Previously students had only to pass a state competency exam in a second language. But expanding the curriculum is not Cibola's characteristic response to perceived inequities or social dissonance. Instead staff try in their small classes and advisories to understand how social conditions affect individual students, and they respond accordingly. In the lower divisions, core curriculum themes of justice, power, and political identity enable them to explore social issues directly. To sharpen their perceptions and reflect on their own behavior, staff debate issues of equity and social justice in a special committee on race, class, and gender (which will be discussed in Chapters Seven and Nine).

Because many of their students live in neighborhoods where social inequity is palpable, Cibola teachers cannot ignore the social context in which their classrooms are situated, and they do not try. In fact, the school deliberately chooses to serve this population.

### Choose Your Own

One of Cibola's most striking advantages is its status as an alternative school of choice with freedom to select its own students. Any family in the city may apply, and those who live in the local subdistrict get priority, but Cibola gives first rights of entry to applicants from its three sister elementary schools, all located in nearby, low-income city neighborhoods. For these students, admission is virtually automatic. Staff estimated that about three-quarters of new students come from this group.

Before any student can be admitted, Cibola requires families to visit and, in Perry Stein's words, "see what we're all about." After meeting applicants from outside the neighborhood, Stein approves admission for students who seem likely to respond to the school's particular demands and with whose parents staff will be able join in an effective partnership of support. In addition to impressions gleaned during the family interview, he considers elementary educators' written assessments of a student's academic abilities, approach to learning, and interpersonal qualities, particularly the ability to deal with adults, authority, and rules.

Parents are expected to attend semiannual conferences in which they review their child's learning plan with the student's adviser. Additionally staff summon parents of students in some kind of trouble to meet with the adviser, other teachers, and a codirector. School policy holds that students must be present whenever their parents meet with school staff. Beyond these commitments, however, parents do not participate much in Cibola's daily affairs. Although they may sit in on staff meetings and retreats, parents have no formal role in governing the school, and they are not especially active as volunteers. According to a veteran participant, their parent association was active in the school's first years but has burned out.

Considering Cibola's ability to select students whose parents accept its approach and relative freedom from district regulations, one may ask how Cibola staff evaluate their programs, how they avoid becoming a closed circle of true believers. They do it, as their students do, by exhibiting their work for an audience of authorities and peers.

### Reaching Out and Looking In

Every year Cibola invites outsiders—university faculty, leaders of other restructured high schools, associates of the Coalition of Essential Schools—to review the required elements of particular graduation portfolios as well as the standards by which they are judged. To review the mathematics portfolio, for example, they invited university mathematicians and mathematics teachers. On one occasion, Cibola alumni joined nationally reputed educators on a panel to examine the whole graduation process. Cibola created these accountability workshops to secure a waiver from state graduation mandates.

"This is a crucial day for our community," Stein explained, "because this lets the public know we are taking care of business and establishing standards. . . . This is the basis upon which we gain waivers on standardized testing. We are judging people here on the basis of their work, so let people come in and take a look at their work."

At the spring 1993 workshop, a reviewer suggested that the science portfolio lacked experimental content; that is, students could demonstrate mastery of scientific method by writing about it rather than applying it. When we visited Cibola that fall, it was clear the criticism still resonated with Cibola staff, who mentioned it repeatedly. "[The reviewer] talked about why every kid should have to do an experiment," said a Senior Institute teacher. "As a result of that, there has been a lot of discussions of experiments, and I know, just from my advisees, I'm seeing all these great experiments the kids have been doing. So something happened, and experiments are definitely occurring now."

Not that staff accept automatically any idea from an outside authority; on the contrary, they value the opinions of review panelists because they respond to Cibola's particular conditions, and are expressed in a climate of informed respect.

According to Donna Melrose, the same attitude, combining solicitude and resolve, characterizes Cibola's stance toward parents and the public at large:

> You hope you have a community outside, some parents who will raise difficult questions for you so it won't be too easy to slip back. We got a letter [from a parent] this fall complaining about one of our courses, and I was enormously grateful because I thought she was right on target. She didn't have all the answers but she posed hard questions for us and it made me aware of something faster than I would have been myself. . . . An enormous amount of the school's work, [our] standards are there for the public to criticize, to ask us to defend, to argue about, but nevertheless we [say], as a community, these are our best judgments. And that combination of external review and internal judgment I think is a very important part of the power of the work we do.

# Island High School
## Calls and Responses

Since the late 1980s, staff at Island High have been roused to change by district and state authorities and by their concern for the welfare of a community embattled by economic decline and social strife. Restructuring has enabled staff to create new programs for particular groups of students and to deliver expanded social services to all students and families. It has also allowed some staff to reshape their professional lives by forming instructional teams. But the ultimate sum of these partial reforms remains unclear.

### The District Initiative

From the mid-1970s on, Island's community suffered from economic decline and from instability in local government and in the school district. By the early 1990s its achievement and attendance data had sunk to the bottom of district ranks as its suspension and retention rates soared. In the meantime, however, the district had pulled together some resources to help schools rebuild. Working with a nearby university, the district established a permanent staff development academy, whose staff trained Island teachers in, for example, cooperative learning strategies and introduced them to the precepts and activities of the Coalition of Essential Schools, which Island joined in 1988. Later the district and university jointly created professional development programs at several schools, including Island.

These incipient efforts were to coalesce for Island when the district superintendent assigned a deputy, Thad Banks, to reorganize both Island and the middle school that shares its campus and name. Banks convened a design team composed of staff, parents, and university advisers to develop a restructuring plan. Dubbed the Island Initiative, the plan brought Island, its sister middle school, and a nearby vocational high school into a single organization. Enacted in 1991, the initiative eliminated Island's traditional principalship, introduced teacher teaming, and created a forum for staff representatives to participate in decision making.

### The State Reform Act

Just as Island's district launched its restructuring programs, its state set forth bold new policies on education. The state legislature in 1990 passed a systemic education reform act that incorporated many current trends in education policy: outcome standards for knowledge and skill in core subjects, coupled with the removal of all curriculum mandates; assessments, including tests, portfolios, and performance measures, keyed to the standards; a formula based on the assessments and other data for measuring progress toward the standards, and the promise of sanctions against schools that fall short of assigned targets; mandates for site-based governance through councils of parents and staff; and professional development programs enhanced and retooled to reflect the standards and assessments. To these, the act added support provisions, including a mandate for school-based social service centers at sites like Island where poverty is most concentrated: 800 of Island's 1,230 students qualify for free or reduced-fee lunch.

### The Call of Community

As hard times settled on their neighborhood, Island staff needed no prompting to respond to students' travails. Enterprising teachers developed several special programs for students beset by socioeconomic conditions that hampered their success in school. Staff thrust themselves into the teenage social fray too by taking up posts in the hallways and grounds during transition times, greeting and directing students, defusing conflict, and exerting a calming adult presence.

A small number of parents also became regular faces in the crowd, contributing, in one parent's words, "a lot of hugging and talking with the students" and other personal support. "We spend a lot of time looking for prom dresses for students who can't afford their own," she said.

Island does what it can to involve parents and foster school spirit in its attendance area. The school dispatches buses to major housing projects during school events. It operates booths at neighborhood fairs and works with community centers to provide spaces where students and tutors can meet at night and on weekends.

Together, the district initiative, the state reform act, and the deteriorating life conditions of many students forced Island staff to overhaul their school. When we visited in 1993–94, staff were still searching for their places in the new order and trying to discover how the structural changes might help them to enrich their classroom practices.

## Divided Divisions

A tripartite leadership team manages Island's complex organization. A campus coordinator hires all staff for both the middle and high schools, oversees the budget, and looks after the several buildings (a new wing to house vocational classrooms, under construction during the Center's visits, was due to open in fall 1994). Within the high school, a building coordinator supervises instruction, scheduling, and community relations, and a coordinator of student services attends to counseling, discipline, and student activities.

High school students are assigned to one of four instructional units called divisions. Most ninth and tenth graders are mixed in the preparatory division, while most eleventh and twelfth graders are in the transitional division. An alternative division for students at risk and a building trades division, which serves as a district magnet program for vocational education, complete the organization.

### *Tendentious Teaming*

Teacher teaming was a central, albeit voluntary, provision of the district initiative, and it remains an important feature, but only of the ninth- and tenth-grade preparatory division. Four teachers share about 120 students, and most teams have a common daily planning hour. Specialists in English as a second language and the education of exceptional students also are assigned to each team. At least one team has experimented with combining classes in different subjects into blocked periods to facilitate interdisciplinary units. In a unit on endangered species, for example, groups of students developed reports on particular animals and constructed dioramas of their ideal habitats. The other six teams retain standard fifty-minute periods. Teachers focus instead on using teams to broaden their knowledge of individual students. "Teams [have] a positive effect because you get to know students better and be in contact with them more often," a teacher reported. "It provides a support system."

But the benefits of teaming to the school as a whole are miti-gated, teachers say, by two forms of discontinuity. Every fall the ad-vent of new stand-alone programs draws some teachers from the main divisions, leaving gaps the leadership team must fill by mov-ing some teachers from one team to another. As a result, team members must start again each year to build cohesive relationships, and students must accommodate to new teachers. When students move into the transitional division, they must readjust to the more conventional routine where each of their teachers operates inde-pendently.

Teaming is a wedge issue that separates preparatory division staff, who tend to be younger and more sanguine about reform, from their colleagues in the transitional division. Some prepara-tory staff consider teaming a necessary step toward deeper reforms in curriculum and instruction, and they view failure to embrace it as foot dragging by teachers in the transitional division. The build-ing coordinator said the charge was credible: "We believe teachers should be generalists, but [veteran] teachers don't accept this idea. I have to support people who want to teach on teams because that is the way we are headed, and that is where the need is."

Designed to promote collective effort by groups of staff within the school, the preparatory and transitional divisions have devolved, in one teacher's estimation, into "two schools in one building."

### Alternative Alternatives

In fact Island already encompasses more than two schools, if one counts its freestanding alternative division for students at risk. Cre-ated under the initiative to serve sixty students, the division has stretched to accommodate seventy-two, with many more standing by. To qualify, students must be sixteen years old and at least one credit year behind their cohort. According to the division director, participants come from the poorest and most troubled families, where "food, clothing and shelter are more important to them than academics."

In the classroom, the division's three teachers run three-hour instructional blocks, morning and afternoon, combining group work on multidisciplinary lessons with self-directed study in courses stu-dents have failed in the mainstream and in a computer-based reme-dial curriculum. Students earn credit also for paid work—fifteen hours a week on average. The director indicated that a main aim of the program is to prepare students for skilled work, not for college. Sixteen students in the division graduated in 1993, while others caught up and returned to the mainstream. A few students were expelled from the division by a review committee of their peers.

To address another condition that leads many students to drop out, the division opened a child care center in 1994, eventually to serve some thirty students who have children of their own.

Beside the official alternative division, Island offers a plethora of special programs targeted to groups of students who share a particular background, condition or goal. Among them are the following:

- An incentive program for about seventy ninth graders, which promises jobs in local businesses to students who maintain good attendance and grades and complete a sequence of competency modules
- A rapid-response program for thirty ninth graders who already are failing, modeled after the alternative division and housed in the same wing of the building
- An elective course for students who plan to attend college but whose grades would be marginal for admission. Staff expected their growing program of tutoring, study skills lessons, and motivational speakers to reach 150 students in grades 9 to 11.
- A half-day multidisciplinary course for eighty tenth graders who lack sufficient credits to advance into the transitional division
- The former vocational school, recast as a "tech-prep" magnet program and incorporated as Island's fourth division. It was still housed separately, several miles across town, when center researchers visited. The division offers classes in the construction trades as well as economics, technical writing, computing, management, marketing, and accounting. It enrolls about three hundred students. Staff work toward integrating academic and vocational activities; for example, students might create a stage property or set design for a play they are reading in English class.

Staff say these special programs keep many students in school who might otherwise be lost to the streets; they help students earn the credits they need to advance or to gain social and trade skills to complement their schooling. Despite their popularity, not all teachers celebrate the proliferation of special programs. Some find them disruptive.

### Complications

Island's building coordinator described teacher scheduling as the most important and difficult issue to arise since restructuring began. Special programs and teacher teams reduce the flexibility of Island's master schedule. The former draws students from the mainstream for irregular portions of the day, while the latter makes it difficult to revise the schedule of any one teacher without disrupting those of several others. The result is that some teachers are assigned sections of courses outside their division or their expertise. A social studies teacher accustomed to teaching U.S. history to juniors and seniors, for example, may be scheduled to teach a section of ninth-grade global studies. Some veteran teachers resist such changes, which they see as a loss of earned privileges. Their protests grew shrill during our spring 1994 visit, when they learned that the leadership team had allowed a team forming within the transitional division to plot their own schedules for the coming year.

Soon after teachers took matters in their own hands. Some motivated by dissatisfaction with the priorities of the leadership team, others by frustrated support for them, Island staff voted to enact a shared decision-making provision of the state reform act. (The act mandated school councils but did not require implementation until fall 1996.) Island's council of three teachers, two parents, and an administrator will be its third governance format in six years. To succeed, council members will have to overcome a double legacy of frustration and distrust.

## Governance: A Checkered History

Shortly after they chose to join the Coalition of Essential Schools in 1988, Island staff voted to create teaching teams and to adopt a limited form of participatory management (which was available to all schools in the district by agreement with the teachers' union).

Both practices are common to many coalition member schools, and their advocates saw them as companion steps toward collegiality and professionalism. But at Island, neither practice produced such unalloyed effects. Many teachers resisted teaming; some also resented that an extra planning hour was given to teachers who did form teams. The extra time has since been withdrawn, and although teaming continues to bring teachers together in the preparatory division, it remains a divisive issue for the staff as a whole. Meanwhile staff voted to revoke participatory management after only three years, amid contentions by some staff that the elected committee it created was stacked with teachers who, in their enthusiasm for new ideas associated with the coalition, slighted the interests and expertise of their colleagues.

The district's Island Initiative arose against the background of these stunted reforms. In 1991 Thad Banks and his design team created the leadership team. By distributing authority among three administrators, they hoped to open a context for direct, informal power sharing with teachers. In this they succeeded, but not, according to staff, with uniformly productive results.

"Last year teachers did not understand each administrator's duties, and therefore [they] resorted to working with the administrator that he or she was most comfortable with," a teacher said.

"You kind of shopped around in the office," another teacher explained. "You knew which administrator to go to get the specific answer you wanted. [But] when one of the other administrators would find out what had happened, he or she would go to that teacher and blow a gasket. There was no communication [between leaders] at all."

Thad Banks's presence as a fourth administrator may have obscured the leadership picture still further. Banks had no formal authority, but he was connected to the district office and staff recognized him as the primary architect of restructuring.

The complexity of Island's organization further attenuated its lines of communication. Preparatory division teams competed with other divisions and content departments for control of curriculum, scheduling, and, most important, teachers' allegiance. Leaders of teams and special programs contended for power against department chairs and other traditional authorities. Additionally, the leadership team seemed to delegate authority unevenly among teachers. One year, for example, the building coordinator invited teachers to join in interviews with job applicants; the next year some teachers were outraged to find themselves excluded from the process.

"The administrators would make decisions and then come and tell us about them," complained one teacher. "We could disagree, but it wouldn't make any difference at all."

In contrast, a colleague located the source of trouble in the teachers themselves: "I would walk out of meetings [between administrators and teacher leaders] and half of the division leaders would walk up to me and gripe and moan about the administrators. I would ask them why they didn't say anything and they would say, 'Because we are afraid.'"

The majority of teachers were not involved in governance meetings and could easily avoid controversy by retreating to their classrooms or by adopting an entrepreneurial approach to restructuring: bringing ideas for new programs directly to an administrator. As one teacher understood it, shared decision making meant teachers were free "to make decisions and run with them" unilaterally.

Finally, in the waning school days of spring 1994, a confluence of the disillusioned and the inspired produced enough votes among the staff to approve the new plan for a governance council as stipulated in the state reform act. Thus, when we left them, the Island staff were preparing to embark on a phase of their restructuring that will both challenge them with new responsibilities and raise the specter of old conflicts. They will assume this challenge without the aid of Thad Banks, who abruptly resigned not long before the staff took its vote. His exit followed closely the arrival of a new superintendent.

## The Act in Action

The departure of Banks marks the culmination of a gradual shift in the emphasis of Island's restructuring from features associated with the district initiative to those stemming from the state reform act. Island's comprehensive social services center, already in place, is one legacy of the act. State mandates for student assessment, also part of the act, are likely to be an important influence on the future course of Island's restructuring, but their influence is not yet decisive.

### Services

By virtue of the hardships faced by its student body, Island has attracted grant support for numerous social service programs, which it administers primarily through an intervention center and a wellness collaborative. Under the state act, schools where more than 20 percent of students qualify for a federal free lunch subsidy receive grants to develop intervention centers. Island's annual grant of $90,000 supports a full-time center administrator to coordinate services in physical and mental health, vocational training and placement, drug abuse, and family crises, which come mainly through community agencies. Center records show that about ninety students participate during a typical week in support groups and personal counseling sessions. Beside various part-time service providers, the center houses a district social worker who, in a role she likened to triage, tries to juggle Island's estimated 150 annual truancy cases, as well as its dropouts and runaways, with cases from other schools she serves. A second social worker, also ensconced in the intervention center but federally funded, organizes support groups for retained ninth graders and their parents, in the hope of preventing the kids from dropping out.

Staff hope that pulling these programs together in the center will make them more efficient in responding to students' needs. Nonetheless, because most of them are on part-time schedules, staff worry that, in a social worker's words, students in crisis "must be put on hold until their counselor will be back."

While its intervention center staff assist students in immediate need, Island tries to prevent further crises by collaborating with the local university on wellness projects, including free immunizations, tutoring by preservice teachers, and the child care center. These programs are held out of the intervention center because their funding through a private source, $250,000 over three years, is temporary.

In addition to programs associated with the intervention center and the wellness collaborative, Island staff work with civic organizations on independent programs to provide internships, work-study classes, a parent resource center, and other services to students and their families. Inevitably some programs and personnel overlap or run on parallel but uneven tracks. For example, the district dispatched a social worker—Island's third—to work full time in the child care center with about a dozen teenaged parents. No one doubts that kids raising kids need support, but when they consider that two other social workers, one full and one half time, are overwhelmed by their case load of some two hundred truant and retained students, among other duties, some staff wonder why help cannot be targeted to deal adequately with selected, critical needs.

### Demands

The state act influences Island mainly through its mandated system of assessments. The system includes tests composed of multiple-choice and essay items in reading, mathematics, science, and social studies, plus a timed writing test based on a standard prompt. But it also emphasizes performance assessment, including portfolios in writing and mathematics and other assessment events in science, social studies, humanities, and vocational studies. These additional exercises involve a sequence of tasks that may take several days and include group work and opportunities for students to revise their work before submitting the final product. The state intends this shift in assessment strategy to push schools toward pedagogies that value practical application of skills and knowledge.

Scores on the various tests are aggregated to the school level and reported as percentages attaining to one of four levels of proficiency, novice to distinguished. Island's building coordinator was pleased to report that students' scores in reading, mathematics, science, and writing showed improvement between 1992 and 1993. She attributed the gains to teachers' efforts to align their practices with the assessments, which led them to assign group projects, emphasize open-ended questions, and initiate student portfolios. "I think it is having a big impact," she said. "Teachers in this building are constantly making an effort by looking for ways to change their teaching. Fewer are lecturing. They are trying to find hands-on activities. They are reflecting [the state outcomes] in the classroom. I see it every day. . . . I see a lot of cooperative learning going on, students teaching students, generating ideas."

Several teachers shared the coordinator's view; one said that the state system "is definitely driving what I do." Another teacher saw the state mandates as a way to reanimate ideas left behind by previous reform efforts. "I see [the act] reinforcing some of the things we were beginning to do under the Coalition. [It's] requiring us to do them, that's the key element," she said.

School leaders hope to nurture the momentum by focusing staff development activities on the state assessments (three days a year on the topic are required under the act). The district's staff development academy has sponsored workshops on, for example, composing open-ended questions and selecting materials for students' writing portfolios. As a result, many teachers said they understood the forms of instruction and assessment they are being expected to emulate. Nonetheless few were able to express a clear notion of how those forms address student mastery of curriculum content.

"I am in favor of authentic assessment, but I am also content oriented, and I believe that students need to know certain content," a science teacher said. "They need to be able to regurgitate it. Now if they can also demonstrate that knowledge, that is great. But I have found it difficult to do that. If I want to know the density of a block of wood, they need to know the formula. I haven't been able to do that with authentic assessment."

Island's restructuring has spawned a diffuse organization where groups of staff respond to different forms and perceptions of student need according to their various professional outlooks. As they struggle to translate their many programs and structures into practices that enhance students' learning, teachers see a need to work within a common framework of means and ends. How may this evolve? Some staff may have found a foundation in the standards and support programs of the state reform act. Island's new governance model, also linked to the act, may provide a mechanism for generating fuller consensus, coordination and collaboration.

**Notes**
1. Boyer (1983); Powell, Farrar, and Cohen (1985); and Sizer (1984) offered comprehensive critiques that have been cited often to support restructuring.

2. In a survey of 3,380 high school principals, Cawelti (1994) found a third or fewer having fully implemented each of the following restructuring features: site-based management, teacher teaming, advisory, outcome standards, alternative assessments, and community-based learning. Among forty-one high schools nominated for the SRS through 1991 and from which the principal was interviewed by Center staff, 22 percent had adopted seven of thirteen indicators of restructuring student experiences, 20 percent had adopted six of eleven indicators of restructuring teachers' professional lives, 31 percent had adopted two of seven indicators of restructuring school governance, and 40 percent had adopted two of seven indicators of restructuring for coordination of community services (Berends and King, 1994).

3. The school actually includes grades 7 through 12, but the SRS focused on the typical high school portion starting at grade 9.

4. The coalition is a national network of about three hundred schools working on reform that began in 1984 under the leadership of Theodore Sizer at Brown University. "Student as worker" is epigrammatic for one of nine principles that member schools hold in common.

# Part Three

# Foundations for Successful Restructuring

The six portraits set out in Part Two reflect enormous diversity in how they and other schools approached restructuring. In Chapter Two we saw that schools varied substantially in their success with authentic pedagogy. In some schools teachers consistently scored above the mean for the whole sample for teaching mathematics and social studies; in others consistently below; and in a few schools teachers scored consistently high in one subject but low in the other. Teachers within a school showed substantial differences in authentic pedagogy, but schools also varied in their success: on a scale of 11 to 43, the actual range of school means was from about 17 to 27. Overall school scores fell closer to the bottom of our scale; none of them came very close to the highest possible score. But in relative terms, some schools were far more successful than others. Since authentic pedagogy is strongly related to authentic student achievement, it becomes important to explain why some schools were more successful in authentic pedagogy than others.

To address this issue, we identified the most successful schools and then asked whether they shared any features that distinguished them from the less successful and would help explain why authentic pedagogy would be more likely to occur in one context than another. To be considered one of the most successful schools, a school had to rank high in its combined pedagogy score for mathematics and social studies and also rank high for each subject. Four schools scored one standard deviation or more above the mean on the combined pedagogy score and also in each subject: Cibola High School, Red Lake Middle, Careen Elementary, and Lamar Elementary.

Center researchers considered the extensive qualitative reports (about two hundred pages) on each school, along with survey data from staff and students. We sought to identify features that seemed critical to these schools' success and were missing in less successful schools. For example, most of the students in all four schools were enrolled through choice, but this was also true of five other schools that were considerably less successful. Three of these four were started as new schools committed to innovation; so were eight other less successful schools. Three of the four schools had principals who pushed for innovation and were highly respected by the staff. But we found impressive leadership in several other schools that did not demonstrate much success in authentic pedagogy. In short, neither structural variables nor strong leadership seemed to be the key that distinguished between the schools that were more and less successful with authentic pedagogy.

The quality that distinguished more successful schools from others was a sustained focus on the intellectual quality of student learning and a strong professional community among staff.[1] These features depend largely on cultural qualities—that is, the values, beliefs, and norms that influence how adults think about the purpose of education and how they work together. Chapters Six and Seven explain each feature and present findings.

**Note**

1. Two Center researchers rated the extent to which a substantial focus on intellectual quality and a strong professional community were evident in each school. All four of these schools received the highest ratings for intellectual quality. Three of the schools received the highest rating for professional community as well. Careen received a "medium" rating for community. Appendix A describes the coding procedure.

# Chapter Six

# Intellectual Quality

*Fred M. Newmann, M. Bruce King, Walter G. Secada*

Advocates of restructuring seem to assume that structural reform—for example, replacing top-down bureaucratic school governance with school-based collaboration among teachers, administrators, and parents; replacing age-graded classes and curriculum tracking with heterogeneous grouping; and planning and teaching courses by teams of teachers, rather than by individual teachers—will improve the quality of instruction, but there is no guarantee. In fact, we found several schools in which restructuring activities did not advance the intellectual quality of student learning.[1]

Why? One problem is goal diffusion. Teachers, parents, and students were seriously occupied with other tasks and goals for schooling. To develop students' intellect, schools must provide a safe and orderly environment, and they must socialize students to behave as responsible members of the community. In addition schools are expected to instill democratic values, to contribute to students' physical and emotional health, to offer engaging extracurricular activities, to provide adult supervision when parents are not available, and to facilitate student placement into jobs and further schooling. Teachers and administrators spent a good deal of time and energy trying to maintain an orderly environment conducive to learning and trying to achieve the other legitimate goals of school. But in less successful schools, preoccupation with these activities deflected attention from the quality of learning. As staff became increasingly involved with issues of student conduct, supervision of extracurricular activity, administrative and managerial tasks, and students' and parents' emotional concerns, intellectual priorities could slip into the background.

We also found that restructuring initiatives themselves generated a host of new issues that could divert staff attention from an agenda for learning. Restructuring introduces substantial departures from conventional practice. New configurations of power and authority challenge educators, students, and parents to perform new roles that require new skills and attitudes. One would expect that the more that new practices and structural tools depart from conventional practice, the greater the difficulties of implementation will be. Overcoming these difficulties, then, becomes a dominant concern of reformers, practitioners, and researchers. The prevailing issue often becomes one of figuring out how to implement the new practice or structural tool.

Although this issue is reasonable, preoccupation with it often diverts attention from the more fundamental question of how the new structural tool is likely to improve the school's human and social resources to increase student learning. For example, adoption of techniques such as cooperative learning groups, use of portfolios, or student independent research projects raised a number of issues about how to manage and supervise students. Adoption of shared governance and team planning expanded the potential for interpersonal conflict and power struggles. When significant reforms were implemented without full faculty support, sometimes reformers understandably became so preoccupied with how to generate support within the school that they lost a focus on the intellectual quality of teacher and student work.

We do not mean to suggest that schools should ignore important nonintellectual goals of school, nor do we dismiss the difficulties of implementing new structures and techniques. But when these concerns became more paramount than the intellectual quality of student learning, authentic pedagogy was less likely to occur. The challenge is to strike a balance that permits attention to a variety of significant issues in educational practice without losing sight of the critical importance of intellectual quality.

In the twenty-four schools studied, we saw many instances of teachers' using innovative practices to move from what they considered to be traditional teacher-centered teaching to more student-centered classrooms. Reflecting an interest in active learning, these activities included small group discussion; cooperative learning tasks; independent research projects; use of hands-on manipulatives, scientific equipment, and arts and crafts materials; use of computer and video technology; community-based projects such as surveys or oral histories; and service learning.

Compared to traditional drill and seatwork, students often showed more animated participation in these activities. But even highly active students can produce work that is intellectually shallow and weak. We observed situations where students worked diligently in small groups to complete routine mathematics or vocabulary assignments, but one student gave the answer for others to copy; students completed interviews of community residents, with all questions prespecified by the teacher and the students merely recorded respondents' short answers, without trying to interpret their cumulative meaning; students used the card catalogue, computers, and mathematics manipulatives to gain superficial exposure to fragments of knowledge without promoting in-depth understanding of an idea; or where students submitted a portfolio of work over a semester filled largely with assignments that asked only for listing of isolated pieces of information.

In several instances, teachers were pleased that these techniques seemed to stimulate students to participate more, work harder, and "construct meaning." All persons, regardless of their formal education, "construct meaning," but the point of education is to improve the quality of the meanings that students construct or to help them to "use their minds well."[2] Without standards for the intellectual quality of learning that defined the difference between authentic uses of the mind versus insignificant cognitive work, instructional reform focused primarily on new techniques for active learning led down an illusory path. Student participation seemed to become an end in itself, regardless of the intellectual quality of students' work.[3]

To be sure, we also found innovative structures and practices used to accentuate attention to student learning of high quality. In these schools, teacher teams offered important support for their peers in crafting more intellectually rigorous and engaging curriculum. Longer class periods afforded important time for students to study topics in greater depth. Small group, cooperative learning activities provided useful venues for students to participate in substantive conversation.

## Criteria for Intellectual Quality

If the merit of any structural or technical reform depends on its capacity to improve the intellectual performance of students, on what grounds should we judge intellectual quality? Recent debates over standards for curriculum and student outcomes illustrate that criteria for quality are highly contested.[4] Judgments of intellectual quality applied to a lesson, assessment activity, or sample of student performance usually imply concern for one or both of two criteria: legitimacy of the content and accuracy.

On the first criterion, legitimacy of the content, the point is to ensure that the subject matter, skill, or disposition is appropriate and significant for teaching and learning according to norms of a discipline, to conceptions of students' cognitive development, or to interests of the political-legal communities that have authority over education. Debates over Western versus non-Western history, basic skills versus higher-level skills, the aspects of science that should be taught to all students, or what values to teach illustrate that consensus on legitimate and proper content is frequently difficult to achieve, especially in a pluralistic society (Apple, 1996; Kliebard, 1986).

Once agreement is reached on the proper content to teach, another criterion to consider is the accuracy of the statements made by teachers, texts, and students. Accuracy usually refers to the extent to which the content or style, or both, of the statements are consistent with authoritative knowledge and competence in the relevant discipline or area of expertise. Public concern with teachers who communicate disproven, outdated, or biased material and with students who make substantial errors in their work illustrates the importance of accuracy as a criterion of quality.

Legitimacy of content and accuracy are both important, but we think a third criterion for intellectual quality should be added: authenticity. Authenticity is the extent to which a lesson, assessment task, or sample of student performance represents construction of knowledge through the use of disciplined inquiry that has some value or meaning beyond success in school. As defined by the standards in Chapter One, authentic intellectual work encompasses the criterion of accuracy but does not resolve the important issue of the specific content and understandings most important to teach. That issue needs to be resolved through continuing discussion among diverse professional and citizen groups. However, even if what is taught is accurate and considered legitimate by the relevant authoritative groups, the authenticity criterion is needed to enrich the intellectual quality of student learning.

These criteria for intellectual quality are offered not as a complete mission statement for schools but as a vision for student learning that should help to establish substantive purpose for the structural reforms and technical practices recommended for school restructuring.

A school faculty shows that it is seriously concerned with the intellectual quality of student learning when teachers talk (and write about) issues of legitimate content, accuracy, and authenticity, but these words need not be prominent in their discourse. The question is whether teachers focus their energies and thinking primarily on the substantive cognitive accomplishments they want to promote in students.

We observed concern for intellectual quality when teachers organized curriculum to include challenging academic content. Serious staff discussion of several topics also signified concern for intellectual quality:

- What cognitive processes to nurture in students
- What subject matter is most and least important
- How material from the disciplines might best be integrated
- How to balance training in basic skills with education for in-depth understanding
- How specific teaching activity accomplishes certain intellectual goals
- What standards should be used to judge the quality of student work
- How to improve assessment

In stressing concern for intellectual quality, we do not intend to dismiss other tasks and goals of schooling, but without a central focus on intellectual quality, there is hardly any reason to implement structural and technical reform. A strong intellectual focus is critical to meet society's demands for more complex cognitive functioning in further schooling and on the job, but also for individual emotional development, physical health, efficient management of personal affairs, and competent participation in democratic civic life.

## Intellectual Quality at Four Successful Schools

The four schools most successful with authentic pedagogy stood out from the others in large part because their faculties showed passionate concern for and complex understandings of their students' intellectual development.

Teachers at Careen and Lamar elementaries, Red Lake Middle, and Cibola High showed concern for the intellectual quality of classroom practice in different ways. They did not use our specific language of intellectual quality, legitimacy of content, accuracy, and authenticity. But we observed commitments to students' cognitive growth, their understanding of exciting and powerful ideas, and mastery of skills that enabled powerful ideas to be grasped and expressed.[5] In short, their descriptions of goals and their professional activity indicated a primary concern for students' substantive cognitive accomplishment rather than the procedures and logistics of reform. This attention to the intellectual quality of student learning paid off in authentic pedagogy.

### Careen Elementary School

Careen provided an environment where students had choices, made decisions, and accepted responsibility for their decisions. Careen's curriculum was built around inquiry-oriented activities that involved real-world application of knowledge. This approach, called Applied Learning, grew out of an initiative by educators and businesspeople to upgrade local standards for education. The project specified seven competencies toward which Applied Learning aims: reading, mathematics, writing, computer literacy, speaking and listening, originality and creativity, and reasoning and problem solving.

Teachers offered different interpretations of Applied Learning, but most pointed to the importance of projects that stimulated student thinking and were connected to life beyond school. Examples included a student newspaper produced by a fifth-grade class;

a museum of state history created by a fourth-grade class; a space museum produced by third graders; a geological museum produced by a kindergarten class; and a schoolwide project to build an improved playground, where fifth graders did research on the costs and benefits of different improvements and parents worked with students one weekend to build the playground.

One teacher described a project in which fifth-grade students studied the sugar content of bubble gum and its ingestion in the body. They observed the stated content on the label and then tasted, chewed, and weighed different gums before and after chewing to estimate how much sugar was lost in the chewing process. The students decided to conduct a school survey to determine the extent to which students preferred gum with different sugar content (including sugarless gum). They formulated the questions, wrote the questionnaires, collected data in the different grades, tabulated and graphed the results, and published the findings in the school paper. Another teacher described a fundraising drive for cancer research where students advertised the drive, collected monies, and mathematically analyzed the results. These activities indicate significant staff attention to students' construction of knowledge and value beyond school: two of our criteria for authentic intellectual work.

Two consecutive lessons illustrated this school's emphasis on intellectual quality. In the first day's lesson, twenty-four fifth graders read a local newspaper article about three high school students who were shot and killed by rival gang members. Students discussed why people join gangs and then examined alternatives, consequences, and possible solutions to the problems of gangs. Solutions to gang activity proposed and considered by students included more and better school programs and after-school programs for youth, a waiting period of a month to purchase a gun, tougher crime watch programs, and more undercover police to infiltrate gangs. For the last fifteen minutes of the class, students began to draft a letter to a local radio station describing their proposed solutions to gang membership.

The next day students continued to work on their letters. About half the class then volunteered to read their letters. The letters gave specific examples of alternatives and consequences of gang membership with some persuasive statements of possible solutions. Students were to prepare a final draft of their letters for mailing within the next two days.

The teacher asked the class to think about what they could do to help other students avoid joining a gang. Students brainstormed: writing a letter to the editor of the local newspaper; creating posters, slogans, songs, and brochures to persuade students to be independent; gathering data on gang crimes to publish in the school newspaper; and producing and videotaping an educational skit to show to the school. Students decided to break up into several groups to work on these projects, and they used the rest of the period to make initial plans.

Both lessons focused on a contemporary and significant social issue. The letters to the radio station and the planning of projects to be presented to other students in the school encouraged students to develop more complex understandings of the issue by explaining possible solutions and constructing persuasive arguments, through creative media, against gang membership. These tasks entailed construction of knowledge for students, both individually and in groups. Consistent with Careen's commitment to Applied Learning, the lessons connected school knowledge to situations outside the classroom and included specific attempts by students to influence audiences beyond their own classroom. This final phase was an aspect of authentic pedagogy rarely encountered in the SRS schools.

Careen's emphasis on student performance in the real world made it appropriate for the school to experiment with new forms of assessment: student portfolios and student self-assessment. Teachers implemented these techniques before they had established standards of quality for assessing the student portfolios but later held serious discussions on standards of quality and on the kind of work to be selected for portfolio entries. Discussions on this issue have been reinforced by Careen's participation in the New Standards Project—a national effort to develop more authentic performance assessments in English language arts, mathematics, science, and applied learning for elementary, middle, and high schools. For one mathematics activity, students constructed a landscape plan for a park and recreational facility that required use of ratio and proportion in scale drawing, collecting and interpreting data, and applying formulas. Faculty groups had begun to discuss assessment rubrics that would distinguish among levels of student performance (for example, from inadequate to exemplary); this effort further signified Careen's concern for the intellectual quality of student work.

## Lamar Elementary School

Emphasis on intellectual quality at Lamar was expressed through a thematic curriculum and through staff insistence that students learn to explain themselves well orally and in writing. One teacher in the grade 3–4 team described what counts most in her approach to assessment:

> The math writing problems are usually a big part of the math. . . . It goes beyond just writing down the solution. It's how they did it, what they did, explaining it. Right now they're working on one that asks them to draw six fractions that are equivalent to one-half and explain why they are equivalent. So it's requiring them to really explain everything they've learned about fractions and equivalencies.

A teacher of grades 4–5 said:

> I like to get a feel of whether the kids are understanding what they are doing by either a project that they are working on, a discussion, or something that they have written. . . . My main thing is to get them to recognize specific details, when they are explaining something, not to be vague about it.

Staff at Lamar shared an educational vision of students as independent thinkers, using academic skills and content to make connections to real-world issues. The curriculum was organized around an overall theme: Survival: Humans and Their Interactions with the Environment. Grounded in concepts of human and physical ecological diversity and interdependence, the curriculum from kindergarten to sixth grade represented a progressive widening of perspective from the child's immediate experience with self, friends, and family to the whole human and physical community of the planet. Teaching of the separate subjects (mathematics, language arts, science, and social studies) was integrated through the study of topics connected to the school's overall environmental theme.

An example of thematic curriculum that integrated the teaching of substantive content and academic skills to understand significant real-world problems was the long-term City of the Future project for grades 3–4. Students predicted what the neighborhood surrounding Lamar will look like one hundred years into the future, and they created a plan to maximize quality of life. Mathematical concepts such as perimeter, area, dimension, and scale were used to construct a large (about 10 feet by 20 feet) Styrofoam topographical map of the neighborhood. Considering population trends and environmental impacts, students set zoning priorities and construction standards. They planned transportation and utilities systems and built a physical model of the community on the base map. The layout, the design, and the uses of the buildings, streets, and public space were based on their studies of issues related to quality of life.

Each spring, fifth and sixth graders at Lamar complete a major ecology research project that poses a challenge in construction of knowledge and disciplined inquiry. The social studies–language arts teacher on the team said this project was the focus "of all of our social studies work this year. We spent a lot of time on research skills, forming opinions, backing up your beliefs with facts, and presenting a logical argument."

Students chose a topic; formulated five initial research questions to answer with their research; found at least two books in the library to address the topic; rewrote the research questions; collected at least five additional sources of information about the topic (which could include articles, books, and videos); took notes on the information; outlined the report; wrote a first draft; revised after getting the teacher's feedback; showed the second draft to a parent; and, if necessary, got some help with final proofreading. The paper was to present specific information and examples relevant to the main question or thesis and a summary and conclusion to review what was learned, with suggestions for solving the problem. The teacher gave students a general outline to follow, illustrated by a student's previously completed outline for a paper on the rain forest.

Students produced computer-printed twenty-page papers on such topics as federal pollution water control laws; whaling; endangered red wolves and Alaskan wolves; environmental consequences of the Persian Gulf War; dangers of ozone; rain forest plants that heal; environmental causes of cancer; pesticides and insecticides; smog; and AIDS. Most of the papers included charts and pictures. Students shared their findings with classmates, and some students presented their research in other classes.

About forty hours of class time were devoted to student work on the project, which lasted the entire semester. The project was the most important factor in evaluating student learning for the semester.

## Red Lake Middle School

In contrast to the other three schools, Red Lake showed no explicit and agreed-on approach to curriculum, instruction, or specific standards for evaluating students' work. But there was a tacit, commonly held belief that all students should master ambitious content. Red Lake achieved reasonably high levels of authentic pedagogy, and Center staff perceived serious faculty attention to the substance of student learning.

Several teachers' statements illustrated concern for intellectual quality. A science teacher said, "I'm interested in the process of science, doing lab work and being excited about science. . . . We can't keep up with the facts. So it's far more important to get the concepts and processes." A social studies teacher reported that he used lots of anecdotal current and historical happenings to illustrate important concepts: "My goal is to try to get kids to think about connections. . . . Even though the assignments I use will focus on concrete information, I will use this as a basis for the thinking and abstraction in discussion." Another social studies teacher described an assessment activity after visiting the Anne Frank exhibit at a museum. It invited creative activity such as drawing posters, composing songs, or writing letters to Anne Frank. Students also "had to use their notes to write an essay on the main idea I gave them."

A mathematics teacher asked "students to communicate what they are learning . . . not the formulas they have learned today, but what is it they understand about what they've done. I'm not going to tell them everything . . . they need to investigate and explore on their own." Another mathematics teacher was excited about some exercises on the new state performance tests that emphasized mathematical thinking, problem solving, and mathematical communication.

Beliefs of this sort translated into lessons like the following Algebra I class for eighth graders. In a seventy-minute class, the teacher first reviewed homework, then asked students to consider the mathematics myth that "it's bad to count on your fingers." They agreed that using fingers could be useful, but sometimes other methods might be better. Students concurred that the point was to find easy or efficient ways to solve problems. The teacher posed problems such as the following which she used to clarify aspects of set theory and principles for counting:

1. Out of 41 frozen dinners, 14 people had beef dinners, 21 had chicken, 5 had broccoli, 2 had both beef and broccoli, and none had both beef and chicken. (a) What is the probability that they had either beef or broccoli? (b) Beef or chicken?

2. If you toss 2 dice 50 times, what is the probability of tossing **E** (an even combination) or **L** (combination larger than 9)?

3. Calvin is giving 10 records to Jorge and Marie. Graph the possibilities [how many each would receive] on the horizontal for Jorge and on the vertical for Marie.

4. If $N(A) = 15$ and $N(A \cap B) = 7$ and $N(A \cup B) = 20$, find $B$.

Throughout the class, the teacher asked students to explain how they solved the problems. Working in groups, students enthusiastically showed one another how they arrived at answers. The kinds of questions raised in discussion of the second problem were typical. As different students explained their work, the teacher asked, "Why did you find the probability of getting an even sum? . . . What are the total possibilities of sums when you roll a pair of dice? . . . What should you get, theoretically speaking? . . . What's the smallest number you can throw on a pair of dice? . . . What's the largest number you can throw?" Putting a number line of 2 to 12 on the board, she noted that with fifty tosses, students would start getting close to the theoretical probability. "What is the probability of getting **L**? How many of you knew you were dealing with eleven possibilities?"

One student suggested that the probabilities could be found by considering only one die. The discussion explained how this would provide incomplete information. As the teacher guided inquiry to focus on the probability of getting **E** or **L**, she showed how this could be understood as the union of two sets (the combinations that produce E and the combinations that produce L).

Red Lake required all students to take interdisciplinary Connections courses, which sought to cultivate the skills of reading, writing, listening and speaking, thinking, research, and studying. Students selected a Connections elective from a variety of topics, usually of contemporary significance related to the academic subjects (for example, Changes and Challenges of Adolescence; Comparisons of Life in 1900, 2000, 2100; A Guide to Social Action; Trials and Forensic Science). Except for a requirement that all sixth graders take the Cultural Connections course, students were free to choose their courses (with guidance from a teacher adviser and parental consent), and faculty designed the courses they wished to teach, according to Red Lake's widely mentioned principle, "Teach to your passion."

Connections courses were developed by two or three teachers working as a team to conceptualize content that addressed cross-disciplinary themes and simultaneously promoted the learning skills noted above. Teams often used $1,000 incentive grants from the district to support course development by paying for release time to meet and resources during the year of the grant. Curriculum planning of this sort concentrated faculty attention on new ways of organizing disciplinary content rather than on administrative-logistical concerns.

In order for Connections and the other courses to be officially offered, they were first approved by the entire faculty after teachers had submitted proposed syllabi for review. Peer review offered an opportunity for faculty to discuss the balance of content among course offerings and their developmental appropriateness for different students (all teachers had advisory responsibility for student course selection).

In short the main evidence of Red Lake faculty commitment to intellectual quality consistent with standards for authentic pedagogy came not from any apparent schoolwide program or approach but from the teachers' commonly held beliefs about the importance of students' learning to understand ambitious content. Given a faculty predisposed to helping students construct knowledge about important real-life problems through disciplined inquiry, the school's structure for "teaching to your passion" reinforced an emphasis on intellectual quality over technique. When both teachers and students were working on topics that intrinsically interested them, both were more likely to be invested in the intellectual substance of the topic than in methodological trappings to enhance student engagement.

Red Lake also demonstrated a schoolwide commitment to student participation in school governance and community affairs, which could explain high levels of authentic pedagogy. Faculty encouragement of students to participate in important decisions on school and community issues and in their own education indicates a respect for students' intellect that probably gives teachers the confidence to challenge students to solve complex problems, demand deep understanding, and encourage students' using their minds to make a difference in the world.

## Cibola High School

Staff at Cibola planned their curriculum, lessons, and assessment activities to promote certain habits of mind. As one mathematics-science teacher said, "We started this school so that students could use their minds well. That was our premise." A humanities teacher said that focusing on habits of mind was typical in his classes, and Center researchers observed one class where he talked with students for about twenty minutes about habits of mind—what they meant and how important they were.

Cibola's staff operationalized habits of mind into five key themes and questions that pervaded the curriculum:

*Viewpoint.* From whose perspective is something being presented?

*Evidence.* How do we know what we know? Is our information reliable?

*Connections.* How are these things, these events, connected with other like events?

*Relevance.* Why is it important? Why are we studying this?

*Supposition.* What if . . . ? Suppose things had been different.

This intellectually challenging agenda was displayed in the classrooms we visited. Teachers targeted lessons and student exhibitions toward "essential questions" that organized disciplinary content to address these themes. For example, Center researchers observed a mathematics-science unit on motion that asked, "What causes something to move; what keeps something moving; what stops something from moving; and how can motion be described mathematically?" Essential questions in humanities classes included, "How do we decide what is just; what is the relationship between law and justice; how can I help bring about justice?" As teachers talked with students they often asked, "Why?" "How do you know?" "Suppose . . . , then what?"

To graduate from Cibola, students completed fourteen portfolio assignments and presented seven of these as oral exhibitions to a committee consisting of the student's adviser, another faculty member, a third adult chosen by the student (often a family member), and a younger student in the school. All staff served on graduation committees, which referred to the habits of mind to evaluate the success of student written and oral presentations.

According to a scoring sheet used by the Senior Institute Graduation Committee, specific criteria corresponding to different habits of mind were used to judge students' oral presentations and written work. For example, Connections was summarized as "The Whole Is Greater Than the Sum of the Parts." To meet this criterion student portfolios were "organized so that all parts support the whole, contain useful transitions, and explain the significance of problems/issues beyond the project." Viewpoint was summarized as "Encompasses Wide Knowledge Base But Is Focused." To meet this criterion, evaluators must conclude that a student's work "clearly identifies and addresses key question and ideas; demonstrates an in-depth understanding of the issues; presents a position persuasively; and discusses other views when appropriate."

Teachers explained these standards to students in class, and they became a significant focus of faculty discussions about the quality of student work. One teacher described an argument he had with a colleague about a student's performance. He felt the student's analysis of one scene in *Othello* was adequate but that the student had not demonstrated an in-depth understanding of other parts of the play. Faculty participation on graduation committees helped to keep them focused on standards of intellectual quality. One codirector observed that "teachers talk about standards over and over again by sitting together and looking at the work of students. Not only in terms of judging it and grading it but also bringing it back to the classroom, bringing it back to habits of mind."

The commitment to intellectual quality at Cibola was consistently demonstrated in lessons and tasks scoring high on construction of knowledge, disciplined inquiry, and value beyond the school. One extended project, which asked students in mathematics-science classes to design a water ride for an amusement park and explain why it would float, involved an extended in-depth investigation into principles of physics and use of appropriate mathematical equations. Students had to take into consideration a number of variables such as properties of different materials for constructing the boat, its shape and volume, the weight of passengers, and how all these parts interact with water.

A project for Humanities, adapted from the Constitutional Education Foundation, required ninth and tenth graders to take the role of a U.S. senator and prepare written arguments for or against a fictitious bill. The purpose of the bill was to make the United States more competitive in international sports and to equalize opportunities and resources for females and males in high school athletics. Students drafted their arguments and received feedback from the teacher and other students for revisions. The class conducted a debate at the local city government building with city officials acting as facilitators responding. The debate was videotaped and shown to another class. In all, students spent fifteen class hours and part of seven days outside the class on this task. They analyzed and developed in-depth knowledge on the meaning of equal opportunity, the role of athletics in education, and the effects of prior court decisions and federal legislation (especially Title IX of the Civil Rights Act).

## Summary

The reform of organizational structure and even of specific teaching practices offers no assurance of improvement in the intellectual quality of teachers' and students' work in school. In some of the twenty-four schools, structural and technical changes diverted staff attention from the quality of schoolwork. Conversely, when a school staff committed itself to improved intellectual quality as the central purpose for structural and technical reform, such reforms assisted the staff in achieving authentic pedagogy. Concern for intellectual quality is represented by staff discussions about and clear conclusions on what is most important to teach (legitimacy of content) and a press for accuracy in what is taught and learned. But concern for intellectual quality can also reach beyond these criteria toward features of authentic intellectual achievement.

We showed how the four schools most successful with authentic pedagogy reflected central concerns for intellectual quality that extended to construction of knowledge, in-depth understanding, and connections to life beyond school. In three of the schools, concern for intellectual quality was grounded in schoolwide principles for curriculum and instruction, but the principles varied. Careen emphasized connecting knowledge to issues beyond school, Lamar emphasized ecological interdependence, and Cibola emphasized specific habits of mind. In contrast, Red Lake's concern for intellectual quality arose more from teachers' passion to teach their subjects in ways that promoted student thinking and understanding.

With these commitments to students' intellectual development, staff in each of the schools used innovative structures and practices such as teaming, flexible scheduling, site-based management, small group work, independent student research projects, and portfolio assessment to support authentic pedagogy. But defining ambitious intellectual goals for a school and implementing pedagogy to achieve them is no easy task.

## Notes

1. In a study of three elementary schools Elmore (1995) and Elmore, Peterson, and McCarthey (1996) elaborate on the inability of structural reform alone to improve teaching practice.

2. Resnick (1989) includes a variety of research on construction of meaning. Sizer (1984) explains the goal of using one's mind well.

3. Regnier (1994) offers a succinct explanation of how preoccupation with technique in education stifles intellectual life in schools. Other

researchers have noticed persistent tendencies of schooling in the United States that subordinate intellectual excellence to other priorities (Goodlad, 1984; Kliebard, 1986; Powell, Farrar, and Cohen, 1984; Tyack and Cuban, 1995).

4. The standards movement elicits controversy over several issues: what is a standard, who should have authority to set them (teachers, parents, districts, states, or national authorities), how are standards likely to improve education and for whom, and if standards are to be set, what content they should include. For diverse perspectives on these issues, see Aiming for Higher Standards (1995); Cohen (1995); Eisner (1995); Lewis (1995); Ravitch (1995); and Struggling for Standards (1995).

5. Meier (1995) presents a compelling argument on the importance of faculty commitment to students' intellectual life.

# Chapter Seven

# Schoolwide Professional Community

*Karen Seashore Louis, Sharon D. Kruse,*
*Helen M. Marks*

The much-quoted African proverb, "It takes a whole village to raise a child," captures the theme of the importance of community support for teaching and learning. Individual teachers and peers in classrooms influence children's learning each day, but the extent to which many adults cooperate over the school years in educating the child ultimately determines whether he or she makes the greatest possible progress in the journey toward adulthood.

Cooperation alone does not guarantee adults' success in building intellectual capacity in children, however. Nevertheless, community among adults, when focused on professional responsibility and the central tasks of education, can reinforce and augment the talent, knowledge, and insight that individual teachers bring to their work. While well-designed school restructuring efforts may stimulate teachers' enthusiasm and satisfaction in their work, without professional community, most individual teachers will find it difficult to sustain the level of energy needed to reflect continually on and improve their practice for the benefit of authentic student achievement.

## The Importance of Schoolwide Professional Community

The school reform movement has emphasized the professionalization of teachers' work. Commonly stated themes include more stringent standards of entry into the teaching field, a national licensing system for more advanced teachers, and better pay and training opportunities to attract and retain skilled, committed practitioners. These reforms may be critical, but researchers and educational reformers should not focus solely on strategies to develop individual professionals.[1] Teachers also need collegial resources for support and refreshment.

Educational networks or other professional organizations beyond the school may provide teachers some forms of technical and collegial support. Discipline-based reform projects, such as those that formulate curriculum standards, can also become the basis for teacher commitment and interaction, particularly in high schools.[2] But professional community, as we define it, offers the more inclusive support of a whole school: An entire faculty comes together around meaningful, shared issues irrespective of teachers' individual disciplines. Schoolwide community does not devalue other forms of collective professional relationships nor is it incompatible with a departmental structure. But it does entail staff members' taking collective responsibility for achieving a shared educational purpose for the school as a whole and collaborating with one another to attain it.

By collaborating on common objectives, sharing developmental activities and concerns, and reflecting together on the technical aspects of their teaching, teachers come to own in common the consequences of their joint work for students' intellectual progress. Professional community reinforces peer pressure on and accountability of staff who may not be carrying their fair share of responsibility for students' learning, just as it eases the burden of other teachers who work hard in isolation but have not found success in helping some students. All of this normative support is helpful in sustaining each teacher's commitment to the difficult work of teaching.

Without the normative climate provided by a school professional community, making major pedagogical change is possible but very difficult. Authentic pedagogy presents a major challenge. It calls on teachers not simply to adopt specific techniques but to make complex judgments about how to promote the intellectual qualities of construction of knowledge, disciplined inquiry, and value beyond school. There are no formulas, textbooks, or training programs that chart the path to success. Instead teachers must build innovative curriculum and assessment, try a variety of instructional activities, and continually revise their practice. School professional community offers the kind of intellectual and social support necessary for success with authentic pedagogy.

## Elements of Professional Community

Five elements appear critical to school professional community: shared norms and values, focus on student learning, reflective dialogue, deprivatization of practice, and collaboration.[3]

### Shared Norms and Values

Through language and action, teachers can develop and reaffirm their common assumptions about children, learning, teaching, teachers' roles, the importance of interpersonal relationships, and commitment to the collective good (Bryk, Lee, and Holland, 1993). Values central to teachers' work include their views about children and children's ability to learn, school priorities for the use of time and space, and the proper roles of parents, teachers, and administrators. When school values are vague or consensus on what is expected of teachers is low, teachers may enjoy more autonomy to pursue their unique interests. But if teachers cannot count on colleagues to reinforce their objectives, individual autonomy can reduce teachers' efficacy.

In contrast, clear shared values and norms, collectively reinforced, increase the likelihood of teachers' success. Shared values find expression in school practices. Where professional community thrives, teachers assume that all students can learn at reasonably high levels. Despite the many obstacles that students may face outside school, teachers are confident they can help them learn (Louis, Marks, and Kruse, 1996). Teachers might require students who are failing to take part in after-school support activities, for example; thus they demonstrate consistency between an appreciation for achievement and the need to offer extra help to ensure that learning occurs.

## Focus on Student Learning

Attentiveness to student learning is a core characteristic of schools where professional community is strong. Faculty discussion and action center on improving students' opportunity to learn and enhancing students' achievement (Abbott, 1991; Darling-Hammond and Goodwin, 1993). Teachers send clear and consistent messages to one another about the objectives and methods of learning. Rather than focusing on activities or techniques simply to engage student attention, for example, these teachers discuss the ways in which their actions promote students' intellectual development. Such mutually felt obligations among teachers emphasize intellectual benefits for students as primary among the many possible goals of schooling.

## Reflective Dialogue

Reflection intensifies teachers' awareness of their practice and its consequences. Commitment to reflection as a group activity leads to extensive and continuing conversations among teachers about curriculum, instruction, and student development (Zeichner and Tabachnick, 1991). In strong professional communities, teachers use these discussions to evaluate themselves and their schools. These critiques can address several issues: selection of subject matter and strategies for presenting it to students, ways to assess student learning and development, the social conditions of schooling, and issues of equity and justice.

## Deprivatization of Practice

Reflective dialogue is often coupled with open discussion about individual teachers' practice. To succeed with authentic pedagogy, teachers must analyze and evaluate their effectiveness in teaching students to construct knowledge skillfully. They must continually devise ways of interacting with students that are not well defined in textbooks or professional literature—for example, how to balance depth of understanding with teaching broad coverage of important information; how to introduce new, unfamiliar material in ways that build on students' prior knowledge;

and how to insist on high standards of performance for all but take into account differences in students' background, style, and pace of learning.

These issues are often too complex to be solved by teachers working alone. Peers become a critical source of insight and feedback to improve reflective teachers' understanding of their own practice (Kruse, 1995). By sharing uncertainties about practice, teachers learn new ways to talk about what they do. At the same time, they kindle new relationships that help to advance their work. In an emerging professional community, the typical norm of individual autonomy is diminished, and teachers become committed to practicing their craft in public ways (Lieberman, 1988).

## Collaboration

Collaboration is a natural outgrowth of reflective dialogue and deprivatized practice. As teachers work with students from increasingly diverse social backgrounds and as the curriculum demands more intellectual rigor, teachers require new information and skills. Sharing expertise with one another can increase teachers' technical competence. Building on the mutual understanding they have established, teachers work together to produce materials and activities for improving curriculum and pedagogy and to devise new approaches to professional development. Collaborative efforts also augment and reinforce the mosaic of socioemotional support within the school (Little, 1990). When teachers collaborate productively, they participate in reflective dialogue; they observe and react to one another's teaching, curriculum, and assessment practices; and they engage in joint planning and curriculum development. All of these forms of collaboration should improve practice.

## How Professional Community Supports Authentic Pedagogy

To examine the extent to which professional community promoted authentic pedagogy in the SRS schools, we used survey data collected from the teachers to construct an index of professional community that incorporates measures of each of the five elements critical to professional community.[4] We compared the level of professional community for each school with its rank on authentic pedagogy (measured as described in Chapter Two).

Figure 7.1 displays the results of this comparison. We found that in schools where professional community is strong, pedagogy tends to be more authentic; where professional community is weak, pedagogy also tends to be weak.[5] Because authentic pedagogy produces high-quality student performance, we can infer that school-wide professional community contributes indirectly to student academic achievement.[6]

The statistical data cannot prove that professional community causes teachers to engage in more authentic classroom practice. A skeptic could plausibly argue that teachers who are making efforts to increase authentic pedagogy are more likely to seek support for this difficult task from their colleagues, thus creating professional community. This issue of causality is like the chicken-and-egg question and could not be conclusively answered through the design of this study.[7] Furthermore, it is possible to imagine a strong professional community focused on refining traditional pedagogy that concentrated only on transmission of knowledge through recitation. Nevertheless, as ensuing examples will show, strong professional communities in the SRS schools enhanced teachers' attention to the intellectual quality of student learning and their commitment to the restructuring effort. The specific form of professional community varied among schools, but the strongest examples reflected the five elements.[8]

## Shared Norms and Values

Red Lake Middle School illustrates how shared values and norms can influence a school environment. School life there centers on the value of individuality embedded in community. Democracy and choice permeate the school's daily processes and long-term goals. The individual is significant at Red Lake, no matter what age or status. Students serve on governance councils, where they participate fully. Teachers share the belief that the school is "here for the kids. . . . [It's a] student-centered school where [we] always ask, 'What do the kids get out of it; what's in it for them?'"

Red Lake teachers design their own courses and are encouraged to teach to their own specific skills and interests. Students,

## Figure 7.1. Professional Community and Authentic Pedagogy.

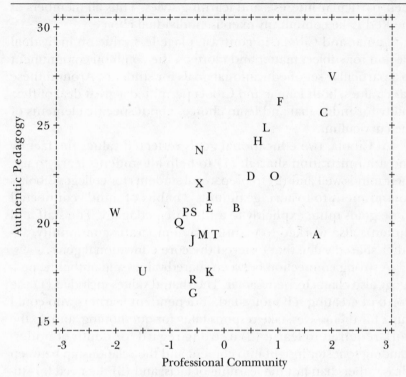

| School Key | Elementary | | Middle | | High | |
|---|---|---|---|---|---|---|
| | A | Humboldt | I | Morris | Q | Fremont |
| | B | Sumpter | J | Selway | R | Wallingford |
| | C | Ashley | K | Baldwin | S | Flinders |
| | D | Eldorado | L | Red Lake | T | Huron |
| | E | Winema | M | Shining Rock | U | South Glen |
| | F | Careen | N | Copan | V | Cibola |
| | G | Falls River | O | Okanagon | W | Island |
| | H | Lamar | P | Ottawa | X | Marble Canyon |

*Note:* Scores for authentic pedagogy are school averages for mathematics and social studies classes, scored according to the standards described in Chapter One. Scores for professional community are school averages for all teachers in the school across the five dimensions of professional community (described in Appendix A), assessed by surveys and standardized across the twenty-four schools.

with guidance from advisory teachers, create schedules to meet their particular interests and learning styles. Thus all members of the Red Lake community exercise individual choice.

Lamar and Cibola, in contrast, place less value on individual passion for subject matter and more on the common commitment to a particular set of educational goals for students. Around these basic values, both Lamar and Cibola permitted a great deal of flexibility for individual and team choices about specific elements of the curriculum.

At Cibola, two educational goals reflected values the faculty and administration shared: (1) to help all students learn to use their minds well and (2) to prepare all students for college. Cibola's commitment to fostering students' "habits of mind" connected these goals quite explicitly to authentic pedagogy. The staff and students also worked to maintain a democratic community, another shared value that fostered the core educational goals.

A strong connection between shared values and authentic pedagogy also characterized Lamar. The shared values included (1) the worth of creating self-motivated, independent learners who could think for themselves, take responsibility for questioning, and do the work required to learn; (2) a strong regard for depth of understanding to foster insight into content and the relationship between ideas rather than just the learning of facts; and (3) the need for students to connect subject matter knowledge with real-life issues and questions, especially those related to human relations and the environment. This set of espoused values is consistent with the dimensions of authentic pedagogy outlined in Chapter One.

To assume that shared norms result in uniformity of opinion would be a mistake, however, even at schools like Cibola and Lamar where teachers exhibited very high levels of cohesiveness around values. The discussion of alternative perspectives within a context of shared values appeared to sustain the commitment to intellectual quality. Such dialogues may challenge the deeply held beliefs of one teacher or contest another's assumptions, while simultaneously advancing each teacher's thinking. A teacher from Cibola noted:

> Given the fact that everybody came here and that everybody is
> a thinking educator, I don't know how you can expect them [to
> agree on everything]—and also in an atmosphere to encourage

people to come with different cultural backgrounds and different beliefs—and to encourage and welcome that. We have discussions about that. . . . I think it's impossible and not desirable to get forty faculty all thinking alike. . . . There are people whom I disagree with most of the time, they just open their mouths and I'll disagree with what they say. But I think that's okay.

Discussions where colleagues offer their views and new information can create opportunities for teachers to consider and change their practice. When exchanges are most fruitful, colleagues air differences in a context of trust and respect for each other's professional skills and contributions to the school community:

> I think that inasmuch as everybody who works here came because they wanted to because of the nature of the work, everybody who works here is a thoughtful, thinking person about education. There's nobody here who doesn't like kids, who's just putting in their time until they retire, or who doesn't at some level think about teaching and learning. Now that's not to say that everybody is actively thinking about what they do in the classroom every day but there's nobody here that said, "Hand me the syllabus and I'll do it." Everybody here has a commitment to design their own courses; that tells you something.

## Collective Focus on Student Learning

A collective focus on student learning means more than setting high expectations for students. Teachers could set high standards but not necessarily organize their work to incorporate collegial analysis of instruction and its implications for student performance. Teachers' collective focus on student learning at Lamar Elementary resulted in setting high standards, and these emphasized students' academic needs. Teachers worked in pairs, increasing peer pressure to ensure that students learned: "You work with another teacher, which means there's some accountability. There's more accountability when you're working with somebody than when you're isolated." The team structure also required that every student spend at least two years with the same team. Working with students over a longer period of time augmented teachers' ability to monitor student progress.

Critical discussions of how students benefit from so much emphasis on individual teachers' choosing what to teach tempered Red Lake Middle's strong emphasis on teachers' autonomy. Like their counterparts at Lamar, Red Lake teachers reported that the greatest pressure to ensure student success came not come from the largely middle-class parents but from within their own ranks.

Red Lake's dual focus on teachers' teaching to their passion and students' choosing their instructional program also reflected a strong commitment to diversity. In some school settings diversity can strain the collective focus on student learning, but at Red Lake the wide range of opinions was not divisive; just as at Cibola, heterogeneity became a valued feature of faculty identity. Red Lake staff's shared respect and commitment to success for all students offered a foundation of support that seemed to withstand considerable variety in educational philosophies, lifestyle, political viewpoints, and teaching strategies.

## Reflective Dialogue

Cibola High provides the most striking example of reflective dialogue nurturing authentic pedagogy. The staff continually used reflective dialogue to create a climate that valued dialogue among staff to advance inquiry-based curriculum, instruction, and assessment for students and to refine their understanding of what it meant to be an innovative school.

Teachers work together on the development of Cibola's curriculum. Team-centered reflection and a schoolwide effort to discuss curriculum, instruction, and assessment publicly supported Cibola teachers in this effort. As one humanities teacher stated: "This is a place where we can disagree without worrying about the wrath of god or falling apart. We're constantly at it, constantly discussing issues. We haven't solved problems but we have addressed them and taken them out of the closet, out of the dark, and looked at them."

Cibola teachers regularly used their common planning time to tackle pedagogical implications of issues often left unexamined in other schools—for example, gender, race, and poor student performance. Workshops and other activities during the year we visited Cibola focused staff attention on gender issues both within the school and in society at large. Teachers claimed that these experiences led to specific changes in their teaching related to issues of gender.

Although few other schools sustained such a high level of reflective dialogue among all teachers, Cibola was not unique. Most teachers at Okanagon Middle agreed that reflection on practice took place most frequently in teams, but a powerful teacher committee stimulated a process of schoolwide reflection on assessment. All teachers took part in developing and scoring authentic English and mathematics tasks that were used to assess students. Colleagues who taught subjects other than English or mathematics graded the student work.

Although the process proved time-consuming, most teachers found it extremely valuable. Teachers discussed in depth both what they expected students to know and be able to do in performance assessments and how their own teaching was supporting these core disciplines. As one teacher pithily put it, "The [schoolwide assessment] is a pain in the butt, but I like it. It gives you a sense of where the kids are relative to the whole school. It gets the whole school involved in where the strengths and weaknesses are."

At Lamar Elementary, reflective dialogue allowed staff to continue to refine their instructional and social goals for students. Unlike teachers at Cibola, Lamar's teachers were most influenced by their daily teaching partners. They extolled the value of dialogue with their trusted partners, who knew their students the best but also reported they would like more time set aside for the faculty as a whole to address shared issues.

## Deprivatization of Practice

Lamar Elementary strongly exemplifies deprivatized instructional practice. The inquiry-based school provides ample opportunities for peers to observe each other's teaching, especially through their two-teacher teams. Teacher teams regularly plan units and lessons, discussing the finer points of curriculum development and students' reactions to previous lessons. Teachers overwhelmingly support the team arrangement. "I wouldn't give my partner up for the lottery," one teacher declared. "We really have it [teaching together] down and really complement and supplement one another.

I couldn't ever imagine teaching without a partner again. It's just so nice having another adult in there." Another teacher underscored her colleague's feelings by adding, "That's what makes it work—the give and take of sharing and having a stake in this place. This is our school, not just a place that we come and work." For Lamar teachers, the opportunity to work with other teachers in an open and public relationship enhanced both the quality of their work life and their feelings of success with students.

In a school where teachers did not team, Ashley Elementary, the principal encouraged teachers to spend time observing in each other's classrooms. Many teachers at Ashley testified to the power of discussions about teaching that emerged from the observations. Other schools were unable to sustain such deprivatization, however, either because of incompatible schedules or because the longstanding norm that teaching should not be open to public scrutiny persisted in the classroom.[9]

Short of peer observation, other significant steps can occur to deprivatize teachers' practice in support of authentic pedagogy. Schoolwide participation in scoring assessment tasks involved Okanagon teachers in evaluating student work from other teachers' classrooms. Having used interdisciplinary groups to develop standards for assessing student performance, teachers learned the value of understanding what constituted a high or low level of performance in disciplines other than their own. Participating in the scoring sometimes challenged teachers' privately held assumptions about what constitutes quality work. Public discussion about the difference in performance of students in some teams and classes was a potentially threatening activity. Nonetheless teachers seemed willing to subject the performance of their own students to public scrutiny: "Well, it could [cause concern], but I think that we all look at it like a training thing for us. I mean, if for some reason all of your kids didn't do too well, then we can help each other."

## Collaboration

At schools with strong professional communities, teachers collaborated. Where they taught in teams, collaboration took place primarily in that setting. Although teams took different forms from school to school, those in the strong professional communities all focused on creating effective learning experiences for students, often through innovative instruction. Through sharing ideas, reflecting on practice, and peer coaching, within-grade and cross-grade teams developed strong collaborative relationships.

At the most successful schools, collaboration extended beyond team planning and curriculum design to committee work aimed at common schoolwide endeavors, usually evident in the school's philosophy of teaching: assessment by performance at Cibola, democracy and choice at Red Lake, inquiry-based programs at Lamar.

## Supporting Professional Community

Schoolwide professional community can sustain intellectual quality and teachers' commitment to the hard work of school reform. However, not all SRS schools achieved such high levels of professional community. If more schools are to advance in developing as professional communities, what school conditions seem to be important?

Strong professional community schools such as Lamar, Red Lake, and Cibola attended to key facets of both school culture and structure. In the following section, we discuss how school culture and structure interact to support professional community.

### Cultural Conditions Supporting Professional Community

Several cultural conditions could conceivably support professional community, but here we emphasize a few that stood out. Schools with the most vital professional communities had two prominent features in common: teachers' dedication to inquiry and innovation, and supportive leadership, typically from a principal or a formally designated teacher leader.[10]

#### A Climate of Professional Inquiry

The culture of emergent professional communities in the SRS schools is decidedly intellectual. Cibola teachers, committed to inquiry, struggled together to define improved practice at both a conceptual and a concrete level. Because Red Lake teachers were engaged with new ideas in the profession, they attended workshops and discussed instruction (despite their limited collaboration). The cultures of inquiry at Cibola and Red Lake welcomed ideas, particularly ideas found outside the school. Conspicuously absent was the "not-invented-here" attitude that deters some teachers from thinking about alternative practices and educational approaches.

Principals at some of the schools served as conduits to new ideas. In other schools teachers, with the principal's blessing, independently brought new ideas to the teams. Under the leadership of the principal, who provided opportunities and expectations for teachers to share new knowledge, teachers at Lamar researched and applied new ideas to complement and reinforce their vision as an inquiry-based school. With support provided by their industry technology partner, teachers took primary responsibility for innovation. Cibola's principal connected teachers to an expanding local network of other educators committed to authentic pedagogy and assessment. By promoting inquiry-oriented school environments, principals at Lamar and Cibola reinforced the role of teachers as generators and consumers of knowledge.

Principals who lead in ways that model and reward intellectual effort help the school environment to sustain the discussion of important ideas, and teachers search beyond the school for new practices and approaches to enrich its program. In short, a culture of inquiry thrives if both principals and teachers build bridges to the world of research and development outside the school or if they actively promote the role of external advisers who can do so.

When colleagues or external sources introduced instructional innovations, for example, teachers in strong professional communities used the collective processes we have described to interrogate the actual value of the innovations: Would the innovation contribute to the intellectual quality of students' learning? When an innovation was judged worthwhile, collegial technical and social support for it often resulted in more focused teaching and more clearly defined assessment methods. As teaching becomes more closely aligned with authentic assessment tasks, student achievement is likely to improve. Visible student improvement, in turn, reinforces teachers' individual and collective commitment to their work and the value they place on collaborative inquiry.

### Can Teachers Take Risks?

Rewards for innovation and tolerance of small failures support intellectual vitality in teachers. But departing from established instructional patterns entails uncertainty and the risk of failure (Rowan, 1994). Yet teachers' and administrators' willingness to take the risks of innovation stood out in all of the most successful schools. These faculties had the capacity to learn from small losses. As with most other successful and vital organizations in other sectors, they acquired knowledge useful for future planning by critically examining small failures as well as successes (Siskin, 1991).

Risk taking and professional community were closely linked at Red Lake. Curricular choice encouraged teachers to design courses and to take on the risk of organizing curriculum and instruction in unconventional ways. To evaluate the effectiveness of their innovations, teachers solicited candid student reactions to their learning experiences. Because Red Lake's principal consistently supported teachers who wished to try something novel, they could openly discuss their uncertainties about the difficult process of translating their ideas into teachable units. Innovation was a norm at Red Lake, but so were expectations for reflection, assessment, and continuous readjustment.

### Reshaping Leadership at the School Level

The formal title for the chief administrator at most SRS schools was principal, but other titles included teacher-director (Cibola), chief educational officer (Okanagon), and coordinator (Island). In some schools, teachers held formal leadership positions, but in all cases, those with principal-like responsibilities had great influence over the quality of professional community.

Leaders in schools with strong professional community differed from their counterparts in schools where professional community proved relatively weak. The more effective leaders took on such new roles as working with teachers to stimulate intellectual inquiry in the school. Confirming the findings of other recent research, we found that the most effective administrative leaders delegated authority, developed collaborative decision-making processes, and stepped back from being the central problem solver (Leithwood, Jantzi, and Fernandez, 1995; Louis, Kruse, and Associates, 1995; Murphy, 1994). Instead they turned to the professional community for critical decisions. In each case the quality of professional community depended more on the way in which leaders enacted their roles than on the formal definition of their roles. A more equitable exercise of power and influence fostered collective responsibility for student learning and instructional collaboration among teachers (Marks and Louis, 1996).

In the more successful schools, individuals in leadership positions defined themselves as at the center of the school's staff rather than at the top. Cibola's teacher-director delegated most of the day-to-day management of the school to others while she provided intellectual stimulation for the faculty. In addition to playing a major role in negotiating the district's bureaucracy, she connected the school to outside resources, including a network of like-minded schools. Okanagon's chief educational officer was a member of most important committees (the curriculum committee and the main governance committee), but both he and the other committee members viewed him as having merely one vote. Nevertheless, as in many of the other schools, he played an important role as keeper of the dream, reminding teachers on many occasions about the key values that were expected to guide difficult decisions.

In sum, although successful leaders of professional community gave up some typically visible leader behaviors, such as running meetings and issuing solutions to school problems, they still maintained a strong presence. They worked effectively to stimulate professional discussion and to create the networks of conversation that tied faculty together around common issues of instruction and teaching.

Our emphasis on commonality, collegiality, and cooperation is not meant to devalue conflict. Without some conflict, professional communities could become resistant to legitimate challenges to established programs and routines. In order for communities to grow, they must occasionally question their own values, a process that inevitably induces disagreement. Thus strong communities encourage debate, but debates engender the potential for division.

In most of the SRS schools, the designated leader effectively managed conflict. Principals in schools with strong professional communities did not often unilaterally resolve differences, but they encouraged a supportive environment and structures for teachers to resolve them. At Ashley, many teachers describe their sense that the principal fostered the norm of continuous discussion but did not demand closure or conformity. One teacher said, "There is no resolution [to our discussions about standardized testing]. You really can't come up with a final resolution. I think in some schools the principal might say, 'This what we're gonna do.'. . . It's not done that way in this school."

Forums for discussion and debate enabled teachers to adjudicate discord and work toward respectful agreement. Safe forums where hard listening occurs allowed teachers to discuss alternatives in ways that reinforce community values rather than individual self-interest. Thus schools could sustain a shared commitment to their restructuring effort, even when members of the staff disagreed.

School leaders must also negotiate the politics of reform within the local context. Reform efforts are highly susceptible to failure, especially when they do not enjoy the support of all the teachers in a school, when they are opposed by vocal parents, or when they are driven primarily by outside agencies. Careful management of relationships within the school and with external groups is necessary so that teachers feel involved with decision making on critical issues and they enjoy support from parents and agencies beyond the school (Beck, 1994; Louis and Miles, 1990). Since many SRS schools were located in large, urban settings, there was a common need for someone who could negotiate the many requirements of the "downtown" district office. Even schools like Red Lake, located in a smaller urban setting, depended on the principal to keep the district office apprised of unconventional developments at the school so as to avoid unanticipated controversy.

Finally, principals and designated teacher leaders often bear the responsibility to ensure that school structure supports professional community. Because they are usually better positioned to negotiate structural innovations (for example, in grade-level and departmental organization, governance systems, scheduling of instruction, or grouping of students), school leaders must understand the potential for organizational structures to support or inhibit professional community.

To summarize, as Louis and Miles (1990) point out, the most effective principals engaged in both transformational leadership activities (maintaining vision, rethinking the organizational structure) and a great deal of detailed management that supported teachers' work (facilitating conflict resolution, obtaining resources, ensuring smooth relationships with the district).

## Structural Conditions Supporting Professional Community

The cultural qualities of professional inquiry, risk taking, and leadership that support professional community can in turn be supported by, and often depend on, important structural conditions, especially school size and complexity, school autonomy and shared decision making, time for teacher planning, and opportunities for professional development.

### Size and Complexity

Large school size adversely affects teachers' ability to know and talk with one another. Meetings of the whole, which can sustain reflective dialogue, become very difficult in large schools. Thus smaller schools and elementary and middle schools tended to be more effective in creating professional community than larger schools, especially high schools. Nonetheless some larger schools supported professional community by repeatedly emphasizing common goals and by creating smaller settings where teachers could work together.

Complexity results when schools maintain specialized academic and student support programs that entail differential staffing assignments and include many nonteaching professionals in staff roles. In complex organizations, subgroups within the staff may develop diverse values and norms.[11] Academic departments in high schools can offer the locus of professional community for teachers, for example, creating, in effect, schools within schools (Siskin, 1994). Cohesive subunits, such as departments or grade-level teams, can develop norms that conflict with the needs of the larger school unless they are effectively integrated into a larger whole (Little, 1993; Talbert, 1994).

Making significant reductions in school size and complexity requires considerable readjustment, but serious efforts along these lines can strengthen professional community and bring significant improvements in student achievement (Lee and Smith, 1995; Lee, Smith, and Croninger, 1995b).

### School Autonomy and Shared Decision Making

The most successful SRS schools shared an important characteristic: considerable autonomy to create their own instructional programs, select their teachers, and organize their staff development programs around local needs. This sort of authority made it possible to form and maintain shared norms and a cohesive school culture. As Chapter Eleven explains, autonomy from external agencies created important opportunities for schools that had established or were poised to establish cohesive cultures.

Because the schools were free from district and state constraints, teachers were also more likely to share in important school-level decisions. Democratic school structures provided fair processes for ensuring that staff members received equitable treatment.[12] Sharing power relations through such structures also permits the experience of associated living: the exchange of ideas, common ideals, and shared concerns and interests. In these ways, democratic school structures provide a critical foundation for professional community.

### Time for Teacher Planning and Analysis

If teachers are to discuss their practice, collaborate, and direct their energies toward common goals of intellectual quality, time for planning and analysis is essential (Wohlstetter, Smyer, and Mohrman, 1994). Reorganizing schools to provide teachers with more noninstructional time is controversial, because it is assumed that this would substantially increase costs that the United States taxpayers would not be willing to bear. Nevertheless, SRS schools with strong professional communities managed to find time for teacher planning through the following strategies:

- Arranging teaching schedules so teaching teams could meet together. For example, teacher teams at Okanagon met almost daily to work on issues related to student advising and curriculum development.
- Reducing the complexity of the schedule by offering fewer courses, an approach that was used primarily in secondary schools such as Cibola
- Enlisting teacher aides and volunteer parents to supervise students, which occurred more often in elementary schools. Lamar obtained more time for consultation between teacher-partners through the use of parents in classrooms.
- Involving students in community internships and service learning, a strategy at Cibola that served both to connect

students with real-world learning settings and move students
out of the school so that larger groups of teachers could meet
for more extended periods during the school day

- Using professional development funds to provide release time
for meetings, retreats, and summer development projects. Red
Lake sponsored all-staff retreats, in some years more than once.

Planning time does not ensure that teachers will develop professional community. In some schools, teams with significant planning time were unproductive because school culture did not
sufficiently emphasize teacher inquiry about the intellectual quality of student learning. Nevertheless the most successful schools
viewed planning time as a critical resource for teachers to develop
and refine the school's particular version of authentic pedagogy.

### Professional Development

To increase teachers' expertise, schools have traditionally participated in professional development activities. Typically these programs vary from opportunities for teachers to enroll in self-selected
university courses to episodic schoolwide presentations by outside
experts. Although individual teachers might profit from such experiences, in general such programs fail to enhance expertise or
school professional community. The one-day or half-day workshop
model was found in most of the SRS schools, but in the more successful schools, we saw alternative approaches that the participants
viewed as more significant.

Professional development tended to be focused on groups of
teachers within the school or the faculty as a whole. Making use of
internal as well as external expertise, staff development activities
took advantage of local skills and sharing of effective practice.
Including internal experts as staff developers reinforced teachers'
sense of commitment to their school goals. Okanagon presents a
strong example of this strategy, because many teachers took advantage of the school's connections to individual conference and training opportunities to learn new skills, but there was a strong norm
that those who did so had an obligation to give back to their colleagues by offering them staff development opportunities in their
areas of special expertise. Faculty tended to view their internal staff
development roles as a privilege and a source of additional per-

sonal growth. One teacher who had been doing the training in Socratic seminars since 1989 found it "incredible to work with [other] teachers. I love that. People can have new ideas, pick your brains, and you learn back from their giving you a scenario, and it makes me think"

In strong professional community schools, staff development responded to the special needs of individual teachers and helped to increase their understanding of instruction and their repertoire of teaching skills, but these advancements were connected to larger collective purposes. The Red Lake principal viewed a grant from the state as part of an opportunity to blend the special "teach to your passion" focus of the school with the need for discussion about ideas among the staff. He deliberately encouraged groups of teachers to take additional courses and seminars in their areas of expertise where these benefited the school, and he used grant monies to develop whole-day staff retreats where teachers would share emerging ideas about pedagogy and curriculum. The retreats were specifically intended for staff development purposes and focused on program development within the school. When grant monies shrank, the principal made an effort to find the resources to maintain intensive, all-school opportunities to connect and plan.

Unconventional staff development strategies were present in a number of the SRS schools. In Ashley, for example, the traditional staff development program had been largely replaced with release time for teachers to organize a full-day conference on curricular and instructional issues for teachers from other schools. Both the principal and faculty agreed that the process of planning for this successful annual event fostered both individual learning and collective growth as teachers worked together on sessions. Teachers' teaching other teachers was a form of professional development in several other schools as well. Cibola introduced another unconventional approach. The director and teachers organized an external review process that included classroom observations of teachers, coupled with individual constructive and nonthreatening feedback. The process offered the school a special professional development opportunity for both specific teachers and the school as a whole, as faculty considered together what they learned from the visitation and report, and what might be changed.

## Island High School: Low Professional Community and Its Consequences

Although the profiles of successful schools make the operation of professional community seem quite simple, developing its core elements, even under relatively ideal conditions, requires major changes in how teachers, parents, and principals think about the operations of schools (Louis, Kruse, and Associates, 1995). Our illustrations have come from thriving, mature communities, such as Lamar, Red Lake, Cibola, and Okanagon. Other schools, such as Island High, struggled. Structure, leadership, and social conditions thwarted Island's ability to develop a professional community.

At one time a traditional high school, Island sought to recreate itself as a restructured school. At the time of our visit, Island's 1,232 students traveled between two buildings to attend classes often taught by teachers who lacked the time and the proximity to meet together to plan for new programs. Unlike Cibola teachers who were able to design a new school for a select population, a district initiative and a state-mandated framework forced Island teachers to adopt a school restructuring agenda. Although Island responded to these mandates with structural innovations, it failed to create a school culture driven by coherent educational goals around which to organize the changes.

Dedicated teachers labored under difficult conditions at Island High School. Faculty disagreement on how best to meet the needs of the increasingly diverse and disadvantaged student population inhibited teachers' efforts to develop unified programs. Individual teachers engaged in efforts to meet the needs of subsets of the student population, but the larger effort was fragmented.

The absence of an academic and instructional focus for staff activity, Island's story suggests, hinders the growth of community within schools. In one innovation, Island grouped teachers across departments, organizing into interdisciplinary teams all the teachers assigned to the preparatory division (grades 9–10). Some faculty appreciated the opportunity to interact with a smaller number of colleagues, but the schedule did not allow all teams common planning periods. Teachers' ability to work together on curriculum and instructional issues was therefore limited—a common problem for a number of the SRS schools.

A substantial minority of Island teachers (25 to 30 percent), who were concentrated in eleventh and twelfth grade, did not buy in to the interdisciplinary team activities and continued to offer more traditionally structured courses. While preserving surface harmony, the strategy inhibited development of schoolwide community. In other schools with higher levels of professional community, dissident groups sometimes formed, but the strong cultures of these schools withstood the conflict. Teachers who did not agree with the reform effort either left or eventually were assimilated into the majority, who favored reform. Island had access to structures of support—such as a relationship with a learning center that provided a wide variety of professional development opportunities and a system of committees that were potential venues for professional conversation—but these failed to enhance professional community. Lacking a schoolwide vision for restructuring, Island teachers reacted to the state reform effort by generating a large number of unrelated innovations. The programs they developed to meet student needs had goals either too vague or too specialized to support the growth of school professional community. Although teachers met regularly, meetings bogged down in confusion over the appropriateness of content or procedural difficulties in reaching decisions.

Lacking an established common vocabulary with which to discuss instruction or curriculum, teachers were unable to reflect collectively on practice or to collaborate productively. Despite their dedication, the faculty lacked shared norms for instruction and curriculum. As a result, reflective dialogue among teachers rarely occurred on instructional teams, governance committees, or a planning committee charged with producing a transformation plan.

## Summary

By looking closely at the nature of teachers' work in the schools more successful with authentic pedagogy, we noticed the importance not simply of individual practice within classrooms but the ways teachers connect to and work with colleagues throughout the school. We identified this positive work setting as school professional community and defined it more specifically through five elements that tended to occur together: clear values and norms, a focus on student learning, reflective dialogue, deprivatization of practice, and collaboration.

Using case study data from diverse schools, we explained how these aspects of professional community supported authentic pedagogy by reinforcing an emphasis on the intellectual quality of student learning, by offering teachers technical help with the innovation that such pedagogy requires, and by strengthening social support that sustains teacher commitment with this difficult work. Teachers in the profiled schools were enthusiastic about their work, found satisfaction in teaching, and believed they were making a difference in their classrooms. They typically reported that elements of school professional communities helped them to improve their teaching.

Finally, we described how professional community is supported through an interaction of cultural and structural characteristics. Critical cultural conditions included a climate of professional inquiry, taking the risks of innovation, and leadership focused on participation, intellectual stimulation, and conflict management. Key structural conditions included reduced school size and organizational complexity, school autonomy and shared power relations, time for teacher planning, and sustained investments in teacher professional development.

## Notes

1. Louis, Marks, and Kruse (1996) expand on this argument.
2. McLaughlin (1994), Rowan (1994), and Siskin (1994) show the importance of disciplinary and departmental communities in high schools.
3. This section of the chapter draws on Kruse, Louis, and Bryk (1995).
4. The survey items are presented in Appendix A, and the methodology is explained in Louis, Marks, and Kruse (1996). Louis and Marks (1996) investigate the relationship of professional community to authentic pedagogy.
5. An exception is School A (Humboldt Elementary), where a lower-than-expected pedagogy score was due largely to missing assessment data. Center researchers reported many examples of authentic instruction from their classroom observations at Humboldt. School N (Copan Middle School), where above-average pedagogy coexisted with lower-than-average schoolwide community, is also an exception. Copan's schoolwide community was affected by the presence of

strong grade-level teams that developed a somewhat competitive stance in relation to each other.

6. The correlation between professional community and authentic pedagogy is .66; between authentic pedagogy and student achievement, the correlation is .68. Correlations are measured on a scale of 0 to 1.0. Researchers consider correlational estimates such as these to be very strong.

7. To conduct a rigorous test of whether professional community causes authentic pedagogy, one might find schools with low levels of both authentic pedagogy and professional community, then select a random sample of schools and expose them to interventions designed to promote professional community but with no explicit focus on authentic pedagogy. After an appropriate period of time, one could see whether advances in professional community were associated with increases in authentic pedagogy and whether schools that continued low on professional community consistently failed to achieve authentic pedagogy.

8. Although our definition of professional community implies that all elements be present to some extent, we do not mean that all schools with strong professional communities must be equally high on all dimensions. Red Lake Middle School, for example, exhibited very strong patterns of shared norms and values, a collective focus on student learning, and commitment to collaborative governance. It exhibited only modest levels of reflective dialogue and deprivatized practice.

9. Little (1990) offers a more extensive discussion about privacy in teaching.

10. For a more detailed discussion of cultural supports for professional community, see Louis, Kruse, and Associates (1995).

11. See, for example, Little's (1994) analysis of the divisions between vocational and nonvocational teachers in comprehensive high schools and analyses of differences between high school academic departments (McLaughlin and Talbert, 1993; Talbert, 1991).

12. SRS findings on this issue confirm and extend the conclusions of Bryk, Lee, and Holland (1993); Bull, Fruehling, and Chattergy (1992); Kymlicka (1991).

# Part Four

# The Interplay of School Culture and Structure

The schools most successful with authentic pedagogy were distinguished from others by two features: a pervasive concern for the intellectual quality of student learning and a strong schoolwide professional community. In this part we examine approaches to other issues that influenced the twenty-four schools' emphasis on intellectual quality, the nature of professional community, and the extent of authentic pedagogy. The schools differed in their extent of support for student achievement (Chapter Eight), how their curriculum and pedagogy responded to student diversity (Chapter Nine), how participatory decision making affected authentic pedagogy (Chapter Ten), and how they used external agents to advance intellectual quality and professional community (Chapter Eleven).

In trying to explain how and why the schools differed in their approaches to these issues, we observed that the degree or type of restructuring in a school contributed only part of the story. For example, many schools had minimized homogeneous ability grouping, used interdisciplinary teaching teams, and formulated school policies through a system of shared decision making. But schools with these structures in common showed remarkable variability in their attention to the intellectual quality of student learning, the strength of professional community, and their success with authentic pedagogy. If structural conditions did not account for variability on these key features, what did?

Our discussions of intellectual quality and professional community suggested that educators' beliefs, values, and group norms about the purposes of schooling and their professional competence have enormous influence on students' education. Careful observation of people's language and behavior in schools (and other organizations) usually reveals a pattern of shared beliefs, values, and competencies that tend to guide the nature of their work and their expectations for success. This pattern of norms constitutes the culture of a school.[1]

Cultural norms are often implicit and taken for granted among the participants, and sometimes go unnoticed. In addition, schools (like other organizations) have official rules, policies, and practices that define the main tasks for teachers, how people and resources are organized to complete the tasks (for example, through the scheduling of work and the grouping of students and teachers), how authority is distributed among staff and between staff and students, and how the school relates to external organizations. These official rules and relationships constitute school structure. Structure is comparatively concrete and amenable to manipulation, but culture is more elusive, because it consists of internalized value commitments and mental constructions or ways of viewing the world, not easily produced through programs or policy. The formal structure of an organization can be defined, charted, and intentionally changed through programs and policy, but organizational culture is more difficult to produce or change through intentional intervention.

Separating school culture and structure analytically can help to explain why structural innovations work in some situations and not others. For example, a school's teachers may have access to teaming and common planning time (structures), but if they are not committed to using these structures to focus on the intellectual quality of student learning (culture), we would not expect to find much authentic pedagogy in that school. Separating the two concepts might suggest that school improvement can be accomplished by first building the appropriate culture and then providing structure to implement it.

This approach may seem appealing, but rarely can real school reform be crafted into such pure stages; rather, culture and structure interact.[2] Structure can influence culture in important ways, and vice versa. For example, structures that force teachers to work alone offer little opportunity for them to reflect critically on their practice. Over a long period of time this isolation can reinforce a culture of professional complacency or resigned frustration, or both, in contrast to a vital interest in continuing improvement. If teaming and common planning time are abruptly introduced into such a culture, the initial discourse will probably be dominated by the existing culture; that is, talk may center on complaints about difficult students, lack of instructional resources, or nonprofessional concerns. With proper leadership, however, more constructive dialogue can be stimulated, and once this catches on, the new teaming structure would serve to invigorate professional culture.[3]

Chapters Eight through Eleven and the Conclusion discuss the ways in which school culture and structure affect intellectual quality and professional community and ultimately how they can support authentic pedagogy and student achievement.

## Notes

1. School culture has been elaborated by others in more detail than we offer in this book. For example, see Bryk, Lee, and Holland (1993); Metz (1986); Sarason (1982); and Spindler and Spindler (1987).
2. Bryk, Lee, and Smith (1990) synthesized research on cultural and structural features of high schools.
3. Research by Lee, Smith, and Croninger (1995a, 1995b) illustrated the interaction between structure and culture in a study of almost ten thousand students in eight hundred high schools nationwide. Initial findings showed that students in high schools with several restructuring practices experienced much larger achievement gains from eighth to tenth and tenth to twelfth grades than students in traditionally structured schools. When subsequent analyses included cultural variables such as collective responsibility among the faculty, academic press, the quality of instruction, and commonality of curriculum, it was found that student achievement gains were more strongly associated with these school qualities than with the presence or absence of restructuring practices.

# Chapter Eight

# Support for Student Achievement

*Helen M. Marks, Kenneth B. Doane, Walter G. Secada*

Authentic pedagogy and achievement demand a high caliber of performance from students. Teachers and schools aiming toward such visions of intellectual quality need to offer a learning environment that at once communicates high expectations for achievement and offers consistent help for students to meet those expectations. This chapter describes what support for authentic achievement entails, illustrates how students experience this support in their schools and classrooms, and summarizes the cultural and structural features of some schools that have succeeded in developing high-quality learning environments.

## Indicators of Support for Achievement

Previous research suggests at least three important dimensions for measuring support for student achievement: the learning environment is orderly and the discipline is fair, teachers set high expectations for student achievement, and students can count on both teachers and peers to help them. We used a combination of survey items from students and the observational measures of Center researchers to identify the extent of these forms of support in SRS schools and classrooms.

### Surveys

Survey responses from 5,943 students documented both their opinions on the learning environment of their schools and the level of intellectual support they received in mathematics and social studies classes. We created a support for student achievement index that combines these two indicators with Center researchers' ratings of the support for student achievement that they observed in classrooms.[1]

### School Environment

We concluded that school environments strongly supported learning when students reported positively on several key features of their schools: their teachers listened to them and disruptions by peers did not infringe on their ability to learn; they made friends with peers from other racial, ethnic, and cultural backgrounds and said that no one felt put down by others; and they could count on fair treatment from both their peers and the adults whom they regularly encountered at school.[2]

### Classrooms

Support for achievement manifested itself in classrooms, as well as in the general school environment. In supportive classrooms, students reported that interactions with teachers and peers were respectful and purposeful and that their teachers conveyed expectations that all students would try hard and master challenging work. The most positive classroom social environments were those where teachers helped students learn but students also assisted each other and where students felt encouraged to try hard, participate, and take intellectual risks.[3]

## Observations

Center researchers evaluated the level of academic support in the classrooms they observed.[4] The criteria for high-support classrooms were mutual respect among teacher and students and a shared expectation that all students, regardless of background or proficiency, could contribute to a rigorous intellectual enterprise. In low-support classes, by contrast, most students found little incentive to concentrate, listen, ask questions, or express their views, either because the tasks failed to warrant genuine intellectual investment or because their efforts were belittled by disparagement or token praise. Just as restructured schools differed considerably in their levels of authentic pedagogy and professional community, they also differed in the degree of support for achievement they offered students, as reflected in the surveys and observations.

## Student Essays

Because schools differed so strikingly in the learning environments students reported, we wanted to understand more concretely how students in the most successful schools experienced support for achievement. Would these students describe their schools differently from students in low-support schools? If so, what might the differences be? We were able to gain considerable insight into how students experienced support for achievement by analyzing essays they wrote for the SRS.[5] By using the student essays, along with classroom observations, surveys, and our close study of other aspects of the schools, we hoped to identify dimensions of school structure and culture that are important in generating strong support for student achievement.

We found that when students were asked to describe the "best things" and "things that could be improved" about their schools, their responses reflected the character of the learning environments they experienced each day. The following comparisons illustrate what students tended to emphasize in describing schools where we found differing levels of support for academic achievement.

### High Versus Low Support

Cibola High students wrote most frequently about instruction, advisory, and the support staff, including administrators. Their comments about these key features of the school were overwhelmingly positive. Although Island High students also were mainly positive about their school (as were the students in all the SRS schools), Island ranked very low on our index of support for achievement. The topics Island students chose to write about most often were extracurricular activities and teachers—interests one might expect in a randomly selected group of high school students. But their comments about teachers showed no consistent emphasis or patterns of concerns about instruction or curriculum. Students' views reflected the diffusion of effort that characterized Island's restructuring.

### High Versus Moderate Support

When we compared Cibola to Flinders High, a large (over twenty-three hundred students) and culturally diverse urban school where students reported moderately high levels of support for achievement, we found a different but similarly revealing pattern among students' responses. Both high schools shared an explicit commitment to prepare all students for college, with Flinders going so far as to declare all of its courses as college preparatory. In their essays, Flinders students wrote copious praise of their teachers' effectiveness but said almost nothing about what they actually did in class. They seemed to perceive positive classroom experiences less as a consequence of the intellectual character of the classroom than of teachers' individual personalities and caring attitudes.

Cibola students also emphasized positive relations with teachers, and in addition they consistently indicated overwhelmingly positive comments about what and how they learned in class. Cibola students' comments about classroom activities reflected the school's emphasis on critical inquiry and in-depth understanding. Students linked social support at Cibola to a schoolwide commitment to intellectual quality, whereas Flinders students regarded social support more in terms of teachers' personal interest in students and respect for social diversity. Predictably the most frequent topics in Flinders essays, in addition to teachers, were other students and extracurricular activities, not classroom experiences.

### A Comparison of Two High-Support Schools

Even in schools where social support for achievement was closely tied to classroom experiences, essays revealed substantial school contrasts in the character and meaning of support. At Winema Elementary, for example, the engine of restructuring was a vigorous program of staff development that supplied teachers with a repertoire of teaching techniques in which graphic organizers, such as the Venn diagram and the tricolumn KWL (what I *k*now, *w*ant to know, and have *l*earned), figured prominently. Accordingly Winema students consistently mentioned classroom activities in their school descriptions. A majority referred to specific techniques students used to organize and present information, skills that they said "help us learn in the best way" and "other schools never do."

By contrast, at Lamar Elementary, where restructuring served a spiraling, inquiry-based curriculum focused on environmental themes, students made firm but less precise statements about classroom activities, such as "We're open to class discussions on almost anything," "They like a lot of questions," and "We think in many different ways." Lamar students emphasized features of their learning environment such as the animals (lizards, turtles, frogs) that lived in their classrooms, their computers, the school garden, and the fact that they were not assigned to desks.

### Summary: The Influence of School Culture

The comments of Lamar and Winema students reflected a contrast between the culture of the two schools. Both groups of students believed that the school had an intellectual direction or purpose that involved them; that is, they experienced support for achievement. But Winema students perceived their school's intellectual purpose enacted in a set of techniques for processing information, while Lamar students recognized an emphasis on inquiry and thoughtfulness. Applying the distinction set out in Chapter Six, we deduced from students' comments that Winema staff focused primarily on teaching technique, while Lamar staff attended more directly to the intellectual quality of students' work. The reports of two weeks of interviews and observations at each school confirmed this contrast.

In short, student essays about their school enriched the data we used to draw conclusions about the culture of each school, particularly the nature of support for achievement. Even the few examples we cited suggest considerable variation in the support for achievement students experienced: caring and personalism on the part of individual teachers at Flinders compared to a schoolwide commitment to a distinctive intellectual program at Cibola; an emphasis on facilitative techniques at Winema compared to a climate of intellectual inquiry at Lamar.

## High Support for Achievement in Classrooms

The analysis of support for academic achievement in classrooms asked, What happens in classrooms where support for achievement is high according to our observations and surveys? Our analysis of all the lessons (seventy-three) that received the top score on our standards for support for achievement identified distinctive features of these lessons related to student tasks, activities, and projects; teachers' attitudes toward achievement; and classroom organization. Several features were common to many high-support classrooms.

## Student Tasks, Activities, and Projects

Complex instructional tasks forced students to cope with intellectual uncertainty. To resolve a problem, they often had to analyze a situation, evaluate incomplete or ambiguous evidence, and assess more than one potentially viable solution. Challenging tasks might require students to produce working models, museum-style installations, graphic displays, or performances. Designing an amusement park ride or building the City of the Future, projects at Cibola High and Lamar Elementary (presented in Chapters One and Six, respectively), exemplify such tasks.

Tasks of this sort also promote cooperation and support among students.[6] By contrast, tasks that ask students only to memorize the necessary facts, definitions, and algorithms involve neither uncertainty nor teamwork. Command of information and procedures was necessary in high-support classrooms too, but basic skills alone were usually not sufficient to address the tasks.

## Teachers' Attitudes Toward Achievement

Teachers in high-support classrooms made relentless demands for students' best efforts. In so doing, teachers established a culture for learning to support student success in performing complex tasks. Teachers disallowed unfounded assertions and flippant generalizations—the familiar classroom discourse that one teacher labeled "studentese." They met answers with calls for evidence or explanation, frequently using phrases such as, "What do you mean?" and "How do you know that?" Whenever possible they invoked school or classroom ideals—for example, "quality over quantity," "student as worker"—transforming these through their own example from mere slogans to behavioral norms.

An eighth-grade mathematics teacher at Red Lake Middle stressed to her class the importance of their own reasoning. "I want you to get in touch with your own thinking," she said. "Don't make it a task of getting a paper in that has the right answers on it. Try to let go of that. Try to see how you *think* about a problem. That's the only thing that develops self-confidence in math, in a mathematics course. How do you think about it? And you *can* do it."

### Active Attention

Although many of them worked with large classes, intellectually supportive teachers were attentive to individuals, interacting personally with as many students as possible in the course of a class period. When students worked in groups, the teachers circulated among them to observe, question, and coach. They listened carefully to students, inquiring to elicit more information about their thinking. When students sought their help, the teachers listened actively; they responded by restating and clarifying the problem, helping the students to think through to a solution rather than providing one on demand. To keep students from falling behind, high-support teachers urged them to identify where they were having trouble and to seek help from the teacher or their peers.

### Shared Responsibility for Achievement

One mathematics teacher at Red Lake Middle framed potential difficulties as shared challenges—part of a learning process—rather than as deficiencies of individual students:

> Let me remind you, I'm dependent on all of you letting me know if you have questions. . . . I hope you're not hesitant anymore to ask in your groups. I listen carefully to what you're saying, and it doesn't seem to me that you're putting anyone down or anything else. Try to facilitate what goes on in your group [and] to take part. . . . And let me remind you that this time is to be used very productively. Try to define in your group what needs to be done first. . . . If there are still questions, please put them up on the board [to be addressed in whole class discussions]. Also remember that I am available outside of class: if there's something that's still bugging you, please come in and let's get it straightened out. One little hurdle is a lot easier to get over than ten all stacked together.

Supportive teachers also made special efforts to ensure that all students felt comfortable contributing to class work—for example, by putting questions to boys and girls alternately, using structured discussion formats that allowed all students equal chance to lead, or asking bilingual students to translate for classmates who felt more comfortable speaking in a language other than English.

## Classroom Organization and Procedure

In classrooms where support for student achievement proved strong, space and time were ordered flexibly, as in a workshop. Nonacademic business such as attendance was handled with a minimum of fuss and distraction, often by the students; for example, in a classroom at Lamar Elementary, students registered their presence as they entered by flipping a card bearing their name and picture from front to back.

Because the lessons themselves were not highly routinized, supportive teachers frequently solicited students' ideas about how to proceed. This reinforced the need for students to reflect both on their own understandings and on effective problem solving in general.

### Problem-Solving Emphasis

Especially in supportive mathematics classes, procedure and substance often coalesced; that is, students came to see themselves as mathematicians working collegially to solve problems. To do this, they had to conjecture, estimate, reason, and explain, and they had to assess their progress continually. Using symbolic notation and appropriate technical terminology reinforced the seriousness of their work. At Red Lake Middle students reviewed homework problems in small groups, copying disputed items on the blackboard where the whole class could consider them. Before they returned a test paper to their teacher, students described on a cover sheet any areas where they had persisting doubts or questions.

Students in high-support classrooms frequently worked in pairs or clusters of three to six, sometimes with designated team responsibilities as leaders or recorders though often without defined roles. Whole class discussions often centered on a broad central question or a set of problems, with students drawing on previous individual work to suggest solutions. Additionally several classes employed a formal workshop format, in which students worked independently with assistance as needed from peers and the teacher. Combined formats characterized other lessons, for example, whole class discussion of a central problem, followed by group work, then reports from the groups back to the whole class.

At Lamar Elementary, the fifth- and sixth-grade class, having just returned from their week-long outdoor education field trip, identified words and phrases to compare the wild and urban environments. They first brainstormed as a large group, then expanded the lists working in pairs. Each pair then contributed the items they thought were the most vivid and accurate to make class lists. Finally, back in small groups, students sorted the items from the lists on a Venn diagram consisting of two partially overlapped circles: one for descriptions of the wilderness, the other for the city, and the overlapping portion for items that could pertain to either environment. The diagram was to be used as a resource as students developed essays and visual displays documenting the relationship between the city and its wild environs.

### Help Among Students

Another hallmark of high-support classrooms was students' speaking directly to one another about the problems at hand, working with one another rather than depending on the teacher as an all-knowing intermediary. On some occasions Center researchers heard students help each other by repeating phrases or questions the teacher had modeled, and sometimes students explained the material in novel ways. Students who struggled seemed reassured by the empathy and assistance of their peers. At Cibola High, for example, an observer noted how a student who had nearly completed her calculations and design of a free-fall ride for the amusement park project spent most of a class period helping classmates who were having difficulty. "Lisa helped Monique as she was working on the deceleration portion of her ride," the observer wrote. "Monique was having trouble thinking of deceleration as negative acceleration. They had an extended conversation about this, and Lisa questioned Monique in much the same way [the teacher] questions students."

In the same class, the observer reported,

Marina explained initial velocity, velocity, and final velocity to
Yvonne. Marina questioned Yvonne to get her to explain it back to
her, much as [the teacher] might, although [the teacher] doesn't
usually explain it first. . . . Marina confided to Yvonne that she also
couldn't understand the formula at first, but when she figured out
that the initial velocity for the free fall was the initial velocity for
the deceleration, then she understood it. She explained it all again,
pointing to appropriate parts of a drawing the class had designed
together. Then she asked Yvonne to explain it back to her. Yvonne
said, "Oh, I get it," and explained it quite clearly.

## School Conditions That Promote Support for Achievement

Our explanation of why some schools were more successful than
others in offering support for achievement of high intellectual
quality relies on two points: The more successful schools had vigorous professional communities, and they used their structural
innovations to support their cultural strengths.

### Professional Community

We found that support for student achievement and professional
community are closely linked.[7] As shown in Figure 8.1, where professional community characterized relationships among teachers,
support for achievement almost invariably existed among students.
Conversely when teachers failed to achieve professional community, support for achievement languished. Schools with very strong
professional communities and highly supportive learning environments for students include Careen and Lamar elementaries
(schools F and H), Red Lake Middle (L), and Cibola High (V).

### *Examples*

Other schools that received less attention in previous chapters also
offered positive learning environments in terms of professional
community among the faculty and support for achievement among
the students. Humboldt Elementary (school A in Figure 8.1) is an

## Figure 8.1.  Professional Community and Support for Achievement.

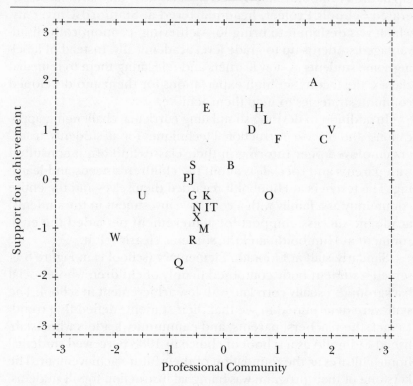

Note: Scores for support for achievement are school averages for the index, standardized across the twenty-four schools. The index, described in Appendix A, combines the reports of all students on school and classroom support with the researchers' ratings of the social support they observed in classrooms. Scores for professional community are school averages for all teachers in the school across the five dimensions of professional community (Appendix A), assessed by surveys and standardized across the twenty-four schools.

example. United through the instructional leadership of their principal, the Humboldt faculty had worked with the national Accelerated Schools Project, headquartered at Stanford University, which was designed to bring low-achieving, economically disadvantaged students up to grade level academically. Instead of labeling some students as slow learners and relegating them to remedial classes, the faculty set high expectations for them and developed common strategies to help them achieve.

In addition to devising stimulating curricula, challenging applications, and diverse instructional techniques for all students, teachers employed peer tutoring in their classes and often consulted with parents and specialists about the children's needs and learning. The teachers at Humboldt regarded themselves and the entire community as a family with a collective investment in the students' academic success. Support for achievement pervaded the environment at Humboldt, and the students clearly felt it.

Similarly, staff at Eldorado Elementary (school D in Figure 8.1) served a student body composed mainly of children whose social backgrounds usually correlate with low achievement in school. The staff were determined to see that their students defied that trend. In fact, the teachers, parents, and community leaders who established Eldorado as a school of choice in 1988 perceived students' home cultures as the foundation of their future achievement. The keystone of their program was bilingual instruction for all students. Admissions criteria for the school provided for linguistic balance and ethnic diversity. At each grade level two classes rotated daily between two teachers, conversing in English with one and in Spanish with the other. Only primary reading was treated exclusively in the native language. Themes of human dignity, solidarity, and social agency permeated the curriculum, and by vigorously soliciting parent involvement in school programs, events, and governance, staff sought to enact these principles within the school community.

When Center researchers visited the school in 1992–93, Eldorado's teacher leadership group spoke passionately of their mission, but they explained that they were struggling to transmit their convictions to other staff so that all could contribute to a more refined, coherent program. Staff turnover was high, and, except for the bilingual program, veteran staff had yet to define specific curriculum and student outcome priorities to help new teachers—and themselves—articulate schoolwide goals. In spite of this problem, Eldorado scored above the mean on our index of professional community, and our measure of support for achievement suggested that the school's fundamental message was getting through to students in both languages.

### Anomalies

Exceptions to the close parallel between professional community and support for student achievement are very few. At Winema Elementary (school E in Figure 8.1), strong social support for achievement appeared to exist despite below average levels of professional community. Similarly, students at Flinders High (school S), were slightly above average in their perception of support for achievement, while professional community there fell below the mean. At Okanagon Middle (school O), the level of professional community was considerably above average but support for achievement among students slightly below.

These anomalies are consistent with other information from the schools. As we have seen, Winema students found the instructional techniques they experienced both compelling and useful, but it was unclear how the techniques enhanced the intellectual quality of students' work. Similarly although teachers who used these techniques believed in their utility for student learning, only a fraction of the Winema teachers had adopted the techniques, and school leaders had yet to articulate a rationale to convince their reluctant colleagues.

Okanagon staff built a strong sense of community around two related commitments. First, they worked to establish a warm social environment conducive to student learning. Okanagon students' survey responses reflected the staff's success. When we visited Okanagon, staff were pursuing their second goal—to prepare all students to succeed in the most rigorous high school courses—by adopting new forms of assessment: portfolios and schoolwide performance events. They placed considerably less emphasis on reforming instruction, which they anticipated would evolve as work on assessment helped teachers clarify what they expected students to know and do. In the classes we observed at Okanagon, both social support for achievement and student engagement were relatively low, which counteracted students' positive survey responses to climate of the school as a whole.

Teachers at Flinders were held accountable for students' academic success, as measured by report card grades and performance on standardized tests. Nonetheless neither a schoolwide intellectual vision nor a particular instructional philosophy united the diverse faculty. Instead Flinders teachers focused their collective efforts on issues of students' self-esteem and respect for diversity. Unless teachers chose to work together, instruction was an individualistic enterprise.

## Integration of Structure and Culture

School structure, as we are using the term, refers to such matters as how schools allocate time and space, organize the curriculum, deploy teachers for instruction and other duties, arrange students into subunits such as houses and advisory groups, and develop links between the school and its community. School culture refers to the goals, norms, and values that inspire the organization and its members, the history and traditions that distinguish it, and the roles and relationships that exist among the members.

Although structure and culture are analytically distinct, in the real world of schools they are closely related. Structures can allow cultures to grow and develop, or they can thwart them. Conversely cultural norms often underlie and reinforce school structures, but they can also motivate staff to circumvent formal rules and boundaries. The human power of adaptation proves so strong that, in unusual cases, a positive culture can develop within the confines of an inimical structure. Teachers and administrators powerfully influence the organizational culture of schools, and agencies, parents, and others outside the school can play important roles too.

To illustrate how structure and culture can interact to nurture support for student achievement, we return to three schools with highly positive learning environments: Lamar Elementary (H), Red Lake Middle (L), and Cibola High (V). Before considering the schools separately, we take note of two structural conditions that were common to these schools: extended instructional time and shared academic experiences.

### Conditions Common in High-Support Schools

Where support for student achievement proved strong, extended blocks of instructional time enabled teachers to plan complex, open-ended activities. Lessons lasted at least an hour, some as long as two hours. Teachers at Lamar used time flexibly rather than breaking the day into discrete, subject-specific chunks. At Red Lake, a seventy-minute period was standard. Cibola employed two-hour interdisciplinary instructional blocks. Projects often extended over two or more class periods. Some, like the City of the Future project at Lamar and the amusement park exhibition at Cibola, comprised many weeks of lessons and activities.

In the most positive learning environments we observed, students shared academic experiences that unified them in a sense of school membership. Interdisciplinary Connections courses brought Red Lake students together, while participation in course selection, service learning, and student government enfolded them in a kind of academic citizenship. Lamar students were connected through a schoolwide environmental theme, and core curricula in humanities and mathematics-science were among several academic experiences all students at Cibola shared. All three schools used mixed-grade classes.

Nonetheless students also experienced block scheduling and common curricula at other schools we visited where support for achievement was comparatively weak. These schools lacked a normative faculty culture aimed at ambitious student achievement. At Lamar, Red Lake, and Cibola, on the other hand, the normative culture was pervasive, built on a shared set of beliefs intended to improve the achievement of students and the quality of their experiences both within the classroom and in the school at large. In the next sections we describe how specific normative commitments in combination with structural features offered high support for student achievement at each school.

### Lamar Elementary School

A philosophy of constructivist learning permeated instruction at Lamar, and its curriculum was organized around an environmental theme. Major team projects such as the City of the Future model and ecology research extended the classroom into the world at large.

Within their classrooms, students of different ages, backgrounds, and abilities worked together every day and saw their teachers do the same. During the City of the Future project, for example, students collaborated on commissions, such as those for transportation and utilities. In the Life Lab, students shared resources with other teams. Thus when interdependence became an explicit focus of instruction in their studies on the ecologies of various environments, students' understandings were underscored by their daily experiences in school. Structure and culture were mutually reinforcing.

### Red Lake Middle School

Teachers at Red Lake focused on building a caring, democratic community. Through strong curricular connections with the external community, Red Lake provided students with opportunities to learn experientially, apply their knowledge, and experience social interdependence and reciprocity. This was exemplified particularly by the year-long interdisciplinary Connections courses. Cultural Connections, the sixth-grade course, focused on cultural diversity in both the local and world community. During seventh and eighth grades, Red Lake students participated in community service learning and mentorships as part of their Connections courses. Building on students' interests, these programs attempted to integrate all Red Lake students with the civic community beyond school.

Parent involvement at Red Lake reinforced home-school linkages around students' education and connected parents with one another. Parents served in various volunteer capacities and sometimes raised funds for school projects. As stakeholders in the school, they participated in governance structures at Red Lake. The house advisory system served to build community not only within the school but also between the school and the larger community, particularly parents. Advisory group leaders visited the homes of new sixth-grade students to meet their parents and to open lines of communication. Advisers and parents kept in contact regularly during the school year about course selection and other matters. In short, the courses, parent activities, and advisory system offered structural support for the norms of community building, which in turn supported student achievement.

### Cibola High School

Cibola High faculty acted in concert to develop in students five "habits of mind," as well as a sense of responsibility to each other and the society at large. Mutual investment in these commitments supplied vital support and energy in relationships among teachers and students. Students entered Cibola High knowing that they were embarking on a serious academic venture that would continually call on their best intellectual efforts. Together they experienced interdisciplinary instruction in core subjects between seventh and tenth grades, and they worked toward the academic review that would determine whether they were admitted to the Senior Institute.

Prior to the academic review, all Cibola students must have fulfilled school academic requirements, completed a community service mandate, and passed state-sponsored academic competency tests. Similarly the Senior Institute required Cibola students to take one college course, complete an internship, assemble portfolios for pregraduation review, and present a final senior project.

Multiple structural supports sustained Cibola students in their academic work. These included teacher teams, who shared responsibility for students over two years, and small advisory groups that met daily. Moreover Cibola's norms served to foster an ethic of collective responsibility among students. To merit a distinguished academic grade, for example, a student must have actively assisted classmates in their learning.

## Summary

Support for achievement thrived where school organizational structures and culture mutually encouraged learning of high intellectual quality. Schools differed in the structural means they used to accomplish collective support for achievement, but several innovations proved significant: extended instructional time; smaller, more personalized school units, such as houses and multiyear instructional groups; a common or core curriculum, with schoolwide curricular themes; structures designed explicitly to support students, such as advisory groups, especially when they offered continuity of relationships over two or more years; the organization of classroom work to foster interdependence among teachers and among students; and well-developed linkages joining the school (students, teachers, and administrators), parents, and the broader civic community.

Certain cultural characteristics also distinguished schools where the learning environments offered substantial support for students. We have focused especially on certain norms, values, and commitments shared by teachers, who then transmit them to their students. Faculty-shared standards of intellectual quality translated into inquiry-oriented curricula and consistent expectations for student performance. And when faculty collaborated to plan, teach, and assess students' learning, they tended to nurture cooperation among students.

Schools with the most supportive learning environments cultivated and practiced democratic values. A communitarian ethos permeated these successful schools, built on respect, trust, mutual concern, and shared challenges. Social bonds were both an important goal or end in themselves and a means to support authentic achievement.

The schools that offered supportive learning environments were socially diverse. Positive relationships among students and teachers who differed considerably in their backgrounds helped to define the missions of these schools.

### Notes
1. These three measures of support are interrelated. Expressed as correlations, the relationship between school learning environment and reported classroom support is .57, $p \le .01$; between observed academic support and reported classroom support, .62, $p \le .01$; between school learning environment and observed academic support, .45, $p \le .05$. The reliability of the index, that is, its internal consistency as measured by Cronbach's alpha, is .79. Observers' ratings of classroom support and students' reports of academic support (in both the classroom and the school as a whole) are correlated at .37, $p \le .01$. The reliability of the combined measure, Cronbach's alpha, is .55.
2. As measured by Cronbach's alpha, the reliability of the school learning environment construct is .66. Survey item indicators are listed in Appendix A.
3. The reliability of the reported classroom support construct, measured by Cronbach's alpha, is .86. Survey item indicators are listed in Appendix A.

4. As part of the classroom observational study, Center researchers rated the lesson according to the academic support evident during the class. As with the instructional standards described in Chapter One, social support was evaluated according to specific criteria on a 1–5 scale (scoring rules are listed in Appendix A). Most of the lessons observed were from three mathematics and three social studies classes, although the Center also invited schools to nominate for observation two additional classes they regarded as having outstanding instruction.

5. Essays written by students, mainly in grades 4, 8, and 10, were collected and scored on a modified NAEP scale by trained readers as a baseline measure of writing ability for the SRS (Appendix A). We then read about forty-five essays from each of eighteen schools and summarized students' responses by organizing them into fourteen topics (for example, teachers, classroom activities, power relations, and social structures) across four categories (curriculum and instruction, administration, social, and nondescript). If a student wrote that she liked to learn about science, for example, we recorded her statement as a reference to the topic "subjects" under the category "Curriculum and Instruction." If she wrote that she liked to learn by experimenting in science, we recorded a reference to "classroom activities" under "Curriculum and Instruction." If she wrote that she had fun doing experiments with friends in the class, we still recorded it as a reference to the topic "classroom activities" but under the category "Social." Each comment was also recorded as either positive or negative. Dayle K. Haglund was instrumental in accomplishing the categorical reading.

6. Cohen (1986) argues that the complexity of the instructional task affects classroom organization. When the instructional task generates uncertainty, for example, students tend to cooperate.

7. The correlation between school professional community and support for achievement is .70, $p \leq .01$.

# Chapter Nine

# Pathways to Equity

*Walter G. Secada, Adam Gamoran,*
*Matthew G. Weinstein*

Just as SRS schools' cultural and structural features affected students' sense of support for meeting high academic standards, these features enabled some schools to achieve equity.[1] Issues of equity arise when schools must deal with student diversity—social class, race, ethnicity, gender, language background, ability—in order to provide equal, high-quality education to all students. In short, the challenge of equity is how to respond fairly to student diversity. In this chapter we address the issue of how some schools were able to meet the challenge of equity.

First we articulate a standard for equity as equal access to high-quality instruction regardless of students' social and academic backgrounds. Second, we examine the SRS schools' structural responses to student diversity. Third, we select two schools that managed to provide high-quality instruction to all students through different structural mechanisms and contrast them to two schools that used similar mechanisms but were less successful in providing high-quality instruction to their students. Finally, we examine the cultural norms of the successful schools and explain that the interaction of cultural and structural characteristics is what enabled the successful schools to create their distinctive pathways to equity.

## A Standard for Equity

Within SRS schools, students' exposure to authentic pedagogy did not depend on their race or ethnic background, although students with higher levels of prior achievement were more likely to experience authentic pedagogy than their lower-achieving peers. Additionally student performance on the SRS achievement measure was no more dependent on students' social background than performance on more conventional test items used in the NAEP. These results revealed little evidence of inequality in access to or benefits from authentic pedagogy for students from varied gender, racial, and ethnic groups in SRS schools.

The absence of inequality, however, does not guarantee equity, for by equity we mean equal access to high-quality instruction. This standard for equity addresses the problem that can result when equity is defined only as the absence of unequal treatment among groups categorized along lines of gender, race, social class, ability, language, or some other demographic characteristic. Under this common definition, it is possible to achieve equity merely by providing equal levels of low-quality instruction among groups of different backgrounds.[2] Our standard insists that equity entails equal access to high-quality pedagogy; there can be no equity without excellence.

By high-quality instruction we mean authentic pedagogy. In the SRS schools the level of authentic pedagogy was not related to students' social background; however, simultaneously with this apparent equality, some schools delivered very low levels of authentic pedagogy, while others delivered high levels of authentic pedagogy averaged across different classes. Only the latter cases reflect equity by our standard.[3]

The schools that we highlight in this chapter distributed high-quality instruction equally across race, class, gender, and prior levels of academic achievement.

## Structural Responses to Student Diversity

Individual students vary in how they experience school, and good teachers adapt their instructional techniques to meet the educational needs and interests of each individual student. In this chapter, however, we are most interested in the learning opportunities offered to groups of students as defined by race, gender, language, social class, and prior academic achievement.

We define responses to diversity as those structures that schools establish and the actions they take to adapt their programs to identifiable groups of students. Ability grouping is one such response.

Student groups are created based on perceived academic ability, and the school conducts programs based on tacit or explicit theories about how best to educate students of different ability levels (Gamoran, Nystrand, Berends, and LePore, 1995; Hallinan, 1994). Other responses to student diversity include categorical programs for poor (Chapter 1/Title 1), limited English proficient (bilingual education, English as a second language), special needs, and gifted and talented students; the creation of all-girls mathematics classes; and the creation of Afrocentric programs and classes designed for African American males.

## Differentiation Versus Commonality of Student Experiences

School responses to student diversity typically fall into those that promote commonality of student experiences across groups and those that differentiate student experiences between groups. For example, between-class ability grouping, tracking, the formation of all-girl mathematics classes or of classes for African American males, and categorical programs create and support the differentiation of student experiences based on students' social or academic backgrounds. Perceived academic ability is used to create curriculum tracking and ability grouping within or between classes; gender is used to create all-female or all-male classes; a combination of race and gender is the basis for classes designed for African American males; and social class, special needs, or language define different instructional groups in the case of pull-out categorical programs.

Alternatively schools may create structures to ensure that diverse groups of students receive common educational experiences. For instance, detracking, full inclusion programs for special needs students, a common core curriculum for all students, and the provision of categorical-program services within regular classrooms are efforts to provide common student experiences.

SRS schools responded to student diversity both by providing common student experiences across demographic variability and by differentiating student experiences. The SRS schools, much like any other organization's response to diversity, did not adhere rigidly to a single response pattern. Within SRS schools, both responses coexisted, sometimes in competition with one another and at other times in a sensible balance.

## Dominant Responses

Although the schools combined commonality with differentiation of student experiences in various ways, twenty-two of the twenty-four exhibited a dominant response—that is, an overall pattern of practice that tended to emphasize either differentiation or commonality. As we probed for the intentions underlying the pattern of a school's actions, we inferred the school's dominant response to student diversity. Table 9.1 provides a school-by-school summary.

Most SRS elementary schools provided common experiences across student groupings, while most of the high schools and the middle schools tended to differentiate experiences, largely because of the pervasiveness of tracking that begins in middle school and to secondary schools' providing more curricular options from which older students could choose. The elementary schools that provided common student experiences were district magnet schools of choice intended to offer a core instructional program as part of district desegregation efforts. Schools whose dominant response was to provide common student experiences enrolled

**Table 9.1.  Schools' Dominant Structural Responses
to Student Diversity.**

| Differentiation of Student Experiences | Creating Common Student Experiences | Ambiguous |
|---|---|---|
| Sumpter Elementary | Ashley Elementary | Lamar Elementary |
| Winema Elementary | Careen Elementary | Baldwin Middle |
| Copan Middle | Falls River Elementary | |
| Morris Middle | Eldorado Elementary | |
| Red Lake Middle | Humboldt Elementary | |
| Selway Middle | Okanagan Middle | |
| Fremont High | Ottawa Junior | |
| Flinders High | Shining Rock Middle | |
| Huron High | Cibola High | |
| Island High | Marble Canyon High | |
| South Glen High | Wallingford High | |

fewer white (34 versus 63 percent) and more free-and-reduced-lunch-eligible (47 versus 33 percent) students than did schools which differentiated student experiences.

Ashley Elementary School illustrates a dominant response of commonality to student diversity (see Table 9.2). Ashley contained a state-mandated program for gifted students in self-contained classrooms. The gifted classes contained fewer students and a smaller proportion of minority students than the regular program. One might assume that the division of classes into gifted and general would signify a major effort on the school's part to differentiate student experiences—that is, the school's dominant response would match its formal structure. In the case of Ashley, this was not so. Teachers in that school made a strong and concerted effort to provide the same high-quality instruction in the regular program as in the gifted program, and they succeeded. Center researchers found similar instructional practices and equally high levels of authentic pedagogy in each program. Thus, the teachers' dominant response in Ashley was to provide common experiences for students, despite a formal structure that differentiated students according to achievement and, de facto, by race.

## Equality and Structure: Two Successful Approaches

By considering four schools, we illustrate that the absence of inequality does not necessarily imply equity and that neither kind of dominant response—toward differentiation or commonality—will in and of itself guarantee or deny the possibility of equity by our standards.[4] First, consider the differences between Wallingford High School and Cibola High School, with average respective pedagogy scores of 17.21 and 27.34, a difference of almost 3.35 between-school standard deviations.[5] In both schools, tracking had been totally eliminated from the grades we studied (grades 9 and 10), and commonality of student experience was the dominant response to student diversity (see Table 9.1). Both schools provided equal levels of authentic pedagogy to students of different social backgrounds across their classes. Yet in Wallingford this cross-classroom similarity occurred at an exceptionally low level of authentic pedagogy—the lowest in our sample. Cibola, by contrast, was characterized by the highest levels of authentic pedagogy across the board. By our criteria, Cibola, but

**Table 9.2. Selected Schools' Structural-Academic Responses to Student Diversity.**

| School Name | Responses That Would Differentiate Student Experiences | Responses That Would Create Common Student Experiences |
|---|---|---|
| Ashley Elementary | Operates a state-mandated gifted and talented track of self-contained classrooms where the student-teacher ratio is lower than for regular classes; Individual Education Plans for gifted students; Reading Recovery for first graders who fall behind in reading, remedial reading programs for others; One third-grade teacher followed her at-risk students to fourth grade; Two self-contained, cross-grade classes for at-risk students | Nonacademic activities combining all students *Equally high-quality instruction provided to students across programs |
| Red Lake Middle | *Freedom for students to make their own schedule *Freedom of teachers to "teach to their passion" *Self-contained special education classes *Self-contained French immersion program *Extant tracking through self-selection | Required connections class Academically recommended schedule Advising all students to take a broad curriculum Serious efforts by one teacher to ensure gender equity in math Reduction of tracks in all disciplines |
| Cibola High | Student choice of the portfolio that gets exhibited Concentration in senior house Evaluation of student performances Different agendas for each advisory group Individualized intern experiences | *Common curriculum during first four years in school *A common set of portfolios to be completed by all students *State minimum competency exams required for graduation No between-class ability grouping In-class support services for special education students |

**Table 9.2.** (continued)

| School Name | Responses That Would Differentiate Student Experiences | Responses That Would Create Common Student Experiences |
|---|---|---|
| Island High | *English as a second language program<br>*ASAP-alternative program that allows student to work and go to school<br>*AVID (Achievement via Individual Determination) targeting average performing African American students to assist in future college attendance<br>*Bridge team to assist students who are not performing academically and are deficient of required academic credits<br>*Urban League Apprenticeship program to assist students to find vocational jobs<br>*Tech-Prep program, a vocational education program<br>Youth Services Center to address personal and family problems | State assessments<br>School attendance area created to pull a large portion of low-income students, both African American and white<br>Heterogeneous grouping of students (within programs)<br>Mainstreaming of special eduation and English as a second language students |
| Wallingford High | Special education classes in math and English | *No tracks, all students take core classes in ninth and tenth grade (except some special education classes) |

*Note:* Starred items indicate the school's dominant response.

not Wallingford, illustrates equity in instruction despite detracking in both.

Island High School created several specialized programs for groups of students seen as having special needs. In this case of providing students with differentiated experiences (see Table 9.2), we observed scattered instances of authentic pedagogy, but the overall quality of instruction was low (20.67 on our authentic pedagogy scale). Red Lake Middle School is another school where differentiation was the dominant structural response to student diversity, in this instance through teacher choice on what courses to teach and student choice on what courses to take. In contrast to Island High, Red Lake offered high levels of authentic pedagogy in almost all the classes (averaging 24.77 or 1.40 between-school standard deviation better than Island). Red Lake thus provided equitable instruction relative to the quality of instruction provided at Island.

Cibola and Red Lake achieved equity through different structural responses to student diversity. At Cibola the dominant emphasis was on providing common experiences, whereas at Red Lake the emphasis was on differentiation through choice. At the same time, both schools exhibited high-quality instruction (as well as high levels of authentic academic performance) for all students. How did one school use commonality and the other differentiation as pathways to equity?

## Cibola High School

Cibola is a school of choice for grades 7 through 12 in a large urban area, with a student population that is 85 percent African American and Latino. The school, particularly in grades 7 through 10, provided a common curriculum for all, even in such traditionally tracked areas as mathematics and English. The school was part of a choice scheme among a subset of schools in the district. Students from a small number of similarly structured elementary schools could choose from among various alternative and regular schools. In addition 20 percent of the student body was selected by the school from students who did not attend the feeder elementary schools but applied to attend Cibola.

The original principal, who later became a codirector, acknowledged that the school's selectivity might be seen as part of a tracking scheme within the district. But she argued publicly for the distinction between choice, which she supported, and tracking, which she opposed. To counter the possibility that choice might lead to de facto tracking, the school selected enough low-income students to ensure a 51 percent low-income population for which they received special funding targeted for low-income students. As one teacher noted, "We want our population to be diverse. About 23 percent of our students are eligible for special ed resources and have been labeled by the system as learning disabled or emotionally handicapped—or whatever the label of the year is. These students are mainstreamed and their support is predominantly in-class as opposed to pull-out."

Most teachers strongly supported this antitracking ideology. Some explicitly insisted that the point of heterogeneous grouping was to ensure high standards for all students. As one history teacher for a ninth–tenth grade class explained, "One of the marvelous things about integrated classrooms is that nobody is putting you in the slow group, so [that] we don't expect anything out of you [the slow group]."

In the seventh- through tenth-grade classes, teachers practiced no ability grouping of any sort.

### Adapting to Individual Differences Within a Common Curriculum

Although the dominant emphasis was to avoid differentiated group experiences, teachers and administrators at Cibola were keenly aware of the need to individualize evaluation within a common curriculum. The codirector made this need clear as she explained the school's need to balance common standards and individual differences: "But we say to kids, you're not going to get out of here if you don't prove [your mastery] to us, and on that, it's a common standard. What kind of evidence [we accept] for meeting that standard differs by kid. No two kids have to meet that standard with the same pieces of evidence."

Thus school staff modified their expectations of individual student performance. Expectations were related to teacher judgments of each student's abilities and basic skills mastery. An English teacher for a seventh-eighth grade echoed this view:

> Clearly not all kids can do the work at the same level. Some of the kids cannot read the same material that other kids read. Or if they

are able to read it, it is with tremendous difficulties and requiring lots of help. What it means is it really does require knowing kids pretty well and giving them work and evaluating their work on an individual basis. By that I mean they do the same exhibition, but with certain kids I expect them to go into different levels of work than I would with other kids. They are able to take multiple viewpoints. They are able to analyze and weigh things, and other students are able to just get at the facts, basically, at least for right now.

This adjustment of expectations extended to evaluation of required graduation exhibitions that students began to work on in the eleventh and twelfth grades. The interpretation and adaptation of the school's performance standards took place on a case-by-case basis. It was not done lightly but rather after serious deliberation of that student. Performance standards were adapted for individuals in the context of high standards for all students; different groups of students did not have different standards.

### Systems for Confronting Diversity: The Race, Class, and Gender Committee

Cibola's attempt to deal with issues of diversity within its overarching approach of commonality extended beyond concern for individual differences. The school established a Race, Class, and Gender Committee to wrestle with issues of difference based on social categories. This group discussed issues of race and gender (social class did not seem to get much attention) among teachers. As the other codirector explained, the committee "is an attempt to give safe places to say wrong things and have your friends tell you, 'If you think that way, it affects me this way.' That to me is the most important role of that [committee] . . . to help understand how words and actions are perceived by other people."

The committee also helped teachers work directly with students. According to one humanities teacher, most meetings "dealt with stereotypes" and "what shapes attitudes, what shapes ideas, how we deal with our kids, how we deal with each other." He explained:

I'm remembering doing some workshop-type activity at a staff meeting that had a profound effect on me. This is what I consider to be real staff development because I was confronted with myself. . . . I pay particular attention to how I treat girls. I didn't realize how that came out of my own philosophy of how I treat women and so forth. That staff meeting gave me an opportunity to talk about it in a strange kind of way. For the first time I got to talk about how I feel about being a male and how that gets played out in class and with my colleagues. I'm doing some soul searching and some self-evaluation that I would never have done in any other kind of forum.

A meeting observed by Center researchers dealt extensively with the role that race and gender played in class activities. The meeting began by describing how authority figures were assumed to be white and male and that this assumption has had an impact on cooperative learning activities in some of the teachers' classes.

These meetings dealt primarily with teachers' personal attitudes and approaches. They did not lead to the school's collecting student data to see how the school program might affect different categories of students. Still, by offering a forum teachers to confront one another on issues of race, class, and gender and to have their own assumptions examined, the school created a mechanism for serious schoolwide attention to these issues.

It is worth reiterating that the high quality of instruction found throughout the school was facilitated through other structural features, among them the staff's opportunity to select teachers, student choice of the school, and the school's use of its resources to run the weekend tutorial sections, which may have freed teachers to engage in more authentic instruction during class time. The school managed to have a relatively small pupil-to-teacher ratio (twenty to one) by not employing typical administrative and support staff (such as counselors and an assistant principal) and instead by having teachers assume those functions. With these student supports, Cibola was able to enact one dominant approach to the problem of student difference: emphasizing a core curriculum and yet maintaining high standards and quality instruction for all.

## Red Lake Middle School

Red Lake Middle School, unlike Cibola, responded to diversity through a system of student and teacher choice. On the one hand students were free to create their own programs with the advice of teachers and their parents. The only requirement was that students take the interdisciplinary Connections course each year. On the other hand teachers were encouraged to diverge from any common curriculum, to "teach to their passions," and to create new courses and work in interdisciplinary teams to expand the number and kinds of Connections classes offered. Student self-selection into courses organized around specific themes supported a high degree of differentiation, particularly in mathematics and foreign language, such that higher-achieving students tended to take different patterns of courses from lower achievers. Even when high-ability and low-ability versions of the same course did not exist, course sequences and prerequisites could lead to a hierarchical ranking of courses, yielding the same effect. Although this approach to differentiation is not the same as deliberate curriculum tracking, student course selection in middle school ultimately leads to student placement in different high school tracks. Especially in mathematics, the prior course choices that a student makes affects the courses into which that student will be placed on entering high school: Algebra Ia, Algebra I, Geometry, Algebra II.

### High-Quality Instruction Within Choice

As at Cibola, the rhetoric of choice at Red Lake Middle School was sharply distinguished from that of tracking. Red Lake's principal explained that the school had worked to reduce tracking while increasing the number of choices for students:

> The commitment of the school is to get rid of [tracking]. When I first came here, the sixth-grade cultural connections classes were leveled [classes were designated high, medium, or low level]. . . . You name it, and there were levels in this building. They had levels 8, 9, 10, 11, 12, 13, and 14. And they had kids, sixth graders, in all those levels. You'd come up to a sixth grader and say, "How are you?" They'd say, "Well, I'm a level 8." And the worst part is, they were keyed to the [school's] reading series. . . . And they had it emblazoned on their foreheads. So I started getting every Jeannie Oakes article [on tracking] and every other article I could get and started inundating people. [Oakes's research is often cited as providing evidence that tracking results in lower-track students receiving an inferior education.] And it became very clear by the amount of paper load where I was on this issue.

The school did reduce the number of tracks in all subjects. One effect of coupling choice and detracking was that no courses were labeled remedial. The levels were not designed to be compensatory but rather, in the words of the Mathematics Department's program descriptions, "All classes . . . include number sense and operation, graphing, measurement, geometry, problem solving, reasoning and estimation skills, statistics and probability, applications and connections. In the different mathematics levels, the topics are covered at increasing levels of difficulty and complexity."

The elimination of the bottom stratum helped to raise teachers' expectations for their students, and these higher expectations produced more ambitious course content. That is, students taking the lower-level courses struggled with the same content as students in higher-level courses, and no teachers focused primarily on basic skills in anticipation of more demanding material to be delivered elsewhere.

Despite the high level of differentiation, especially in comparison to Cibola, Red Lake Middle School offered high-quality instruction to all students. All mathematics teachers, regardless of class level, received 4s and 5s on the Center's standards for authentic instruction at some time during our observations of their teaching. These scores occurred on a remarkable eight of the twelve lessons we saw.[6] In social studies (which included several of the interdisciplinary classes that are a hallmark of the Red Lake program) the scores were somewhat lower. But even these levels placed Red Lake's pedagogy in the top third of the SRS schools as a whole.

### Compensating for Choice

Red Lake Middle School's system of choice was not without equity problems. As one teacher described it, students often "group themselves," against their teachers' recommendations. At least occasionally girls overselected courses that would place them in lower-track classes. Three teachers—one each in mathematics, social studies, and physical education—were particularly concerned about gender inequalities produced by the choice system, so they imposed enrollment requirements in their classes to ensure a balance of boys and girls. Although some other teachers questioned their colleagues for taking this step, they were supported by other teachers and the principal, and their enrollment requirements prevailed.

Red Lake did not have a forum for systematic reflection on inequities (as in Cibola's Race, Class, and Gender Committee). Hence concerns about equity were addressed only on an ad hoc basis, depending on the individual teacher's initiative. Nevertheless when individual teachers expressed such concerns, they were taken seriously, as in the case of the teachers who placed enrollment requirements on their courses to redress inequities.

Red Lake represented a successful example of equitable distribution of high-quality instruction to all, using a mechanism of differentiation rather than a common curriculum. It should be noted that Red Lake Middle School worked with a relatively prosperous and racially homogeneous community. Staff did not face many of the issues that teachers at Cibola wrestle with daily. At the same time conditions at Red Lake could hardly be described as ideal. About 15 percent of their students received free or reduced lunch, and about 20 percent were considered special education, but most were mainstreamed into regular classrooms, and class sizes averaged thirty students (compared to twenty at Cibola).

## Interaction of Culture and Structure

The qualities that distinguished Cibola and Red Lake from many other SRS schools, including Island and Wallingford, that minimized inequality but had not achieved equity in instruction by our standards do not lie solely in the choice between structures of commonality or differentiation, since Cibola's dominant structural response was common experiences and Red Lake's was differentiation. Part of the answer may lie in the culture that supported each school's particular blend of differentiation and commonality. Both Cibola and Red Lake managed to combine features of difference and sameness that fostered high levels of authentic pedagogy schoolwide. Within the differentiated context of Red Lake, we observed a commitment to equity expressed as the desire to minimize tracking, to keep content common in mathematics classes, and to equalize the gender makeup of classes. In addition we found a reliance on teaching and learning to one's passion as a way of ensuring excellence in all learning contexts. Conversely, within the context of common experiences at Cibola, teachers found ways to individualize curriculum and assessment and to set goals that students could meet, in essence adapting their standards for performance within a framework of equal opportunity. This too fostered high levels of authentic pedagogy in all classes.[7]

To complete the picture, we return to the two key elements of school restructuring: an emphasis on intellectual quality and a strong professional community. Clearly intellectual quality distinguished Cibola from Wallingford, two high schools that addressed diversity by providing common experiences for students. Cibola was also characterized by a strong community, whereas Wallingford was not. Similarly the strong professional community of Red Lake contrasted with Island, though both schools responded to diversity with differentiated programs for students. And the emphasis on intellectual quality we observed at Red Lake was absent at Island.

Intellectual quality and community are essential for school restructuring to succeed with authentic pedagogy. Those characteristics support the higher standard of equal access to high-quality instruction to students from diverse groups. In responding to student diversity, schools tended toward a dominant pattern emphasizing either common or differentiated student experiences. But in the more successful schools, dominant responses were not adhered to in a rigid manner; they were adapted and modified in the light of individual cases. Cibola and Red Lake may have differed in their dominant responses to diversity, but each found an effective balance between differentiation and commonality. Other schools also blended these two approaches to some degree (see Table 9.1). But the additional focus on intellectual quality and professional community set Cibola and Red Lake apart and enabled them to minimize inequality at a high level of authentic pedagogy and performance. This accomplishment distinguished them as providing model pathways to equity in instruction.

**Notes**

1. Patricia Berman, Donna Harris, and Carol Wright provided helpful research assistance on this chapter.
2. This dilemma has been discussed by Coleman (1975). Also see Brookover and Lezotte (1981) and Campbell and Klein (1982).
3. One could also adopt a standard for equity based on student outcomes. That is, equity of outcomes would entail high levels of

achievement regardless of student social or academic backgrounds. Chapter Two reported that authentic academic performance in the SRS schools was relatively weakly related to social background. In some schools that small inequality occurred in the context of very poor performance; in others small inequalities occurred in the context of much higher performance for all groups of students. Only the latter cases would count as equity. The design of the SRS study did not permit application of an outcomes-based standard for equity because it did not assess change in student achievement over the period of schooling and the extent to which achievement could be attributed exclusively to school practices, to initial differences in student populations, or some other variables. Since we found that authentic pedagogy is strongly associated with student achievement, we decided that the distribution of authentic pedagogy could serve as an important criterion for educational equity.

4. Differences in levels of authentic pedagogy between schools that provide commonality (20.86) versus those that differentiate (21.86) was 0.33 between-school standard deviation. Differences with respect to overall levels of student performance were 0.40 between-school standard deviation (6.47 for commonality schools versus 6.11 for differentiation schools). Hierarchical Linear Modeling analyses contrasting levels of authentic pedagogy and of achievement between the two groups of schools found that these differences were not statistically significant.

5. Generally researchers consider a difference of 0.8 or more standard deviations to represent a large difference, whereas 0.4 and 0.2 standard deviation differences are considered moderate and small, respectively. Combining scores for mathematics and social studies classes, the highest possible pedagogy score for a school was 43, the lowest was 11.

6. We did not observe any low-track mathematics classes at Red Lake. The regular-level mathematics class scored slightly lower than did the high-level mathematics classes, though it still scored higher than most mathematics classes in other schools. The teacher responsible for the regular track class was considered the department's most traditional teacher. With another teacher in charge of that class (which would happen the following term since teachers frequently switch classes each term in the mathematics department) the scores might well have been higher.

7. Research by Bryk, Lee, and Holland (1993), Coleman and Hoffer (1987), and Lee, Smith, and Croninger (1995a, 1995b) suggests that schools, especially high schools, that provide common curricula are more likely to achieve outcomes-based equity. That is, they narrow

the within-school achievement gap among students of different socioeconomic class, race, and gender. Our results suggest two possible explanations for their findings. First, we hypothesize that the schools in these studies that were organized to provide students with common experiences tended to have the cultural characteristics that would ensure equitable pedagogy (and therefore result in more equitable outcomes) for students. Of primary importance, as shown in the case of Cibola, is staff willingness to adapt to individual differences (especially in the case of high-stakes outcomes) but still maintain high standards. Second, and conversely, we hypothesize that the schools in the studies cited above that differentiated student curriculum tended to lack the cultural characteristics that would be necessary to achieve high-quality instruction for all students in a differentiated setting. As the case of Red Lake suggests, these characteristics include efforts to ensure strong content and high-quality instruction across tracks and mechanisms by which individuals who notice the unequal distribution of students across tracks can take steps to equalize that distribution. Strong content and high-quality instruction in lower tracks, and the mechanisms to ensure that course enrollments reflect a school's social makeup, are notoriously missing from tracked high schools.

Additional support for our second hypothesis comes from schools in Success for All (Slavin and others, 1994), a program that differentiates students' initial reading experiences and leads to equitable distribution of high-quality instruction. This seems to occur in part because of a central cultural feature: a schoolwide (some would call it, a relentless) insistence that no student be allowed to fail. Several structural features help staff to implement this commitment: cross-age ability grouping that is limited to reading instruction; the flexible re-creation of reading groups every eight weeks; smaller reading groups for lower-level students, including individual tutoring for non-readers; and the use of paired-peer reading.

# Chapter Ten

# Participatory Decision Making

*M. Bruce King, Karen Seashore Louis,*
*Helen M. Marks, Kent D. Peterson*

Schools can offer curriculum, instruction, and other kinds of
support for students to achieve at high levels. Aspects of school
governance can contribute as well to the intellectual quality of
teaching and learning. Shifting from traditional, hierarchical
bureaucracies to participatory governance and decision making is
a major theme in school restructuring, with two distinct strands.
The first emphasizes the shift in authority from the district office
to individual schools, often calling for increased accountability at
the school level.[1] The second emphasizes changes in the decision-
making roles of teachers, parents, principals, and students within
a school.[2] In this chapter we focus on the involvement of teachers
in key aspects of school decision making (the role of parents and
districts is considered in Chapter Eleven).

The SRS schools all made efforts to change governance, but not
all were equally successful in providing effective classroom experiences for students, that is, authentic pedagogy. And although all
schools changed the formal structure of governance roles and
processes, the ways in which power was actually enacted varied considerably among schools. We found that schools illustrated four distinct types of power relations, only one of which appears to hold
promise for the promotion of authentic pedagogy. We illustrate this
conclusion with examples of how the changes in power relations
supported teachers' sustained focus on improving the intellectual

quality of their own and students' work. The chapter also examines the crucial roles of school leaders and external agencies in sustaining altered power relations.

## School Decision Making and Instructional Improvement

Advocates of participatory decision making for teachers assume that it will enhance individual and organizational performance, thus improving the quality of instruction in schools. Decentralization of school districts and schools, they argue, enables those closest to classrooms and students to make decisions that can most benefit learning and achievement.[3] Participation in decision making, advocates contend, will enhance opportunities for teachers to use professional expertise to improve school effectiveness, leading to more innovative and vital school environments. Additionally democratic processes will motivate faculty to exert greater effort and demonstrate more commitment as they work toward common goals.[4]

Despite the promise of participatory decision making, research investigating its relationship to change in classroom practices has established no clear relationship (for reviews, see Conley, 1991; Fullan, 1991; Malen, Ogawa, and Kranz, 1990; Murphy and Beck, 1995; and Smylie, 1994). The investment of time in governance can intensify teachers' work, initiate and escalate conflict, and slow the pace of reform (Hannaway, 1993; Hargreaves, 1994; and Weiss, Cambone, and Wyeth, 1992). Where site-based management, shared decision making, and other strategies shift formal authority to the school, administrators' attentions are often deflected away from altering power relations in actual practice. Although the self-managing school is ostensibly more democratic, traditional school authorities may use such reform initiatives to maintain their control (see Bimber, 1994; Bryk and others, 1993; Smyth, 1993; and Weiler, 1990).

Although restructuring governance will not automatically alter the quality of teaching and learning, it can be a facilitative condition. In the next sections, we describe four types of power relationships within innovative governance structures and explore the ways in which shared power relations promoted one of the central principles of successful school restructuring: sustained attention to the intellectual substance of student learning. This, in turn, supported authentic pedagogy.

# Formal Structures and Power Relations

Taking as our focus decision making within schools, we examine the extent of teachers' involvement in decisions traditionally outside their scope of influence. We consider decision making in whole school governance bodies and also in committees and teams, which typically have more specific responsibilities. Central to our analysis is the distinction between the governance structure, reflected in changes in the organizational chart and defined responsibilities for decision making, and the culture of power relations, that is, the norms, values, and commonly accepted behaviors that affect the operation of the formal structures.

## Formal Structures

Unlike private sector models advocating participatory decision making, the literature on school governance reform has not provided how-to-do-it blueprints. Thus the SRS schools implemented diverse approaches to altering decision-making structures. These included decision making by whole faculties, steering committees, cabinets, or improvement teams; community or parent advisory councils; teacher management teams in lieu of a principal; extensive faculty committee structures to support aspects of restructuring; and semiautonomous teaching teams. Schools varied in decision-making roles for parents and students, in their use of schoolwide versus decentralized decision making, and in consensus or voting models for decision making. In all of the schools, however, participants viewed structural changes as important elements of their reform efforts.

## The Culture of Power Relations

Regardless of structural changes in governance, schools differed in the way that they altered actual power relations from the traditional pattern. Putting participatory decision making into practice requires a difficult shift in the actual exercise of power and influence by teachers and others in these settings. Consistent with the emerging literature on the micropolitics of schools (Ball, 1987; Blase, 1991), we analyze actors' use of power and influence in their specific contexts. We focus on critical issues such as individual and collective autonomy, the extent of cohesiveness among teachers, norms about how decisions should be made and by whom, and the degree to which group decisions were binding. Our examination of the actual exercise of power in the SRS schools revealed four types of power relations: consolidated, balkanized, laissez-faire, or shared. Twenty-two of the SRS schools could be classified as clearly falling into one of these categories.[5]

## Consolidated Power Relations

When power was consolidated in schools, the principal, district personnel, or a small group of teachers limited broad participation in decision making. Thus most teachers were unable to influence key policy and programmatic issues. Cohesiveness in the school was viewed as important but controlled by the power holders. Of the eight schools we classified as consolidated, Selway Middle School is the clearest example.

Selway, initiated in 1989 as a small school focused on technology and individualized learning, was a school of choice for parents, children, and teachers in the district and surrounding communities. Formally governance was to be in the hands of teachers and shared with a school council consisting of parents, students, staff, and representatives from the community. Although there was a part-time principal, a lead team of four teachers had primary responsibility for school policy, administration, and curriculum. From the beginning the lead team teachers made all important decisions, including final judgments regarding interpretations of school philosophy and climate, as well as actual policy determinations. Their actions tended to inhibit other teachers' opportunities to talk freely about schoolwide issues and to undermine the confidence of new or inexperienced teachers, making them vulnerable to criticism and uncertain of whether they were "teaching right." To illustrate this point, a staff member discussed why one teacher had left the school: "The message from the lead staff was that 'we welcome ideas, we welcome change; if you've got ideas, let us know.' [But] what happened after her first day here was a roadblock when it came to her ideas and her inventions and her hopes. . . . She was just banging her head [against] these people."

## Balkanized Power Relations

In balkanized schools, teachers and administrators coalesced in multiple subgroups, which typically communicated poorly with each other. Power was dispersed among these smaller groups, each of which guarded its increased influence and autonomy. Disagreements and intergroup conflict often made schoolwide decision making very difficult, and individuals in the school believed that cohesiveness in school practices was neither necessary nor possible to achieve. Four schools exhibited this pattern, and Fremont High illustrates many common characteristics.

Fremont had one of the most elaborated formal decision-making structures of the SRS schools. A steering committee, whose meetings were open to anyone, including parents and students as well as teachers and the principal, made policy and programmatic decisions after hearing from the whole faculty or other bodies. A variety of subcommittees fed into the steering committee, including interdisciplinary grade-level teams and curriculum, budget, and student service committees. In addition to these organizational forms, Fremont retained traditional subject matter departments. Although decisions in all these structures were to be made by consensus, staff disagreements about restructuring undermined schoolwide cohesiveness and high levels of participation. As a result the steering committee became reactive, rejecting proposals that had broad teacher support but lacked unanimity, such as a plan to place all teachers on teams. Fremont teachers formed independent groups associated with various aspects of reform. The mathematics teachers, for example, retreated to their department when their attempts to influence schoolwide issues were defeated. Committed to NCTM standards, they saw proposals to extend an interdisciplinary curriculum as undermining their content goals. These teachers also pushed unsuccessfully for rapid evaluations of new programs while others (including the principal) opposed them. Members of the mathematics department, while persisting in their own vision of improved educational quality, rejected all-school restructuring.

## Laissez-Faire Power Relations

We observed laissez-faire power relations at schools where teachers prized individual autonomy and acted independently to achieve disparate goals. In these schools we saw a great deal of restructuring activity, but staff used decision making to increase personal autonomy. The individualistic culture resulted in a proliferation of programs that undermined any common vision of curriculum and pedagogy. Arguing that the pursuit of their individual interests would benefit students, teachers did not value cohesiveness in the school. Sumpter Elementary exemplifies the three laissez-faire schools we found.[6]

Sumpter, like Selway, was a teacher-run school. Staff elected a teacher facilitator and three coordinators (for academics, evaluation, and building and grounds) for two-year terms. The facilitator was relieved of teaching responsibilities, but the three coordinators accepted administrative duties in addition to their regular teaching assignments. This team carried out the major administrative affairs of the school, and the whole staff convened weekly to make major policy decisions. The culture of the school strongly reinforced teacher innovation and rewarded teachers who initiated programs. Typically teachers presented a rationale for a program or effort they believed in, and they received authorization to act from the faculty as a whole. Innovations generally involved one or two teachers, but even when initiatives had implications for the whole school, no teacher was required to participate. For example, faculty narrowly passed an inclusion program that mainstreamed special education students by forming teaching teams of regular and special education teachers. Since some staff strongly advocated the policy and the nonparticipating majority felt they should not stand in their way, they added the proviso that no teacher had to team. One of the teachers summed up the broad-based yet individualistic exercise of power evident at the school: "All I have to do is submit a plan; if I can support it, I can teach it."

## Shared Power Relations

When power was shared, decision making involved participation throughout the staff, equal access and voice, reciprocity, and a focus on issues relevant to the collective good. Unlike the consolidated power schools, influence here was distributed relatively equally. And in contrast to balkanized and laissez-faire schools,

schools with shared power relations focused on key elements of a schoolwide restructuring plan and frequently made binding decisions about curriculum and pedagogy. Most teachers agreed that they had both a right and a responsibility to participate in decisions; they valued and nurtured shared power and paid attention to strategies to maintain broad involvement. These schools used decision-making opportunities to reinforce both common values and coherent practices in classrooms. Seven schools exercised shared power relations. Because this pattern of participatory decision making is the basis of our ensuing discussion, we examine two different examples, Ashley Elementary School and Okanagon Middle School.

As part of its improvement plan, the district instituted site-based management at Ashley in 1988. The school promoted shared decision making through a twelve-person advisory council, which included parents, teachers, community members, support staff, and administrators. Teachers exercised influence and responsibility in decision making through a variety of groups and committees. Although the principal retained final responsibility for and veto power over school decisions, she rarely exercised it. Rather than viewing the principal as the decision maker, faculty saw her as the school's advocate, describing examples in which she fought and won battles with the district over site-based budgeting, hiring, waivers on standardized testing, and grading policies. Teachers took considerable initiative as well. For example, three teachers formulated and won district approval for a proposal to create a combined fourth- and fifth-grade class for at-risk students and a waiver on burdensome district requirements for special education documentation. The hiring process for new staff involved the relevant grade-level teachers and the principal in interviewing candidates. Consensus decision making among teachers was the rule. In one instance when teachers could not come to agreement and wanted the principal to decide, she refused, delegating the issue back to them.

Okanagon, a large middle school designated as a magnet school in the district's desegregation plan, obtained status as a charter school in 1994. A community council, composed of faculty and professional staff, parents, and students, met biweekly and was responsible for schoolwide policy. Other formal decision-making bodies included staff committees, teams, and whole staff. Overall the school had a decentralized decision-making system without a consistent process for delegating issues to various bodies, although the staff exercised considerable power in these groups and arenas.

The instructional team at Okanagon was a primary arena for influence. Each team was responsible for making curriculum decisions, grouping their 160 students, and creating the weekly schedule. Teams varied considerably in how they operated. The principal discussed the philosophy of decision making at the team level: "The empowering piece is simple. The people closest in proximity to teaching and learning must have most of the power. . . . The only way to know how to intervene differently is to know the children. . . . Basically we say there are two levels of decision making at this school: the educational [team] and the community council. And it's sacred, that all decisions that have to do with teaching and learning are made only by [teams]. . . . They do whatever they need to do to get the dream on earth."

Each teaching team designated a team leader who served on the community council and attended weekly team leaders' meetings. One team leader explained, "I am responsible for the administration of the [team] as well as meeting with other leaders and formally deciding on strategies for schoolwide things. I have never felt more empowered as a teacher to deal with school issues." A faculty committee illustrates teachers' influence on schoolwide issues. The curriculum committee, consisting of representatives from each of the teams, had formal responsibility for policy decisions and implementation on curriculum issues. At a curriculum committee meeting researchers attended in the fall, the committee continued their work of setting schoolwide performance standards as they discussed guidelines for completing the homeroom section of progress reports. In terms of actual influence, the committee set the benchmarks against which all homeroom teachers in the school were to evaluate their students.

## Shared Power, Intellectual Quality, and Authentic Pedagogy

The different types of power relations we have outlined help to explain the connection between participatory decision making and authentic pedagogy. We will first show how the typology is related to the school's scores on authentic pedagogy and then discuss how some forms of power relations contributed to improved classroom practices.

Figure 10.1 illustrates the association of schools clustered by type of power relations and authentic pedagogy. This figure suggests two conclusions. First, some of the schools with consolidated, balkanized, or laissez-faire power relations were making progress toward more authentic pedagogy and achievement. In particular, three of the consolidated power schools appear among the top group in promoting student learning. However, six of the seven

**Figure 10.1. Distribution of Restructured Schools on Authentic Pedagogy and Power Relations.**

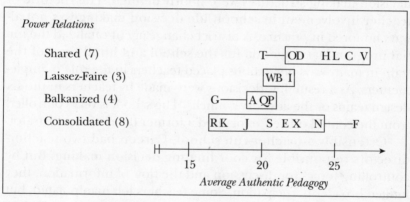

| School Key | | Elementary | | Middle | | High |
|---|---|---|---|---|---|---|
| | A | Humboldt | I | Morris | Q | Fremont |
| | B | Sumpter | J | Selway | R | Wallingford |
| | C | Ashley | K | Baldwin | S | Flinders |
| | D | Eldorado | L | Red Lake | T | Huron |
| | E | Winema | M | Shining Rock | U | South Glen |
| | F | Careen | N | Copan | V | Cibola |
| | G | Falls River | O | Okanagon | W | Island |
| | H | Lamar | P | Ottawa | X | Marble Canyon |

*Note:* Two schools with ambiguous relations are omitted. The outlier schools in shared, balkanized, and consolidated types reflect means on authentic pedagogy that were more than three-quarters of a standard deviation from the closest school, thus lying outside the cluster.

shared power schools were among the most successful in terms of authentic pedagogy. Thus we are led to explore further the ways in which shared power relations and some forms of consolidated power relations support teachers' focus on intellectual quality for student learning.

## Consolidated Power Relations and Sustained Focus on Intellectual Quality

Careen Elementary exemplifies a highly successful school with consolidated power. Chapter Six described in detail how a focus on intellectual quality supported its development, and the portrait description in Chapter Three of the prominent role of the district administrator suggested the possibility of consolidated power.

At Careen, in contrast to many of the other schools, formal decision-making structures were poorly defined. The rhetoric of teacher involvement in schoolwide decision making was not always honored in practice. A district change agent catalyzed the initial programmatic agenda for the school and hired most of the staff. In many ways her actions placed teachers in the role of implementers. As a result few decisions were made by teachers in the six design teams or the advisory council. "The school is very controlled from the central office," explained a former district administrator.

Ostensibly a teacher-run school, Careen had two teacher-directors responsible for coordinating decision making. But by controlling topics for discussion and the flow of information, they limited broader participation. Some teachers felt manipulated, but the consolidation of power was not absolute or inflexible. Teachers did make decisions on the curriculum and were developing criteria for portfolio assessment. In some cases teacher consensus resulted in upward influence—for example, when they convinced the district administrator to permit teachers, in addition to students, to select materials for portfolios.

Because a vision of school reform, as reflected in the tenets of Applied Learning, was a criterion for hiring decisions, teachers' individual efforts were especially focused on student learning. Nevertheless the district program involved unique and demanding tasks (such as developing narrative student reports instead of grades), so teachers felt the district agenda controlled their work.

In short, teachers embraced Careen's vision but did not want to be manipulated in their practice of it.

This case suggests that where administrators and teachers share values and objectives for student learning, teachers can achieve high-quality instruction under fairly heavy-handed administrative control. However, the unresolved tension between the district's agenda and teachers' concerns might eventually undermine their focus on intellectual quality.

## Shared Power Relations and Sustained Focus on Intellectual Quality

Change in power relations is no guarantee of improved teaching and learning. But the broad participation, reciprocity, and collective focus on important issues characteristic of shared power facilitated further success in schools where staff concurred on the goal of intellectually demanding pedagogy. We illustrate how this occurred in three such schools.

At Ashley, teachers engaged in extensive curriculum planning in grade-level teams under teacher leadership. A focus on whole language guided their deliberations for curriculum, instruction, and assessment. Teachers' definitions of whole language included such dimensions as "real-world experiences," "higher-order thinking," and "in-depth work and problem solving," corresponding closely to standards of authentic pedagogy.

Teachers' exercise of power also included teacher-initiated programmatic efforts that sustained their intellectual focus. Three activities exemplify this. First, each year the school sponsored a one-day in-service conference for state educators. Most of Ashley's teachers participated as presenters. In addition to raising significant sums of money, the conference validated individual and school efforts and prompted teachers to reflect together on their work. Second, a group of Ashley teachers were involved in Reading Recovery, an intensive intervention program for students struggling with learning to read, which has been adopted by schools nationwide. In so doing, they conducted peer observations and critical discussions of pedagogy, and they also discussed the Reading Recovery principles with other teachers in the school. Finally, the faculty study committee, comprising teachers and the assistant principal, directed staff development throughout the school. Monthly meetings focused on whole language for grade K–2 teachers and self-esteem and thematic units for grade 3–5 teachers, further supporting their focus on student learning.

Ashley illustrates an important feature of shared power relations in practice. The emphasis in this school was not on the formal decision-making process (although teachers were involved in this as well) but on teachers' implementation of and responsibility for the school's curriculum and instructional programs, as well as their own professional development.

Ashley's medium size permitted a high level of all-school participation in several critical activities. As we turn to a much larger middle school, we see how the principles of shared power relations can operate in a more complex setting through a system of faculty committees and subcommittees that took charge of critical aspects of pedagogy:

At Okanagon the portfolio committee met every other week. Seven core members—all volunteers from the curriculum committee—participated regularly. Many of these seven were active in one or more of the national or state-level assessment projects. The committee developed the Student Personal Reflection sheet used throughout the school for self-analysis and peer review of portfolio submissions. On this sheet, students respond to questions about what they learned, what strengths they exhibited, how they would improve the piece, and what they would like feedback on. The committee also decided on quarterly schoolwide performance assessments in mathematics and language arts, developed the scoring rubrics, and trained the rest of the staff in using the rubrics. The emphasis on extended writing across the curriculum, problem solving, and in-depth learning reinforced the school's focus on intellectual quality for student learning. The training and use of scoring rubrics provided the substance for ongoing programmatic development consistent with that focus.

Interdisciplinary, thematic units and long-term projects often dominated grade-level team discussions. For example, in one team, teachers developed a multidisciplinary curriculum project, Design a House, calling for a design on paper and a constructed model. The house was to be ecologically sound and appropriate for the particular biome the student groups decided on. Team meetings thus offered opportunities for collective faculty decision making that contributed to their focus on intellectual quality.

Many of Okanagon's staff dedicated out-of-school time to decision making that focused on improving student learning. Much of this effort emphasized the development of common standards for assessment, including designing and scoring schoolwide authentic tests in English and mathematics. Because it was a large school, many critical decisions were delegated to powerful subcommittees whose work the staff viewed as binding. Not all schools would want or be willing to engage in such a time-consuming process, nor would they tolerate such broad exercise of power by colleagues. Red Lake Middle School illustrates a faculty whose model of shared power relations confronted the tension between individual participation and consensus:

At Red Lake teachers, individually or in teams, designed their own courses, "teaching to their passion." Department reviews of courses helped to ensure broad-based understanding of the total school program and provided a means for the staff to act on a tacit instructional philosophy that supported intellectual quality. Much of the consensus at Red Lake occurred because the staff was constantly involved in conversation about the intellectual focus of their work, not only through the committee structure but through persistent informal conversation. Unity of intellectual purpose evolved largely though informal discussion in a decisively participatory decision-making culture of the school.

An incident involving the faculty curriculum committee demonstrated the unique commitment of Red Lake's staff to democratic governance. Based on his perception that staff wanted to examine and improve the school's overall curriculum, the principal formed the committee (consisting of himself, six teachers, two students, and two parents) to make specific recommendations for improving the curriculum. But during their process of study, research, and reflection, the committee incurred staff resentment. One nonmember explained, "Over the period of time they worked, for nearly a year, it was kind of a mystery as to what they were doing. I don't know if that allowed for some of the mistrust or suspicion or whatever to germinate without having further input [from the rest of the staff]." After a year, the curriculum committee members attempted to report on their work at a regular staff meeting, but other teachers objected to the process, and the committee subsequently disbanded.

Participatory governance, through a combination of formal and informal decision making, had become such an integral part of the culture at Red Lake that teachers' disenfranchisement nullified a year of reflective, perhaps productive, effort by the curriculum committee. A committee that oversteps its bounds and fails to create a compromise consensus among all staff members at Red Lake will not succeed.

## Sustaining Shared Power Relations

Teachers in many of the SRS schools reminded us of the fragility of altered power relations in school restructuring. They noted that their ability to sustain new practices of decision making depended largely on the principal's commitment to shared governance and on the district's willingness to support school autonomy. In other words, they did not believe their involvement in participatory governance was well institutionalized. In this section, we discuss how school leaders continued to be crucial and how external agencies can limit a school's authority and influence.

### School Leadership

In contrast to early rhetoric concerning restructuring, the roles of principals have not disappeared, but they have shifted. Principals in schools with shared power relations provided stable facilitative leadership committed to the school's mission. Their actions encouraged teacher leadership and contributed to the school's persistent focus on intellectual quality.

Principal leadership took several forms. First, principals nurtured decision making by teachers. As secure and energetic leaders in their own right, they were able to cultivate the nascent leadership of teachers in a variety of arenas. They found time and resources for teachers to discuss and develop new instructional approaches. At Red Lake, for example, the principal thought of himself, and was perceived by others at the school and in the district, as a "process person." He described it this way: "My job is to facilitate the group's figuring it out. I'll have a voice in that and share my thoughts. But I just don't believe you change by telling people what to do." His use of power, viewed as a key element in Red Lake's restructuring, helped others, including parents, teachers, and students, to exercise power. Overall, principal leadership provided motivation and ideas, as well as symbolic and managerial support for teacher leadership and activism in decision making.

Second, principals encouraged experimentation. As one teacher at Ashley reported, "I think the thing about this school is that everybody wants everybody to succeed. And our principal wants us to succeed. If I make a mistake, she would never fuss; she would just say, 'Let's see how we can make it better.' And she gives us so many opportunities to make it better." The principal at Ashley took an active role in issues of curriculum and instruction. For example, she helped them to define expectations for whole language instruction and to construct an environment that encouraged teacher leadership and risk taking in the classroom. One teacher noted that the principal "draws people out and then she turns it over to you." Another explained that "participation in decisions . . . contributes to an atmosphere here of teachers caring about each other and helping each other out."

Third, principals were entrepreneurial and spurred the same quality in teachers. They secured not only ideas but grants and external recognition, which sustained their school's focus and development. At Red Lake, for example, the principal's initiative helped to bring in a number of state grants that provided time for teachers to develop the curriculum. At Ashley the principal encouraged all teachers to write proposals to obtain resources for their classrooms (and most did), and she actively supported their yearly conference, which brought in a substantial flexible income for the school.

Fourth, these principals buffered the school from the pressures, demands, and rules of the local district and state. The principal at Ashley, for example, obtained waivers from state and district regulations that conflicted with the school's mission, and she encouraged her faculty to push the envelope of rigid district regulations. At Okanagon the principal encouraged teachers to apply for charter school status. Such buffering protected the school and teachers while they implemented new ideas.

Finally principals often reminded teachers of the school's vision when they became distracted with the hectic day-to-day pace of the school year. At Okanagon this role was evident in the principal's name tag, which reflected his title as "Keeper of the Dream." For him, his role was to continue to develop the culture of the school, which embraced an advanced academic curriculum for all students, a family atmosphere, and staff empowerment. He regarded his meetings with team leaders as a place "to practice team-building activities, so that leaders could model the behaviors of leaders—of caring, of focusing on learning, . . . of keeping the dream alive."

## External Control

Several of the SRS schools showed a depth of experience with shared power relations indicating lasting changes in the culture of the school. Such cultures were supported by considerable autonomy from potentially burdensome state and district requirements. The autonomy helped insulate the schools from shifts in district leadership and priority and to maintain sustained efforts toward their missions. Ashley and Okanagon, for example, each had authority to hire new staff. Principals and staff at these schools also developed impressive credibility with district officials, which allowed them great discretion in interpreting district and state guidelines to fit their missions. Red Lake's high levels of student achievement and its strong faculty cohesion provided credibility and power, which led the district to leave it alone. In fact each of these schools was considered to be sufficiently successful that district authorities tended to praise them as models.

In other schools, however, sharing power was fragile—not because teachers became disinterested or unwilling to step up to the challenges of managing a school but because external constraints, poor leadership, and traditional tendencies either vitiated their collective will to manage or undermined basic principles of self-governance. Problems typically occurred not because some were deliberately trying to alter the new power arrangements but because diverse goals and priorities could not be resolved. Two examples illustrate these points:

School-based management was the official policy of the district that included Copan Middle, and teachers there enthusiastically pursued heterogeneous grouping as a vehicle for increasing equity of outcomes among their students. State mandates, however, required them to reintroduce pull-out programs for gifted and talented and special education students.

At Humboldt Elementary different approaches to teacher teaming and student grouping helped to implement the strong faculty commitment to the principles of the Accelerated Schools Project. But with the departure of the principal who initiated this work, the vitality of shared decision making waned. Whole faculty decision-making meetings and other weekly meetings were not sustained. The school became more balkanized with two relatively autonomous teams, one traditional and one innovative. The new principal regained considerable influence from teachers in the areas of budget and staffing.

Those schools that experienced reenactments of traditional, hierarchical relations of power reflected a salient feature of the states and districts in the study. Most still operated under the basic principles of bureaucratically organized public agencies. In several cases state departments of education, legislatures, and districts proposed and mandated policies that applied to all schools and constrained activities at the school level, even when those activities were sensible from a state or district perspective. Districts tended to view principals not as members of the school team but as middle-level managers responsible primarily to the central authority, who could be moved or replaced based on central personnel policies. Shared power relations and more democratic processes within schools were not viewed as critical to schools' success.

## Summary

Our analysis of decision making in restructuring schools revealed that many schools that appear to be in the forefront of efforts to involve teachers in decision making have made only superficial changes in their underlying power relations. Teachers may have gained formal positions in governance, but structural changes do not guarantee increased and more equitable influence over school-wide issues.

Restructuring school decision making in terms of either structures or power relations does not necessarily improve the quality of pedagogy provided to students. Although all twenty-four schools implemented innovative structures of shared decision making, they exhibited significant variation in authentic pedagogy. Not every school with altered power relations was successful in authentic pedagogy.

When power was shared, participatory decision making could facilitate more authentic pedagogy and learning. Patterns of consolidated, balkanized, laissez-faire, and shared power relations all contained examples of schools that scored close to or above the sample mean on authentic pedagogy. However, within a school culture that values intellectual quality, shared power in decision making reinforced that priority and helped to support sustained programmatic efforts to achieve instructional goals more than the other three patterns. Principal and teacher leadership played a key role in facilitating the sharing of power and advancing the school's vision for high-quality teaching and learning.

In showing the importance of shared power, this chapter has illustrated how cultural aspects of a school's power relations interact with formal structures of decision making. Shared power relations are valuable because they can help support intellectual quality and authentic pedagogy and strengthen the professional community in a school. The quality of power relations within a school can also depend substantially on the school's relationship with outside authorities, such as the district, parents, and other agencies.

## Notes

1. Hannaway (1993) discusses district decentralization processes and their consequences in two districts. See Chubb (1988) and Meier (1995) for examples of arguments for more school autonomy.

2. See Elmore and others (1990), Maeroff (1988), and Shedd and Bacharach (1991) for examples of arguments for altered roles in school governance.

3. This assumption is based on a long line of noneducational experiments, in which work redesign that increased the influence of all members of the organization was shown (in some settings) to lead to more effective performance. See Cotton, Vollrath, and Froggatt (1988) for one review.

4. For various expressions of these claims, see Darling-Hammond (1988); Elmore and others (1990); Maeroff (1988); and Shedd and Bacharach (1991). Theories of organizational productivity in the private sector, and their applications to schooling, also make similar arguments; see, for example, Wohlstetter, Smyer, and Mohrman (1994).

5. According to procedures explained in Appendix A, power relations in each school was initially coded as one of the following: consolidated–principal; consolidated–small group of staff; shared–teachers; and shared–teachers and administrators. Through further analysis of

the reports for each school, we coded the schools into consolidated, balkanized, laissez-faire, and shared power relations. Coding by each researcher was done independently, and after initial codings, any discrepancies were discussed until consensus was reached.

6. Island High, described in Chapter Five, also had laissez-faire power relations.

# Chapter Eleven

# Support from External Agencies

*Gary G. Wehlage, Eric Osthoff, Andrew C. Porter*

Nested in a complex environment of expectations, regulations, professional standards, and historical traditions, schools are the object of many influences. Initiatives advanced by districts, states, federal agencies, independent reform projects, parents, and citizen groups aim to help schools improve. These external agencies have critical financial, technical, and political support to offer, yet they do not always speak with one voice. Competing demands and sometimes rapid shifts in leadership and policy can pull schools in different directions, making it difficult for schools to maintain a constant course of reform. The main question of this chapter is this: To what extent and under what conditions did external agents help schools develop intellectual quality and strong professional communities?[1]

The SRS looked at the impact of external agencies through the eyes of local educators, from the school outward. Those agents identified by informants and observers most often as having some important impact on these schools were districts, states, parents, and independent developers (private nonprofit organizations dedicated to promoting school reform and restructuring).

Our analysis of the four most active external agents provided additional insights into the relationship between school structures and the schools' professional cultures. We found that by itself an external agent could not successfully transform an unfocused, fragmented school into one characterized by intellectual quality and professional community. Rather schools with a culture that was predisposed to consider, or already focused on, the principles of intellectual quality and professional community provided the most productive responses to initiatives from external agencies. These schools were inclined to find productive ways of using new resources and opportunities.[2] In short, success in reform depended on interaction between positive aspects of culture and structure.

Three forms of assistance by external agents had the potential to promote intellectual quality and professional community: sustained schoolwide staff development, standard setting aimed at learning of high intellectual quality, and deregulation that increased the school's autonomy to act on a well-defined vision.

## Staff Development

Staff development programs have great potential to help educators focus on the intellectual quality of student learning, and if the programs stimulated staff to work together collectively to examine their goals and improve their practice, then staff development also strengthened professional community. Our analysis indicated that whether staff development programs offered by external agents promoted attention to intellectual quality and professional community depended on three general factors. The first two were whether staff development was sustained for a sufficient time to have an impact on teachers and whether the whole faculty was involved. Unless all staff shared in a long-term experience, the outcome was likely to have uneven, fragmented results. These two factors—sustained over time and staff inclusiveness—were structural.

The third factor in the success of staff development programs was the underlying purpose of the program. Cultures in the restructuring schools differed in the extent to which staff focused on the substantive goals and values required for providing students with high-quality pedagogy. Introducing new administrative and teaching techniques, procedures, and structures produced little change in the quality of student learning if teachers failed to address intellectual issues concerned with student learning. For example, ninety-minute classes (a structural change sometimes advocated as part of reform programs) had little payoff for higher intellectual quality if teachers continued to cover large amounts of material, rely on drill and practice, and remain satisfied with students' reproducing only isolated facts, definitions, and algorithms. But ninety-minute class periods offered a significant structural aid for promoting authentic pedagogy when teachers used the time for students to go into greater depth through inquiry, extended conversation, and thoughtful writing.

To illustrate the importance of structure and culture in staff development programs, we describe some reform efforts advocated by the Coalition of Essential Schools. Eleven SRS schools had membership in the coalition, which offered a general framework of common principles to guide restructuring, a process for planning school change, and opportunities for a school's educators to interact with other practitioners engaged in school reform.

The coalition conducted national staff development activities. Typically a school sent two or three teachers to an intensive summer workshop on instruction. Following the workshop, teachers were expected to share their expertise with others in their school and also to be available to visit other schools as coaches to help with reform. Many schools also sent two to five teachers to an annual national coalition conference where practitioners had an opportunity to exchange ideas and rekindle their commitment to reform.

Many teachers in the SRS schools, however, were exposed to the coalition primarily through local professional development efforts to implement practices advocated by the national organization. For example, local retreats stressed inquiry to identify schoolwide issues and goals. Ideally this process was intended to promote consensus and planning for organizational changes needed to implement reform. In some cases teachers formed voluntary study groups to continue to investigate restructuring issues and to learn from teachers' experiences at other schools. In a few of the eleven schools, staff development activities like these helped to strengthen professional community and produced greater staff clarity about the intellectual purpose of the school and how it might be promoted. However, generally such efforts tended to be highly episodic, consisting of one or two sessions on a topic with little or no follow-up. In most cases, staff development was not schoolwide; it was optional and attended only by interested teachers. Such activities had little chance of building consensus on a school's vision or in promoting professional community.

Few teachers in the coalition schools reported having participated in any professional development focused on the intellectual quality of pedagogy. Instead they attended to procedural knowledge needed to make administrative changes (such as how to implement block scheduling or heterogeneous grouping) or technical changes in classroom practice (such as using cooperative grouping or having students keep portfolios). These technical and administrative topics were important, but staff development on them apparently did not help faculties establish clear visions of pedagogy designed to promote learning of high intellectual quality. The common rhetoric that accompanied staff development devoted to technical and procedural issues was sometimes mistaken as evidence that staff had arrived at a shared set of educational goals and practices. But use of common labels to describe teaching procedures did not produce a vision focused on intellectual quality.

Of the eleven schools with coalition membership, only Cibola was driven by a vision that included a focus on the intellectual quality of student learning and the importance of building a strong professional community. It was not clear exactly how this clear vision about learning and professional community developed. To some extent, it appeared that these characteristics preceded staff development by the coalition. However, it was also apparent that staff used coalition ideas and resources to consider how best to refine instructional practices to promote student achievement of high intellectual quality. In contrast, other coalition schools addressed instruction and learning in such general terms that teachers could justify almost any instructional practice with one or more of the coalition's principles. Differences in impact from staff development based on the Coalition of Essential Schools are illustrated by comparing the responses of Cibola High and Winema Elementary.

Interviews with Cibola's teachers revealed that they had a sophisticated understanding and interpretation of the coalition's vision of learning. Many of them came to the school because they saw it as a place receptive to their beliefs. Others, identified as having a set of values and skills that Cibola wanted, were recruited to the school. Cibola's teachers shared a core set of standards for judging the intellectual quality of curriculum and students' work.

The standards were consistent with and used some of the language of the coalition. They also participated in formal sessions and networking sponsored by the coalition, but this was only a small part of the staff development effort at this school. Professional development occurred primarily in team planning periods and departmental and division sessions where teachers shared their expertise through discussion and debate that helped them to clarify and implement their standards.

In these informal staff development sessions, discussion commonly centered on goals for instructional practices such as student portfolios, interdisciplinary curricula, student internships in the community, and graduation by exhibition. Internalized standards for high-quality learning allowed teachers to draw from the coalition principles and staff development opportunities without getting distracted from their own vision. Cibola illustrated how the culture of the school was essential for productive use of staff development resources provided by an external agent such as the coalition.

At Winema Elementary, a large suburban school with only a small percentage of poor and minority students, the district officially endorsed the coalition and allocated $250,000 to support staff development based on the Coalition's ideals. Winema staff conducted a week-long retreat, as prescribed by the coalition, to build consensus for restructuring. About a dozen of its fifty-four teachers participated in either national conferences or summer training sessions during three years.

Winema's staff development nevertheless lacked a sustained focus. During one year, for example, the school hosted thirteen staff development activities under the coalition's banner focusing on such issues as Total Quality Management, management information systems, whole language instruction, cooperative learning, and study skills. But no consistent theme guided the work, and these topics tended to direct teachers toward management procedures and teaching techniques rather than toward defining standards for intellectual quality. Certainly technique is important, but in this case staff development did not help most teachers to address the intellectual content of the work they expected from students.

Even with the principal's leadership and the commitment of a dozen or so teachers, staff development at Winema failed to produce a schoolwide vision of pedagogy and learning. Coalition supporters at the school were unable to persuade many of their peers to change their thinking and practices. In fact, the high profile occupied by coalition advocates had some negative effects on the school's professional cohesiveness. Because the advocates had access to professional travel opportunities and a higher professional status in the eyes of the principal, some colleagues resented them. In retrospect, this weakening of the school's professional community problem might have been avoided if staff development had been inclusive, sustained, and focused on the issue of clarifying the school's primary intellectual goals for teaching and learning.

## Standard Setting

High standards for student learning are central to successful school restructuring. Without clear, high standards to guide teachers' selection of content and goals for learning, the school is like a rudderless ship tossed aimlessly about in an educational sea. But what role do external agents play in helping schools develop a vision of high intellectual standards for curriculum and student achievement?

We found evidence of educators' standards being influenced by a number of external agents. Districts, states, professional organizations, and independent reform initiatives all contributed to the standard-setting process. Teachers reported being influenced by books and reports from professional organizations, such as the National Council of Teachers of Mathematics (NCTM), and by independent developers, such as the Coalition of Essential Schools and the Accelerated Schools Project. Some states and districts mandated curriculum or achievement standards for public schools. Whether mandated or voluntary, we found that an array of external agents had stimulated professional dialogue to help schools define and implement standards for increasing the intellectual quality of student performance. Such dialogue usually resulted in reflection about goals and practices that strengthened professional community.

States employed a range of standard-setting strategies. Several relied on more traditional competency and achievement tests, which in many cases provoked questions about their intellectual value. Other states initiated new forms of assessment and curriculum frameworks that more clearly reflected efforts to raise the intellectual quality of student performance. More traditional forms of standard setting came from state testing programs such as New York's Regents Competency Test, the Texas Assessment of Academic Skills, and the California Test of Basic Skills. Standards that showed more attention to demands for enhanced intellectual quality were included in the now-defunct California Learning Assessment System, the Kentucky Instructional Results Information System, and the Vermont Assessment Program.

Since state-sponsored assessments aimed at higher intellectual quality were relatively new, they had yet to produce a broad impact on instruction or on student achievement. Although California, Vermont, and Kentucky each experienced political or technical problems, or both, with their assessment efforts, these states did succeed in stimulating discussion at the school level of the importance of high standards as the basis for reform.

Although only recently implemented (beginning in 1993), the Kentucky Education Reform Act (KERA) had the potential to elevate the intellectual quality of instruction because its framework and assessment techniques called for students to use complex academic knowledge and skills. For example, at the high school level students were assessed through three strategies: problem solving using state-developed paper-and-pencil tests, portfolios in mathematics and writing, and state-administered performance events that emphasized applying knowledge and solving real-world problems in group settings. These tasks call for more demanding intellectual performances by students than conventional competency and achievement testing.

Independent developers such as the Coalition of Essential Schools, the Accelerated Schools Project, and the New Standards Project also helped schools to emphasize and clarify intellectual standards for student work. Sometimes these independent developers had positive effects on the quality of instruction, depending on conditions such as those already described. An example of standard setting by a professional organization was NCTM's standards for mathematics, which influenced a number of SRS schools. For example, at Careen Elementary serious discussion of NCTM standards elevated mathematics teachers' knowledge of their field.

Adopting standards issued by professional organizations and independent developers was, of course, voluntary. Not surprisingly schools that made the best use of such standards were already inclined to see the need for them and to incorporate them into a larger schoolwide framework. In general, these schools had created a culture in which staff were encouraged to search for help and draw on ideas and insights from external resources. Standard setting by external agents helped to refine school visions already in place.

## Deregulation

Deregulation by states and districts is a structural tool that can give schools a substantial degree of autonomy to pursue innovation. Chapters Seven and Ten described how autonomy sometimes promoted professional community by engendering a sense of local investment and ownership. The right to engage in participatory decision making characterized by shared power relations can enhance a school's ability to focus on intellectual quality and professional community. Here we discuss in greater detail how different forms of deregulation helped schools address the two features central to successful restructuring. In some cases the district granted new schools a significant degree of independence from district regulations. In others, schools obtained a state charter to gain nearly complete deregulation from both state and district. In still other districts, schools struggled with their administrations to gain freedom to depart from conventional practice.

### District Demonstration Schools

Two districts authorized special demonstration schools to advance restructuring. The immediate purpose in each case was to test and refine innovations in teaching, learning, and school organization. In the long run administrators in the two districts hoped to establish models that could be implemented districtwide. To create a demonstration school, a district assembled a core staff and then gave them general directions, resources, and permission to engage in practices not authorized at other schools. In effect such schools were born deregulated, but they were also closely monitored by the district's central office. Deregulation by the district to foster inventiveness and experimentation was constrained by pressure for the school to demonstrate success.

### Selway Middle School

Selway was created to demonstrate how to teach children to become inquirers. The superintendent, convinced that schools of the future had to look and act much different from those typical of the district, argued that students should not be locked into textbook learning. Instead they should learn to use the kind of technology that retrieved, organized, and linked information worldwide. The superintendent persuaded several central office staff, the teachers' union, a group of business executives from the electronics industry, a number of influential parents, and community leaders to design a school around inquiry-based learning and technology. Several local foundations and businesses provided financial support and contributed state-of-the-art instructional technology. Students had frequent and easy access to computers, and each teacher had a personal computer with services such as e-mail and access to the Internet. The school's existence depended on financial and technical support from these sources beyond the district.

As an urban school of choice, Selway served 280 students, with about 40 percent from minority groups. The district obtained waivers from the state to free the school from state requirements in curriculum and staff certification. The school minimized the role of the traditional principal. Instead a group of four lead teachers had substantial decision-making authority to manage the school in accordance with its mission. Lead teachers were hired on an eleven-month basis to facilitate and reward their leadership responsibilities. A major responsibility was to provide direction to the general staff in matters of curriculum and instruction.

The core vision of the school was to teach students how to inquire. Staff frequently referred to this vision with the claim that "students should learn how to learn." The vision emerged from the planning group who encouraged the teaching staff to consider new conceptions of how and where children learn. Featuring a highly flexible curriculum with minimal use of traditional textbooks, the school was sometimes described by students as well as staff as a textbook-free school.

A number of those who helped to found the school believed that learning should take place not only in the school building but also in the places where adults work and live. The curriculum emphasized problems and topics that encouraged students to learn through the rich set of resources in the community. For example, the school was located near major art and science museums, which students visited regularly to do research; they used the large city library (there was no school library); and they had internships with professionals in such fields as law, medicine, and aeronautics to extend learning in ways schools usually do not consider necessary or feasible. Selway students constructed knowledge by using a wide variety of resources and technology, all of which were expected to increase students' engagement in authentic learning.

Two major problems developed at Selway, and these eventually led to its demise as a demonstration school for the district. The first difficulty arose over a central feature of restructuring: differentiated staffing, in which some teachers have official responsibilities to lead or train or produce curriculum for others. The four lead teachers had substantial authority and responsibility for the success of the school, including directing the work of general staff. But in exercising their authority, the lead teachers failed to build a strong professional community among general staff and between general staff and themselves. Disagreements over who should make decisions eventually led to open, bitter conflict. On several occasions the lead teachers also ignored the wishes of parents, who expected to have a genuine role in decision making, and this increased the level of conflict. Reports of stressful working conditions for teachers weakened the union's support for differentiated staffing.

Evaluating the effectiveness of the school posed the second problem. Given the lack of assessment devices sensitive to the special kinds of curriculum, instruction, and technology found at Selway, favorable outcomes for students were difficult to demonstrate. More serious was the requirement imposed by the central office that regardless of the kinds of assessment offered by the school, student achievement must also be measured by standardized tests. The district assumed that documenting the achievement outcomes of Selway's students with conventional measures was necessary to demonstrate publicly the benefits of such a school. When results on these tests showed relatively low performance, especially in mathematics, some parents (and the central office) expressed their concerns.

When the media picked up the story about disappointing test scores, the school faced a serious public relations problem. Then

Selway's founding superintendent left the district, and the central office weakened in its resolve to support the school. Without district support, the school could not sustain the thrust of its initial mission. In this case, deregulation, a vision of intellectual quality for student learning, and district and community resources all proved inadequate to create a successful demonstration. The school's vision of student achievement and standardized testing proved to be a mismatch, at least politically. The absence of a strong professional community among the staff made the school more vulnerable, and eventually the district office abandoned this promising venture.

### Careen Elementary School

Another district-created school for demonstration and development, Careen, served as a district experiment to test innovative ideas and practices with the intent of diffusing them to other schools in the district. Careen proved much more successful than Selway.

Careen's origins lay in concerns by the business community and district leadership over the competence of public school graduates. In response the school board and superintendent decided to develop a site to test what some described as a blend of progressive education and the application of academic skills and knowledge to real-world problems and settings. The particular name given this concept of teaching and learning was Applied Learning.

Careen was a school of choice for both students and staff. A central office administrator recruited a group of teachers from the district who were selected because of their skills and previous success in teaching. These teachers indicated general agreement with the premises of Applied Learning, and they saw an opportunity to teach in a stimulating educational environment and try new practices on the cutting edge of their profession. To assist the school's development, a local foundation funded a program of staff training, including stipends for teachers to attend summer workshops and Saturday sessions during the school year.

The district authorized Careen to engage in site-based management, a departure from conventional practice. The school had use of central office resources to develop its plans, the opportunity to recruit skilled and committed teachers from throughout the district, and a special publicity campaign to recruit students. The school was exempted from using district textbooks, and because of plans to develop new forms of authentic assessment around portfolios and narratives, Careen did not have to use the district's report card. The central office also paved the way for the school to establish its own year-round calendar, a unique option in the district. Through all of these facets of deregulation, the district afforded Careen a level of support not available to any other school in the district.

Careen succeeded overall in creating intellectual focus around the theme of Applied Learning. Moreover, teachers had sufficient competence to implement the concept in ways that professionals and most parents judged successful. Sustained attention to Applied Learning had strong political support because the key central office administrator supporting the school dedicated herself to making it work well, and she generated financial and human resources to this end.

Teachers enthusiastically supported Applied Learning, but they struggled to build a strong professional community, mainly because the school was new and all of the teachers were transplanted from other schools. Except for the ongoing staff development program, no structures (such as common planning time) were designed to ensure frequent face-to-face interaction among staff that could serve to strengthen shared norms and expectations. Careen provided an example of a deregulated school that succeeded in creating a focus on intellectual quality without a foundation of strong professional community. In this situation the staff's prior commitment to Applied Learning provided the important element of cohesiveness to promote successful restructuring.

## Deregulation as District Policy

Cibola High grew from a grassroots movement headed by local educators whose concern for intellectual quality guided the school from the beginning. This concern was sustained in part because of the strong staff recruited by the principal, the presence of support networks such as the coalition on which the school drew, and the intellectual and political leadership of its principal, all of which helped to sustain the school's mission. In addition Cibola had the significant benefits of membership in a special category of alternative schools established by the district to free them from bureaucratic rules and constraints.

The origins of this special status date back to 1984 when district administrators saw the need to grant autonomy to selected secondary schools that were small, innovative, and promising models of reform. As an alternative school, the district and the union allowed it to bypass seniority rules in recruiting teachers. Staff testified that without the freedom to select teachers who were both skilled and convinced of the school's intellectual purpose, Cibola could not have developed as it did.

The autonomy gained from alternative school status gave Cibola time and permission to develop its own educational vision. Autonomy allowed Cibola to define its own curriculum. It chose not to offer physical education and music; students obtained experiences in these areas through extracurricular activities. Teachers taught interdisciplinary courses even though they lacked certification in all disciplines covered by the course. Portfolios and exhibitions became the central strategy for assessing the competence of students. Moreover, to establish accountability the school invited external reviewers, from other schools, universities, and the Coalition of Essential Schools, to participate in the assessment of graduating students; the intent was to ensure that students were competent, especially that they were qualified for college entrance. As a school of choice, it attracted many students who fit the staff's interest in intellectual development and authentic pedagogy.

An important factor contributing to Cibola's success was the financial support it secured. Extra start-up money came from the district, but this funding proved to be only a small portion of what the school subsequently raised from a variety of foundations and private contributors. That grant money came largely without strings attached gave the school important flexibility to develop its program. Staff at Cibola helped to establish a local consortium of schools engaged in similar reform efforts, and the consortium served as a conduit for raising grant money to support these schools. The funding from external agents provided Cibola with additional staff and release time to develop new curricula and assessment materials. Innovations in these areas gained the school national visibility as a development site for successful school reform.

## Wresting Autonomy from the District

Eldorado Elementary served 350 students (63 percent Hispanic, 22 percent African American, 15 percent white), about 70 percent of whom qualified for free lunch. The school was conceived when the district announced plans to close a traditional, poorly performing elementary school occupying the same building. Community members and parents responded to the threatened loss of their neighborhood school by banding together with a small group of teachers to plan a new school. This coalition led to the founding of a school with a unique vision designed to serve the multicultural population of a particular neighborhood. The school featured a two-way bilingual immersion program. On alternate days, English and Spanish are used as the language of instruction for all students, whether dominant in English or Spanish. The intellectual focus of the school is on multicultural issues intended to promote racial and social class tolerance.

The district and the school had an uneasy relationship from the beginning, and Eldorado's story illustrates some of the barriers that an external agent such as the district can put in the path of reform. One of the school's founders described negotiations with district office staff as punctuated with a lot of "yes, but . . ." language. The district's administration concurred that proposals for Eldorado were interesting, even creative, but they were impractical, or cost too much, or violated some rule. Eventually after prolonged negotiations the school district authorized and supported a national search for a bilingual principal. The district office recommended a person who spoke German, but both the staff and the Hispanic community refused to concur. Parents from the school community organized and picketed the district office; they attended a school board meeting where they succeeded in persuading the newly hired superintendent to direct his office to find a Spanish-speaking principal. Eventually a Spanish-speaking principal was appointed.

Parents continued to lobby school board members and the superintendent to promote the legitimacy of Eldorado's bilingual and multicultural vision. Parents' advocacy helped the school to obtain a fair share of the district's resources. Teachers built strong relations with parents, and the leverage that parent activism created played an important role in wresting greater autonomy from district regulation.

Staff believed that they were ahead of the district on school restructuring issues, and part of their task was to push the district to allow further innovations. At times staff had to find ways to work around bureaucratic problems. For example, the school wanted parents to have a majority on the governing council, but union rules stipulated that teachers must be the voting majority in site-base-managed schools. Although Eldorado observed the letter of the law, staff appointed a set of alternate parent representatives to increase the number participating in discussions, if not actually voting. Further, staff permitted parents to constitute a majority on the committees appointed by the council.

Another bureaucratic struggle developed when the school wanted to establish a new schedule that allowed for dismissal of children at noon one Friday a month to provide staff with additional planning and meeting time. The proposal sat in the district office and with the union for months. Apparently neither wanted to act on the request. The school began its lobbying, and at the next round of contract negotiations, an "Eldorado clause" was included in the contract to permit special scheduling arrangements.

As a site-base-managed school, Eldorado took advantage of the district's offer of waivers. For example, the school developed its own report card, and it secured an exemption from district curriculum guidelines. Because site-based management allowed for control of its budget, the school used funds to hire a parent participation coordinator and paraprofessionals to help English-dominant students better learn Spanish. As a magnet school, Eldorado received some of the federal money given to districts with magnet programs, but otherwise the district did not provide additional funding to promote Eldorado's restructuring.

Eldorado's staff and parents joined hands in a long struggle for the legitimacy of their unique academic vision: bilingual instruction grounded in a multicultural curriculum. In spite of initial district and union resistance, the hard-won fight for a degree of district deregulation helped to create a strong professional community. Because of the school's strong support in the community, accommodation by the district became politically necessary. The

Eldorado experience shows the potential for parents and staff to overcome initial resistance by a district.

## State Charters

Our study included schools from sixteen states, but only one granted charters, at the time a relatively new form deregulation. We studied two charter schools in that state, Okanagon and Lamar, to determine how charters helped to strengthen the intellectual quality of student achievement and professional community in these schools.

To obtain a charter, the state required a school to write a proposal that described school governance procedures, instructional practices, and student outcomes. Each school's application built on a vision that was already largely implemented, but the need to describe and justify it in a logical and elaborated framework helped to clarify the path of development.

Charter status legally deregulated the schools, exempting them from most state and district rules. The main benefit from the schools' perspective was protection from interference by the district. It also served as a guarantee to educators that the investment in reform would become less vulnerable to sudden changes in local political leadership and policy.

### Okanagon Middle School

Okanagon served 1,350 mostly poor and minority students: 34 percent African American, 17 percent Hispanic, 8 percent Anglo, and 41 percent Asian. Fifty-four percent qualified for free or reduced-price lunch. The school was recreated when the district gave a principal the authority to select a core group of teachers and plan a new neighborhood school. This group secured grants from the state and from foundations to support planning and implementation. With these funds, the staff purchased books on school reform, held retreats, discussed ideas about the kind of school that would best serve the poor and minority children from the school's neighborhood, and visited other restructuring schools. External support made possible a rich dialogue that eventually forged consensus around the intellectual goals and practices of their school.

From the outset, the district had granted the staff considerable authority to invent a new school. Still, staff found that some district regulations impeded their work. Consequently when the new state law offered the possibility of increased autonomy through charter status, Okanagon staff voted to pursue it.

The charter application process required Okanagon's staff to clarify the school's intellectual goals. Staff developed formal written academic standards to guide students' and teachers' work and created a set of campus and classroom behavior standards for students. These two sets of explicit standards subsequently shaped the day-to-day language and expectations of students, parents, and staff who saw the standards as important guides to teaching, learning, and personal behavior.

With the granting of the state charter, Okanagon was ensured the authority to make decisions in several areas crucial to carrying out its vision. Most important from the school's point of view was the freedom to select new staff who embraced the school's vision without being restricted by seniority rights stipulated in the district-union negotiated agreement. The school used its authority to eliminate counselors from the staff, because the school's vision called for teachers to undertake an extended role that included counseling.

Okanagon is an example of a school that was poised to use deregulation to act more consistently on its self-defined mission. The charter helped to build and consolidate a staff that had already developed a strong professional community, and the charter helped staff to clarify and strengthen the intellectual quality of teaching and learning.

### Lamar Elementary School

Lamar Elementary, also a charter school, was initially founded to maintain progressive educational ideals and practices of the 1960s amid the back-to-basics movement that followed. Child-centered instruction focused on students' cognitive development through inquiry-based, interdisciplinary, thematic units. As an alternative school of choice, it initially had an important degree of independence from the district, but it nevertheless experienced cumbersome, bothersome constraints. When the possibility of obtaining a state charter appeared, the staff and parents of Lamar jumped at the chance. Like Okanagon, Lamar's charter proposal required elaborating in writing the conception of teaching, learning, and school governance the school had practiced for a number of years. Obtaining a charter guaranteed that the vision and its practices could continue despite likely changes in district politics.

Parents and staff said that before the charter, the relationship between Lamar and the district had been a constant tension-filled struggle. Having obtained a state charter, the school had the right to develop its own assessments of student achievement in order to demonstrate effectiveness as required by the charter. As with Okanagon, Lamar was able to hire staff outside the negotiated agreement between the union and district. Any certified teacher could be hired, and in special areas such as music, art, and coaching, a teacher need not be state certified. Such autonomy gave the school much greater flexibility in staffing nontraditional classes. Lamar was also exempted from district and state regulations governing curriculum content. While defining its own curriculum had long been a trademark of Lamar, this now became officially accepted practice. The charter eliminated time-consuming paperwork formerly demanded by the district's central office. For example, it freed the school from having to seek specific waivers from the district for each deviation in the way it used in-service days or evaluated staff.

Charter status and parental involvement intersected to produce positive results for Lamar; deregulation freed the school to spend private funds raised by parents. Since its beginning, Friends of Lamar, a nonprofit organization run by parents and community supporters, raised money from private contributions to supplement instructional programs—approximately $85,000 annually to support special enrichment programs in the arts, music, and horticulture. The money paid for supplies and field trips, and to hire full-time aides for teachers, but paying for personnel was controversial. District officials interpreted regulations to permit the use of private contributions for materials, equipment, and field trips but not to hire supplementary teaching staff. With charter status, Lamar's principal believed this restriction had been eliminated.

For Lamar, charter status was the icing on the cake. It helped the staff to achieve a tighter focus on academic purpose, built a stronger professional community, and reaffirmed the essential link between parents and the school.

## Parent Involvement

Parents, though not formally organized as an agency, are potentially an important source of external influence at any school. We have already documented their crucial roles at Lamar and Eldorado. Lamar offered the premier example of parents' participating in significant ways in all phases of the school, from involvement in hiring staff to raising money and influencing the content of curriculum. Eldorado parents helped to found and govern the school, but possibly more important was their role as lobbyists with the school board and superintendent to protect the school's mission and to increase its autonomy. In fact each of the twenty-four schools included numerous examples of parent participation, if not always as significant as at Lamar and Eldorado. In other schools parents helped to build a new playground, conducted student registration for courses, taught other adults, raised scholarship money, and helped to make policy governing the school.

Fourteen of the twenty-four schools had some form of shared decision-making council that included parent membership. But in only six of the fourteen did actual shared power relations provide parents with the opportunity to influence decisions. In the other eight schools, participation remained largely symbolic; informal arrangements maintained hegemony by professionals on important decisions.[3]

Seven of the twenty-four schools stood apart as schools with high parent involvement; compared to other schools in the SRS study, parents participated with greater frequency in one or more of three areas: decision making through school governance; developing curriculum, pedagogy, and assessment; and providing technical support for the school (such as fund raising or helping teachers in the classroom). The seven schools with high involvement were four elementary schools—Falls River, Careen, Eldorado, Lamar—and three middle schools—Morris, Selway, and Red Lake.

Three of these seven schools also demonstrated a high degree of consensus: Lamar Elementary, Eldorado Elementary, and Red Lake Middle. In these schools, parents and educators held common beliefs and shared expectations about schooling. High consensus helped these schools to maintain a clear vision for intellectual quality and to strengthen professional community. Lamar and Eldorado, examples of both high involvement and high consensus, demonstrated significant parent involvement in areas such as governance and fundraising, stimulated largely by a strong commitment to a shared school vision.[4]

Most schools experienced some mixture of consensus and conflict, but consensus generally prevailed. For example, Careen Elementary sometimes faced an element of conflict when parents raised doubts about the purpose and value of certain school practices, such as assessment by portfolios and teacher narratives evaluating student skills and achievement. However, in contrast to those schools characterized by consensus, a few experienced significant conflict between parents and staff over school practices. In some cases, high parent involvement consisted of parents' trying to change policies or practices with which they disagreed. For example, Morris Middle, an urban school created to address the needs of poor minority children, felt pressure from middle-class parents who wanted the school to make a greater effort at preparing their children for tests that would get them into the city's "good" high schools.

Two schools had both high involvement and high conflict—Selway Middle and Falls River Elementary—because parents and staff disagreed strongly about specific practices. Selway Middle began as a new school devoted to testing a number of innovations, including a role for parents in shaping curriculum and governing the school. Initially parents supported the school with strong involvement, but the school soon encountered a number of divisive issues that disenchanted some parents. For example, some parents believed that student discipline was too lax; others wanted their children to spend more time learning through direct experiences in the community. When staff appeared to resist parental suggestions, several dissatisfied parents pulled their children from the school.

Falls River Elementary also faced strong parental dissatisfaction because of children's low reading scores. Parents organized to protest against the school's program of whole language instruction, which they believed was responsible for low reading performance. Some parents advocated a return to phonics instruction. When the principal resisted, parents organized and drove her from the school. In the short run this conflict destroyed community support for the school. In the long run such conflict could conceivably, under certain conditions, strengthen the school. But as the Falls River case suggests, if conflict is to be productive, a fair and respectful process of dialogue between parents and educators must occur. If parents are to have a meaningful right to influence school decisions, the staff must remain open to rethinking their professional views and responsibilities.

Like other external agents, parents had the potential to influence a school to pay attention to the intellectual quality of student learning. Where consensus existed between parents and teachers over the purpose of schooling, powerful alliances emerged. Lamar stood out as the clearest example of parents reinforcing a vision of schooling with intellectual quality at its center. At Falls River and Selway, on the other hand, parents challenged educators' professional views, and the resulting conflict destroyed order, harmony, and purpose in these schools. We saw no examples where serious conflict was managed in ways that eventually strengthened intellectual quality and professional community for a school.

## Conclusion

The study did not discover an example of a school once characterized by fragmentation, disorder, and confusion about its educational vision and practices that was subsequently transformed by the work of external agencies. External agents may not be powerful or skillful enough to accomplish such transformation. However, independent developers, districts, states, and parents provided important technical assistance, funding, and political support. All twenty-four restructuring schools experienced some positive influence from external agents. Those schools whose culture already predisposed them to address issues of intellectual quality and professional community found productive ways to use the resources and opportunities offered by external agents. But external agents alone did not guarantee that schools productively focused on intellectual quality and professional community.

External agents may offer new resources or performance standards or pressure schools for accountability, but unless schools have the cultural capacity to strengthen intellectual quality and professional community, additional resources or new standards can easily fail to generate successful restructuring. Pressure for strong external accountability was unrelated to organizational capacity in the SRS schools (Newmann, King, and Rigdon, 1996).

The most successful schools in the study had basic cultural features that combined with structural autonomy to allow them to flourish on the margins of their educational systems. The special character of these schools enabled them to mobilize human and material resources and structural innovations productively. If external agencies and their policies can find ways to assist all schools in the task of addressing intellectual quality and professional community, then successful restructuring is more likely to move from the margins of education toward becoming the heart of the American educational system.

## Notes

1. Appendix A describes the method of data analysis used in this chapter.
2. This conclusion is consistent with a large body of research on site-based management (Odden and Wohlstetter, 1995).
3. For more detailed analysis of parent participation, see Wehlage and Osthoff (1996).
4. Not all schools that focused on intellectual quality and professional community had high parent involvement. For example, Cibola had only modest levels of parent participation. Shared power relations in the school did not extend to the parents. Reinforcing the school's messages at home was the main role for parents. This role was probably acceptable to most parents because they appeared to trust the school to do what was best for their children.

# Conclusion: Restructuring for Authentic Student Achievement

*Fred M. Newmann, Gary G. Wehlage*

When we began the SRS in 1990, the restructuring movement was only a few years old. By the end of the study in 1995, we hoped to learn what school restructuring had accomplished for students in twenty-four public schools in the United States. We were particularly interested in the conditions under which restructuring contributed to authentic student achievement. This chapter summarizes the three main contributions of the book, synthesizes what we learned about cultural and structural features needed to promote the kind of intellectual quality and professional community associated with authentic student achievement, and discusses implications of the findings for widespread improvement of schooling to promote authentic student achievement.

## Summary of Findings

The first contribution of the study was to offer a definition of authentic intellectual achievement. The ensuing set of standards for pedagogy and student achievement, derived from that definition, can be applied to diverse teaching techniques and curriculum content.

The second contribution was to show that in spite of much skepticism and many obstacles, some American public schools offered students much higher levels of authentic pedagogy than others. When teaching was more consistent with the standards for authentic pedagogy, students achieved at higher levels. Moreover, in this diverse sample of restructured schools, authentic pedagogy was delivered equally to students of different races, classes, and genders, and the effects on authentic achievement were equal across students of different social background.

In spite of this positive news, the schools we studied varied considerably in their success in delivering authentic pedagogy. Several schools, though highly restructured, showed low ratings on the standards. The examples of pedagogy and student performance and the in-depth portraits of six schools illustrated both successes and problems. Whether the more successful schools were good enough, we leave to the reader's judgment.

The third contribution of this study was to explain why some schools were more successful than others in offering authentic pedagogy. There are two parts to the explanation. The first is that the more successful schools constantly worked at two themes: advancing the intellectual quality of student learning and nurturing professional community in the school. The second is that the promotion of intellectual quality and professional community depended on a complex interaction of cultural and structural conditions.

In short, innovations in the restructuring movement should be seen as structural tools to be used for specific purposes in particular situations. Tools such as hammers, saws, and sandpaper can substantially enhance or diminish the value of the materials to which they are applied; their effectiveness depends on how they are used in specific contexts. Similarly the effectiveness of each restructuring tool, either alone or in combination with others, depends on how well it organizes or develops the values, beliefs, and technical skills of educators to improve student learning. We found that a number of structural conditions can be useful in promoting authentic student achievement—if they reinforce key cultural features of the school.

## Cultural and Structural Foundations for Authentic Student Achievement

Prior chapters have indicated how a variety of cultural and structural features helped to promote authentic pedagogy and student achievement by keeping schools focused in a sustained way on intellectual quality and professional community. We summarize these features in Table CON.1. We list the main cultural and structural conditions in separate columns for analytic clarity, not to suggest that they be should pursued as separate objectives. Nor do we intend to indicate any particular connection between items appearing in the same row. Success with authentic pedagogy seems to depend on integrating all the items to promote intellectual quality and professional community.

We illustrated a variety of ways in which some schools placed the intellectual quality of student learning at the center of their restructuring efforts. Staff demonstrated through words and actions their serious commitment to student work of high intellectual quality. The language of student learning became the currency of daily discourse in the school. But staff aspirations for more ambitious learning were not restricted to traditionally high-achieving students. The commitment extended to all students, based on the belief that all students could meet higher standards and staff willingness to take special actions to bring this about. This commitment translated into authentic pedagogy that contributed to higher levels of achievement for all students.

The cultures of successful schools included not only these demanding expectations for student learning but also norms for professional conduct that increased the chances for meeting the expectations. Because research on teaching offers few clear recipes for how to proceed with authentic pedagogy, staff searched continually for ideas and materials to improve their practice and to test new possibilities through discussion, observation, and study. We described the importance of norms that support innovation and continued professional growth.

All of this is difficult work at which neither adults nor students are likely to succeed working alone. Successful schools met the challenge by providing an ethos of trust, respect, and sharing of expertise and power that made it possible to put the full resources of the school community into cooperative effort, focused on the school goals. The cultures of these schools reflected neither "shopping malls" where individuals "did their own thing," nor bureaucracies where everyone complies with the dictates of superiors. Instead they represented democratic communities, insisting that

**Table CON.1.  Cultural and Structural Foundations
for Authentic Student Achievement.**

| Cultural Conditions | Structural Conditions |
| --- | --- |
| Primary concern for the intellectual quality of student learning | Sustained time for instruction, planning, staff development, and student advising |
| Commitment to maintain high expectations for all students, regardless of individual differences | Interdependent work structures for staff, especially teaching teams and committees for schoolwide decision making |
| Support for innovation, debate, inquiry, and seeking new professional knowledge | School autonomy from regulatory constraints |
| Ethos of caring, sharing, and mutual help among staff, and between staff and students, based on respect, trust, and shared power relations among staff | Small size for school and instructional units |

staff and students cooperate and take collective responsibility to support individual achievement.

Structural features helped to support these cultural foundations. Schools found ways to make time for working and learning more sustained and continuous than is typical. Time to exert sustained effort is required for teachers to craft effective schoolwide goals and standards, to gain new professional knowledge and reflect on innovative practices, and, of course, to gain the trust and knowledge of students that make it possible to teach more complex material. We saw in various schools how class periods were extended beyond the common fifty-minute episode, how students were placed in groups for instruction or advising that continued for more than one year, how time for common planning among teachers was arranged during the school day and beyond, and how staff development remained focused for a year or more on critical topics.

To carry on the collaborative work critical to professional community, key decisions about instructional program, hiring, and allocation of resources were often made in teaching teams or committees. Such structures reinforced interdependence within the teaching staff, and when combined with the cultural commitment to intellectual quality, they facilitated authentic pedagogy.

Missions oriented clearly toward intellectual quality and strong professional communities thrived in schools that had significant autonomy from centralized bureaucratic constraints. We explained how decision-making authority allowed school leaders and staff to craft a school vision, to hire staff committed to it, and to organize curriculum and assessment consistently according to that vision. Of course, site-based management alone was insufficient to promote authentic pedagogy, but when school culture leaned toward intellectual quality and professional community, this autonomy assisted the development of authentic pedagogy.

Finally, we found that smaller schools or instructional units organized to personalize teaching and learning offered striking support for professional community and for building respect and trust between students and faculty. The study design did not allow calculation of an ideal size for a school or an instructional unit, but the schools most successful with authentic pedagogy varied in size between about three hundred and eight hundred students.[1] Smaller size and the reduced organizational complexity that often accompanied it made it much easier for people to communicate and to develop collective responsibility for success. When the educational challenge for both students and staff is as demanding as that posed by authentic pedagogy, the need for sustained face-to-face interaction among most members of the organization seems especially important.

Identifying the key conditions that promote intellectual quality and professional community still leaves open a major implementation question: how does a school—or how do tens of thousands of schools—lacking these conditions attain or develop the key cultural and structural conditions?

## Making It Happen

We summarize here how key cultural and structural conditions were facilitated through particular forms of leadership and access to external support, and conclude by addressing the implications of our findings for teachers, administrators, and policymakers.

# Leadership

Several chapters pointed to the critical role of school leaders, both administrators and teachers, in helping to establish the cultural and structural conditions for successfully restructuring schools. It is well documented that leadership is critical to helping schools improve (Fullan, 1991; Leithwood and Montgomery, 1982; Louis and Miles, 1990). The SRS did more than identify the need for strong leaders; it helped to specify some of the most significant characteristics and practices of successful leaders in restructuring schools.

First, leaders in successful schools gave central attention to building a schoolwide, collective focus on student learning of high intellectual quality. Leaders understood that promoting intellectual quality required more than increasing the knowledge and skills of individual teachers. They also acted to build the capacity of the organization by placing issues of teaching and learning at the center of dialogue among the entire school community.

To nurture professional community leaders helped to express the norms and values that gave substance to a school's vision; they did this concretely, in language and action. Effective leaders initiated conversations about the kinds of classroom experiences that promoted students' intellectual development. Leaders continually emphasized that staff needed to maintain high expectations for all students, and they provoked staff to consider how they could best pursue the school's vision. For example, Okanagon's principal described his responsibility as helping staff continually to clarify what the "Okanagon Way" meant in practice. At Cibola leaders regularly discussed the implications of the goal of helping students develop "habits of mind" that would make them critical thinkers.

To support these conversations, leaders created time for reflective inquiry and opportunities for substantive staff development. By creatively organizing retreats and meetings, leaders found additional time for professional growth. To give substance to these activities, leaders helped to connect teachers to new ideas through reform efforts such as the New Standards Project, the Coalition of Essential Schools, the Accelerated Schools Project, and a variety of state reform initiatives. By linking their schools to these sources of ideas, leaders helped to set norms for acquiring new knowledge and skills.

Where principals provided the main source of leadership, they were at the center rather than at the top of their schools' organization. To facilitate consensus building and collective effort, they shared power with staff and often with parents. They invited faculty and parents to participate in decisions on hiring new staff, setting budget priorities, and allocating staff development funds. They kept key issues in focus, such as the performance standards to set for students or whether to become a charter school, leading the school to reflect carefully on its collective purpose and vision. Power sharing frequently brought conflict to the surface, both within the faculty and in some cases between parents and the faculty. In these situations, successful principals functioned as conflict managers, using negotiating skills to find common ground.

Principals also applied important political skills to relationships beyond the school. They negotiated for waivers from district or state regulations; buffered the staff from unreasonable intrusions by parents, visitors, and the press; and helped the staff to take advantage of new policy initiatives, especially those that strengthened school autonomy and offered funding for program development. Principals acted as entrepreneurs in securing outside financial support. As illustrated at Lamar, Careen, Red Lake, Okanagon, and Cibola, principals secured grants for innovation and staff development from the district, state, foundations, corporations, and independent developers.

In summary, effective leaders worked to improve teaching and learning not only by motivating teachers to examine and try new teaching practices but by addressing central issues in school culture and structure that lie at the heart of teaching practice. They cultivated a school culture that placed high priority on intellectual goals of schooling and staff collaboration to achieve it, and they acted to secure the structures and resources that would reinforce these cultural norms.

## Access to External Support

Support from a variety of external agencies helped schools to promote intellectual quality and professional community when they were poised to take advantage of it. A school's access to professional and political support from beyond the school depended both on the actions of school leaders and their staff and on the priorities of the external groups themselves.

Professional support included staff development sessions to help the school advance its mission (for example, Lamar's five-year relationship with a computer company, Careen's summer institutes and in-service workshops on Applied Learning, Red Lake's staff retreats sponsored by grants from the state), and opportunities to consider new standards for student performance proposed by professional organizations, state agencies or independent developers, or a school's outside reviewers.

Political support came in the form of deregulation by the district (for example, at Cibola, Lamar, and Okanagon) and by the state, which enhanced schools' ability to establish programs, hire staff, and spend funds pursuant to goals that the school community supported. Some districts also played a more active role in helping some schools to accomplish their work (for example, Careen). In addition to political support from formal agencies, schools need help from parents. Theoretically school choice should maximize the opportunity for parental support, but Selway Middle School demonstrated that school choice offers no guarantee of parental support if faculty do not respond to the interests of active parents.

## Facing Reality: Questions from the Field

Effective leaders and support beyond schools are critical to building cultural and structural conditions that promote authentic student achievement. The ultimate challenge for leaders and agencies is to help staff within each school resolve difficult issues in implementing more authentic pedagogy. Consider the problems posed in the following hypothetical letter:

> Dear Center Researchers:
>
> You've made a good case for the importance of sustained attention to intellectual quality and professional community to school restructuring that promotes authentic student learning. I can see that none of the many reforms being advocated are worth the trouble unless each is somehow guided by these principles, but I don't see how to do it in our school.

In our school, intellectual quality seems to come last. Getting kids to behave, responding to their emotional needs, and just teaching the basics often take priority. Some of our staff really don't believe all kids are capable of more ambitious performance, and some are just marking time until retirement. To be honest, I think many adults have not even experienced the kind of in-depth intellectual work you're talking about, so how can we be expected to teach it to others?

As for professional community, several teachers feel more comfortable working alone and resist collaboration. Even those of us who want to work together to improve the school have serious differences in educational philosophy. We have virtually no time to meet together to iron these things out. And leadership? For several years we had a principal who was happy with the status quo. But in the last ten years, we've had three principals, and they seemed more concerned with adopting some innovation to make a name for themselves and then moving on to a better job.

I guess we're one of those schools with a pretty low base of resources. What can we do?

Sincerely,

Concerned Teacher

The teacher raises tough questions. We wish we could respond by pointing to many schools that began like hers and turned themselves around, producing high levels of authentic pedagogy and authentic student performance through a focus on intellectual quality and school professional community. If such examples could be found and if they reflected a common set of steps to success, we would be delighted to share the formula. But we found no such schools. The most successful schools in our sample had either started anew fairly recently with well-defined missions aimed at intellectual quality or had been pursuing such missions for many years. In short, they seem to have begun their innovative work with a higher level of cultural and structural resources than this teacher's school. Nevertheless, the diverse experiences of the twenty-four schools do suggest some guidelines for action.

# Guidelines for Action

Here is our response to the concerned teacher:[2]

> Dear Concerned Teacher:
>
> In the less successful schools we studied, we noticed many of the difficulties you face. We found no easy solution to the problems you mention, but here is what we would do if we were in your spot.
>
> Find a few colleagues in your school, and hopefully some parents and people in the district office, who you think might be interested in discussing the importance of intellectual quality and the need for school professional community to make it happen.
>
> These discussions should be exploratory and informal, not aimed at school restructuring or implementing any new practices or structures. The assumption should be that there is no point in thinking about such changes until the school achieves reasonable consensus about its intellectual mission for children. As we have emphasized, adopting new structures first puts the cart before the horse and is likely to generate unproductive division.
>
> The point is to develop a group of people who really understand these ideas and are committed to working together to confront the very problems you have raised. In short, you must become the initial leaders to organize the resources you do have to build a larger effort to work toward the principles.
>
> As you begin to formulate a vision for intellectual quality, don't try to reinvent the wheel; don't just brainstorm a long list of student outcomes. Consider the essential principles behind notions of intellectual quality that have been previously argued and tried; for example, the Great Books, the *Foxfire Journals,* recent standards documents (American Association for the Advancement of Science, 1993; National Council of Teachers of Mathematics, 1989; Quigley and Bahmueller, 1991), materials from school reform groups (such as the Coalition of Essential Schools), and, of course, the standards we formulated.

Try to apply specific criteria for intellectual quality in your classrooms. Analyze your instructional activities, materials, tests, and how you grade student work to become more aware of the priorities that you currently support. If you think more attention might be given to some principles, such as depth of understanding, try some new forms of instruction or assessment consistent with the principle and evaluate the results. Discuss all this with colleagues, and use the results of these inquiries to inform broader discussion in the school.

As the initial group begins to hammer out a vision for intellectual quality, you must consider when and how to expand the group to maximize possibilities for consensus. You don't want to be seen as an elite club making secret plans for the school. However, the point of expanding the circle is not simply political. Seriously considering your colleagues' notions of educational excellence will strengthen the power of your conclusions. As your discussions become more inclusive you will confront the continuing dilemma of trying to build consensus and unity without paying the price of compromises that diminish the substance of your vision or that undermine the principles of community and sustained effort to support it.

Support from the outside can be a big help. In these initial stages, and later as well, try to connect with people from other schools that might be working in compatible directions, as well as regional and national reform efforts that seem consistent with the principles. At first you might want to shop around to learn how different projects try to elevate students' intellectual work. Later, however, you should connect external help to a clear, more focused vision. The clearer you are about your purpose, the more able you will be to ask critical questions about new ideas, and this will increase the probability that external assistance will serve you well over a sustained period.

Once you arrive at a solid notion of intellectual quality that most staff agree with, then think about one or two changes in practice or structure that might help to move in that direction. Before making these into a

formal proposal, anticipate and seek out the resources
and cooperation you will need to accomplish it.

Eventually you'll need to consider when and how
to put your work into a public agenda and when to
make formal proposals for the few changes you want.
These changes could be a formal mission statement, a
new schedule, a staff development series, a change in
governance, or hiring or transferring of staff.

Once you begin to initiate actions of this sort, you
can probably expect a long and complicated effort to
gain the technical and political support and autonomy
you'll need. Most of the effort should be concentrated
in your school, but you will need cooperation and
resources from the district. If you can find a skilled
principal committed to these ideas, this will help
enormously. At this stage, it will be important to think
of ways of minimizing resistance from staff who have
difficulty with the school's newly defined intellectual
mission or its new procedures.

We know we haven't given all the answers, but we
hope our vision of authentic achievement and our
finding that authentic pedagogy pays off in student
performance helps you define an intellectual mission
for your school. We hope our standards for authentic
intellectual work and the findings on professional
community, support for student achievement, equity,
participatory decision making, and external agencies,
give you additional ideas about how to use school
restructuring to help all kids learn.

Good luck,
Fred and Gary for the Center staff

Our letter addresses the challenge of restructuring an individual school from within that school, and this is the perspective that
guided our research. At the same time we recognize the perspective of administrators, policymakers, and citizens beyond schools
who are interested in improving systems of schooling. Instead of
assuming that the initiative for reform must rest with each school,
a systemic perspective assumes that leaders beyond schools—for
example, in districts, states, or national reform projects—can craft
programs, policies, and incentives that spur improvement in many

schools simultaneously. We did not study directly whether some programs, policies, or incentives of districts, states, or reform projects by independent developers were more effective than others in promoting successful restructuring among many schools. But the considerable data we gathered within schools tell us that efforts toward systemic change are likely to succeed only to the extent that they fortify the cultural and structural conditions at the school level that we identified.

Teachers will need help from middle-level administrators, superintendents, and policymakers. Assuming that leaders at these levels wanted to push reform in the direction of authentic student achievement, intellectual quality, and school professional community, we can also imagine letters from them posing complex problems of implementation and asking for advice. What can they do? We think they can make a substantial contribution if they use their leadership and the resources at their disposal to promote the cultural and structural features summarized in Table CON.1. We illustrate how superintendents and policymakers can promote these specific points, but in doing so we do not suggest that separate strategies should be devised for each cell in the figure. To the contrary, systemic reform aimed at promoting intellectual quality and professional community must be deliberately aimed at connecting the various features. For example, school autonomy alone is not likely to be helpful unless it is accompanied by an ethos of sharing among staff, and a culture that supports innovation is likely to be stifled without adequate time and other resources for teachers to act on their commitments.

Superintendents should communicate with middle-level staff, principals, teachers, board members, the business community, and parents about the crucial importance of these cultural and structural features. They should take the lead in helping to establish a districtwide vision for education that places high priority on intellectual quality. District-sponsored meetings, planning activities, curriculum development, staff evaluation, and especially staff development should all be aimed at this central target.

Mindful of the difficulties of raising intellectual quality without strong professional community in schools, the superintendent can encourage schools to develop teaching teams and schedules that offer more time for planning and professional development.

The superintendent can clear away bureaucratic constraints to innovation, encourage the development of small schools, and provide funds for school-based innovation and professional networks.

Careen Elementary illustrated how district leadership gave high priority to innovations promoting authentic student achievement supported by sustained staff development. The Careen portrait also illustrated how the central office helped to organize community support for a major innovation. The superintendent, spurred by criticism that high school graduates lacked the competencies to fill many of the jobs available in the community, initiated talks with the business community and school board about the need to improve student achievement. Out of this dialogue came a study by the district, supported by the business community, of the kinds of skills and knowledge required of workers in complex but typical work settings. District office staff discovered that a mismatch existed between the demands of many jobs and the competencies taught in school. The recommendation was to connect academic work to real-world problem-solving activities through the pedagogy called Applied Learning, and Careen became the demonstration site. Successful implementation there led to extending the pedagogy to a middle school and selected departments in a high school. The district's plan was to extend successful aspects of Applied Learning to other schools as well.

Other districts in the study demonstrated leadership from the superintendent and middle-level administrators who created opportunities and allocated resources for schools to become educational entrepreneurs. Often leadership in the district office communicated to the public a vision of high-quality intellectual achievement and negotiated community political support for promising innovations.

State and national policymakers, especially those interested in the work of independent developers, also helped to shape school reform toward higher-quality intellectual achievement. But the policy agenda can easily veer from this goal. Issues of school choice, vouchers for private schools, funding formulas for special programs, national goals, or desegregation plans sometimes became ends in themselves as they dominated policymakers' discourse—to the neglect of how to help schools promote students' intellectual development.

To promote intellectual quality and professional community, policymakers could focus educators' and the public's attention on efforts to improve instruction, curriculum, textbooks, tests, assessments, preservice and in-service teacher education to emphasize more ambitious intellectual work for all students. Kentucky's educational reform act (KERA) offered a systemic response to reform and innovation that touched many if not all of the key features of schooling. Although the results of the reform were still in doubt at the time of our research, KERA was the product of long and careful deliberation aimed at improving the achievement of the state's children in directions consistent with some of the standards we describe.

To encourage large-scale reform, policymakers could offer incentives for local districts, national professional organizations, and networks of schools to focus on the intellectual quality of student learning. And as they have done in the past, they could offer special resources for the education of students who have the most difficulty reaching high standards. To support professional community, policymakers could sponsor conferences and long-term institutes to help schools create organizations characterized by trust, mutual help, shared power relations, and reflective dialogue about innovation. Policymakers could offer incentives for breaking down larger schools into smaller ones. And they could launch studies of burdensome regulatory constraints and encourage states and districts to offer opportunities for greater autonomy as a way to stimulate innovation.

These examples represent a variety of leadership activities from the teacher to the policymaker. At all levels the work requires inspiration, argument, and evidence to focus school culture on intellectual vision and professional community. Leaders need imagination and persistence in devising and winning support, both political and financial, for concrete structures, resources, and policies. To be sure, the guidelines we present cannot resolve all the tough practical questions of large-scale implementation, especially how to gain the cooperation of hesitant or recalcitrant professionals, parents, policymakers, and other stakeholders with important influence. The material in Part One, however, provides a detailed definition of authentic student performance, along with new argument and evidence that this goal is worth pursuing, through authentic pedagogy. We hope this substantive material will be a useful resource in the effort to win broader support among those who doubt that U.S. schools should or can achieve authentic intellectual quality.

While we take these questions of systemic implementation seriously, we must not lose sight of the initial questions of this study and the findings on those issues. Our main question was, Under what conditions can school restructuring promote authentic student achievement? Part of the news is positive: in spite of much pessimism about the prospects for authentic pedagogy in this nation's schools, some teachers and schools are reasonably successful in offering authentic pedagogy that pays off equitably in authentic student achievement in elementary, middle, and high schools in mathematics and social studies. Part of the news is negative: even in restructured schools, many teachers are not very successful with authentic pedagogy; that is, school restructuring alone does not guarantee authentic student achievement. Yet after five years of study we conclude with optimism. If educators can concentrate on the cultural and structural features that we found to support intellectual quality and professional community, they will strengthen the prospects for authentic pedagogy and help students generate authentic intellectual work.

## Notes

1. Lee and Smith (1995) and Lee, Smith, and Croninger (1995a, 1995b) persuasively document the positive effects of smaller high schools on student achievement gains from grades 8 through 10 and 10 through 12 in a national sample of about eight hundred high schools.
2. Sizer (1992) offers a more detailed hypothetical scenario of how a high school developed a plan for reform consistent with the principles of the Coalition of Essential Schools.

# Design of the School Restructuring Study

The goal of the study was to understand how organizational features of schools can contribute to six valued outcomes: authentic student achievement; equity for students; empowerment of the school's teachers, parents, and school administrators; sense of community among staff and students; reflective professional dialogue; and accountability.

## Sampling

### Schools

Twenty-four public schools, equally divided among elementary, middle, and high schools, that had demonstrated substantial departures from typical organizational features were selected through a national search. Nominated schools indicated by questionnaire which of thirty-six criteria for school restructuring they had adopted (see Exhibit A.1). Follow-up telephone inteviews were conducted with the 301 nominated schools. Preliminary site visits were made to 57 schools from which the final 24 were selected.

Innovations common to many of these twenty-four schools were school-based governance councils, teachers working in teams with common planning time, abolition of ability grouping for students, instructional periods lasting from one to two hours, extensive use of small groups in instruction, and special programs to address students' social and emotional needs. The schools included those that were newly founded, hiring new staff to fit a

## Exhibit A.1.  Criteria for School Restructuring.

To study the effects of restructuring, the Center is searching for public schools with comprehensive restructuring according to the criteria listed below. Please answer yes (Y) or no (N) to each item, and elaborate if you wish. Further information will be requested from schools that answer "yes" to twelve or more of the questions on the nomination form.

*Student Experiences*
1. Is learning time more equally distributed among whole class instruction, small group work, and individual study rather than dominated by whole class instruction?
2. Do students spend most of their time in heterogeneous groups?
3. Do learning and assessment tasks emphasize student production rather than reproduction of knowledge?
4. To complete their work, do students usually speak and write in full sentences and continuous sequences rather than in few-word fragments?
5. Do learning tasks aim for depth of understanding rather than broad exposure?
6. Do learning tasks emphasize "multiple intelligences" and multiple cultures?
7. Are academic disciplines integrated in the curriculum?
8. Is time for school learning flexibly organized rather than in periods of standard length?
9. Do students participate in community-based learning?
10. Do students relate to adult mentors, either teachers or persons outside the school, in a long-term programmatic way?
11. Is student work assisted by extensive use of computer technology?
12. Do students serve as and have access to peer tutors?
13. Do students have substantial influence in the planning, conduct, and evaluation of their work?

*Professional Life of Teachers*
1. Do teachers function in differentiated roles such as mentoring of novices, directing curriculum development, and supervision of peers?
2. Do staff function in extended roles with students that involve advising and mentoring?
3. Do staff help to design ongoing, on-the-job staff development based on local needs assessment?

## Exhibit A.1. *(continued)*

4. Do staff participate in collegial planning, curriculum development, and peer observation-reflection, with time scheduled for this during the school day?
5. Do teachers teach in teams?
6. Do teachers exercise control over curriculum and school policy?
7. Are there specific organizational incentives for teachers to experiment and to develop new programs and curriculum that respond more effectively to student diversity?
8. Do teachers work with students in flexible time periods?
9. Do teachers work with students as much in small groups and individual study as in whole class instruction?
10. Do teachers work closely with parents and human services professionals to meet student needs?
11. Do teachers receive financial rewards based on student outcomes or evaluation of teaching performance?

*Leadership, Management, and Governance*
1. Does the school exercise control over budget, staffing and curriculum?
2. Has the school been divided into schools within schools, divisions, or houses?
3. Is the school run by a council in which teachers and/or parents have control over budget, staffing, and curriculum?
4. Does the school receive financial rewards based on student outcomes?
5. Does the school make program decisions based on systematic analysis of student performance data disaggregated by student subgroups (such as race, gender, socioeconomic status)?
6. Does the district provide special incentives for the principal to participate in restructuring?
7. Do students enroll in the school by choice rather than residential assignment?

*Coordination of Community Services*
1. Does the school have a systematic program for parent involvement in the academic life of students that goes beyond the normal activities of parent-teacher organizations, parents' night, and attendance at extracurricular events?
2. Does the school have formal mechanisms for coordinating with community agencies offering services dealing with child care, drug and alcohol abuse, family disruption, homelessness, sexual abuse,

teen pregnancy, crime and delinquency, economic welfare
assistance, and parental employment and training?
3. Does the school participate in an external mentoring program,
such as "I Have a Dream," which follows students for several years?
4. Does the school have formal arrangements with local employers to
place students in career-ladder jobs during the school year,
summers, and following high school graduation?
5. Does the school have formal arrangements with institutions of
higher education to assist students to continue their schooling?
6. Does the school have formal arrangements with institutions of
higher education to assist with staff development and curriculum
design?
7. Does the school offer adult education programs and recreational
opportunities for the community at large?

---

particular mission, as well as long-established schools trying to
restructure around a newly defined mission. The schools were
located in sixteen states and twenty-two districts. Compared to a
national sample of schools of all grade levels, these schools generally enrolled more students (average 777 students per school) and
higher percentages of African American (20.6 percent) and Hispanic students (21.7 percent). About 37 percent of the students
were on free or reduced lunch. Comparisons within grade level
indicated pronounced differences from a national sample. For example, the SRS elementary schools enrolled three times more Hispanic students than other public elementary schools; the SRS high
schools enrolled about twice as many African Americans; the SRS
middle schools enrolled somewhat lower proportions of both
African Americans and Hispanics.

## Subjects, Grade Levels, and Classes

Research focused on two core subjects, mathematics and social
studies, and selected grade levels. The grade levels studied most
thoroughly were grades 4 and 5 for elementary schools, 7 and 8
for middle schools, and 9 and 10 for high schools. Within these
grades, three classes each for mathematics and social studies were
selected. For each subject, at least one of the three teachers was
to have been clearly involved in the school's innovative efforts,

and the classes were to reflect the range of student achievement in the grade as a whole. Each of the classes was observed four times during one year. Two additional classes—those considered to be taught by the better teachers in the whole school—were selected for single observations on the second of two one-week visits (fall and spring). Across the twenty-four schools, 556 lessons were observed.

## Assessment Tasks

Each of the mathematics and social studies teachers was asked to send from the class we observed two examples of assessment tasks. We requested tasks that could provide valid and important indicators to them of students' proficiency and understanding of the subject. One task was sent in the fall and one in the spring. The teacher was also asked to complete a short questionnaire describing the conditions under which the task was administered ("teacher task description"). Across all schools about 235 assessment tasks were received. About 95 percent of the teachers provided at least one assessment task, and 65 percent provided at least two.

## Student Performance

The mathematics and social studies teachers were also asked to send a full class set of student work completed in response to the assessment tasks they sent. Thus the study tried to obtain two samples of student performance for each student in each observed class. Each student was also asked to complete a short questionnaire (student task description) describing his or her perceptions of the task and the work. Across all schools about fifty-one hundred samples of student performance were received. At least two samples of performance were received from about 45 percent of the students.

## Data Collection and Scoring Procedures
### Classroom Observations

Each class was observed four times during the year by a Center researcher who scored the lesson according to the standards for authentic instruction presented in Chapter One (Exhibit 1.2) and who completed descriptive notes to document evidence of high ratings. The complete scoring rubrics are presented in Newmann, Secada, and Wehlage (1995). One example follows:

*Standard 2: Deep Knowledge*

Instruction addresses central ideas of a topic or discipline with enough thoroughness to explore connections and relationships and to produce relatively complex understandings.

Knowledge is deep when central ideas of a topic or discipline are explored in considerable detail that shows interconnections and relationships. Knowledge is deep when, instead of being able to recite only fragmented pieces of information, students express relatively systematic, integrated, or holistic understandings of central concepts. Mastery is demonstrated by students discussing relationships, solving problems, constructing explanations, and drawing conclusions.

Knowledge is superficial or thin when it does not deal with significant concepts or central ideas of a topic or discipline. Knowledge is also shallow when important, central ideas have been trivialized or when knowledge is presented as nonproblematic. Knowledge is thin when important ideas are covered in a way that gives students only a surface acquaintance with their meaning. This superficiality can occur when teachers cover large quantities of fragmented ideas and bits of information that are unconnected to other knowledge. Evidence of shallow knowledge exists when students do not or cannot use knowledge to make clear distinctions, arguments, solve problems, and develop more complex understandings of other related phenomena.

Depth of knowledge and understanding can be indicated by the substantive character of the ideas that the teacher presents in the lesson and by the level of understanding that students demonstrate as they consider these ideas. It is possible to have a lesson which contains substantively important, deep knowledge, but where students do not become engaged or where they fail to show understanding of the complexity or the significance of the ideas. The criteria below ask observers to consider both the depth of the knowledge presented by the teacher and the depth of understanding that students develop of that content.

5 = Knowledge is very deep because during the lesson almost all students do at least one of the following: sustain a focus on a significant topic; or demonstrate their understanding of the problematic nature of information and/or ideas; or demonstrate complex understanding by arriving at a reasoned, supported conclusion; or explain how they solved a complex problem. In general, students' reasoning, explanations, and arguments demonstrate fullness and complexity of understanding.

4 = Knowledge is relatively deep because either the teacher or the students provide information, arguments, or reasoning that demonstrate the complexity of an important idea. During the lesson many students do at least one of the following: sustain a focus on a significant topic for a period of time; or demonstrate their understanding of the problematic nature of information and/or ideas; or demonstrate understanding by arriving at a reasoned, supported conclusion; or explain how they solved a relatively complex problem.

3 = Knowledge is treated unevenly during instruction; i.e., deep understanding of something is countered by superficial understanding of other ideas. At least one significant idea may be presented in depth and its significance grasped, but in general the focus is not sustained.

2 = Knowledge remains superficial and fragmented; while some key concepts and ideas are mentioned or covered, only a superficial acquaintance or understanding of these complex ideas is evident.

1 = Knowledge is very thin because it does not deal with significant topics or ideas; teacher and students are involved in the coverage of simple information which they are to remember.

About 25 percent of the lessons were observed by a second Center researcher who made independent ratings on the standards. The overall level of agreement between two raters on each standard is indicated in Table A.1. When ratings on the four standards were added, the overall level of agreement between the two raters on the total score was estimated as a correlation coefficient of .89.

## Table A.1.  Interrater Agreement for Instruction and Student Performance on Authentic Standards.

|  | Exact Agreement (%) | Exact or Off by 1 (%) | Pearsonian Correlation |
|---|---|---|---|
| *Instruction* | | | |
| (*N* = 132 mathematics and social studies lessons)[a] | | | |
| Higher-order thinking | 58 | 96 | .79 |
| Depth of knowledge | 67 | 97 | .79 |
| Substantive conversation | 68 | 91 | .78 |
| Connection to world beyond classroom | 67 | 91 | .77 |
| | | | |
| *Student performance* | | | |
| Mathematics (*N* = 637 papers)[b] | | | |
| Analysis | 60 | 94 | .62 |
| Concepts | 57 | 92 | .51 |
| Communication | 57 | 95 | .54 |
| Social studies (*N* = 685 papers)[b] | | | |
| Analysis | 45 | 90 | .59 |
| Concepts | 49 | 88 | .49 |
| Communication | 54 | 92 | .62 |

[a]Lessons were rated by over twenty different observers in more than twenty combinations of two-person teams.

[b]*N* = number of student papers, randomly selected, scored by two independent raters. For mathematics this represents 27 percent of the total papers scored (2,380) and for social studies 26 percent of the total papers scored (2,675). Raters were randomly assigned and rotated among numerous two-person combinations.

## Assessment Tasks

Each assessment task was scored in Madison according to the standards presented in Chapter One (Exhibit 1.1) by a Center researcher and a currently practicing teacher in the subject, trained by Center staff who also had experience teaching the subject. To make judgments about the teachers' demands and expectations for students, the raters also examined the teacher task description and teacher comments on samples of student performance. If the two-person team did not agree on their initial independent ratings, they discussed the matter until they reached consensus. The complete scoring rubrics are presented in Newmann, Secada, and Wehlage (1995). One example follows:

*Standard 3: Disciplinary Content*

The task asks students to show understanding and/or use of ideas, theories, or perspectives considered central to an academic or professional discipline.

To what extent does the task promote students' understanding of and thinking about ideas, theories, or perspectives considered seminal or critical within an academic or professional discipline, or in interdisciplinary fields recognized in authoritative scholarship? Examples in mathematics could include proportion, equality, central tendency, geometric space. Examples in social studies could include democracy, social class, market economy, theories of revolution. Reference to isolated factual claims, definitions, algorithms—though necessary to inquiry within a discipline—will not be considered indicators of significant disciplinary content unless the task requires students to apply powerful disciplinary ideas that organize and interpret the information.

3 = Success in the task clearly requires understanding of concepts, ideas, or theories central in a discipline.

2 = Success in the task seems to require understanding of concepts, ideas, or theories central in a discipline; but the task does not make these very explicit.

1 = Success in the task can be achieved with a very superficial (or even without any) understanding of concepts, ideas, or theories central to any specific discipline.

# Student Performance

Each sample of student work was scored in Madison according to the standards presented in Chapter One (Exhibit 1.3) by a currently practicing teacher in the subject, trained by Center staff who also had experience teaching the subject. The complete scoring rubrics are presented in Newmann, Secada, and Wehlage (1995). One example follows:

### Standard 2: Disciplinary Concepts: Mathematics

Student performance demonstrates an understanding of important mathematical ideas that goes beyond application of algorithms by elaborating definitions, making connections to other mathematical concepts, or making connections to other disciplines.

This standard is intended to measure the extent to which the student demonstrates use and understanding of mathematical concepts. Prior to scoring the student's work, the rater should identify what mathematical concepts, if any, a student must use and/or understand to succeed in the task. Low student performance scores may be due to tasks which fail to call for understanding of mathematical concepts.

A guiding question for using this standard is, "Does the student show understanding of the fundamental ideas relevant to the mathematics used in the task?" Correct use of algorithms does not necessarily indicate conceptual understanding of the material. Such understanding can be demonstrated, for instance, by elaborating upon the concept through definition or by making connections between the core concept and other related ones.

If work is not shown, correct answers can be taken as an indication of conceptual understanding, if it is clear that the task or question requires a conceptual understanding to be completed successfully.

Completion of the task is not necessary to score high.

4 = The student demonstrates an exemplary understanding of the mathematical concepts that are central to the task. Their application is appropriate, flawless, and elegant.

3 = There is substantial evidence that the student understands the mathematical concepts that are central to the task. The

student applies these concepts to the task appropriately; however, there may be minor flaws in their application, or details may be missing.

2 = There is some evidence that the student understands the mathematical concepts that are central to the task. Where the student uses appropriate mathematical concepts, the application of those concepts is flawed or incomplete.

1 = There is little or no evidence that the student understands the mathematical concepts that are central to the task, or the mathematical concepts that are used are totally inappropriate to the task, or they are applied in inappropriate ways.

About 26 percent of the papers were scored independently by a second rater, randomly assigned. The overall level of precise agreement between two raters, indicated in Table A.1, was 54 percent, and agreement within one point was 92 percent. When the three standards for performance were added, the overall level of agreement between two raters on the total score was estimated as a correlation coefficient of .70 for mathematics and .77 for social studies.

## Student Baseline Tests

All students in the observed classes were asked to complete tests of basic knowledge in the fall. Students in observed mathematics classes were given a test composed of selected items from the National Assessment of Educational Progress (NAEP) mathematics tests for the appropriate grade level. Students in observed social studies classes were given a test composed of selected items from the NAEP reading tests, along with a short test of writing scored by Center staff according to NAEP standards. The overall response rate for these tests was about 85 percent. SRS student scores on these tests at the elementary level were at the national average in mathematics and slightly above in reading; at the middle level, above the national average in both subjects; at the high school level, below national averages in both subjects (but this could be due to the fact that the high school NAEP norms used were based on twelfth grade and most SRS students were not above tenth grade).

## Student Survey

Students in the observed classes, along with other classmates in the same grade, were asked to complete a survey asking about their experiences in the class and the school. This included items on student engagement, teacher expectations, school climate, and parent involvement. The overall response rate was about 82 percent.

## Teacher Survey

All teachers in the school were asked to complete a survey asking about their instructional practices, their expectations for students, their professional activities and environment, the school's approach to restructuring, and the influence of outside agencies. The overall response rate for the teacher survey was about 81 percent.

## Interviews

Semistructured interviews dealt with each of the six initial questions of the study and with the role of external agencies in supporting or inhibiting school restructuring. The mathematics and social studies teachers, four other teachers, and the school principal were interviewed during both the fall and spring research visits. Additional teachers, administrators, parents, and other persons connected with the school's restructuring efforts were also interviewed. Approximately fifteen interviews were held in each school on each of the two research visits.

## Team Reports

Observation and interview data were summarized in extensive (150- to 200-page) reports for each school, organized according to the six initial questions of the study, and a section on the influence of external agencies. Draft reports were revised into final versions, based on reviews by both the three-person team of researchers and two additional researchers. The reports provided a major database for analytic conclusions, along with the quantitative data available in class observations, surveys, and the scoring of assessment tasks and student performance.

## Coding

To help synthesize the extensive information assembled, two members of the Center research team for each school completed a standardized coding work sheet on each school. The coding asked for researchers' conclusions on the following topics: restructuring practices implemented, intellectual quality, program coherence, curriculum differentiation, professional community, staff development, leadership, governance/empowerment, parent-school relations, accountability, and influence of external agencies. Coders completed individual work sheets, then negotiated responses to items on which their initial responses differed. The coding work sheet included more than one hundred items; examples are given in the next section.

## Construction of Selected Variables

### Intellectual Quality

Researchers' conclusions described in Chapter Six were based primarily on information from the team reports, but the coding sheet also provided the following indicator:

> How would you characterize the overall dominant emphasis in this school (check the best answer):
>
> A. The staff's primary concern is the intellectual substance of student learning; that is, construction of meaning around important ideas.
> B. The staff's primary concern is how to implement or deal with procedural/administrative innovations; for example, teaming, shared decision making, cooperative learning techniques, new scheduling, new grading systems, etc.
> C. The staff shows no primary emphasis on either A or B. That is, they might show equal concern for each or perhaps a different primary emphasis such as offering a trusting environment for students.
>
> In making this judgment, do not consider actual scores of lessons or quality of observed assessments. Instead, consider teachers' reports of their individual concerns, priorities and activities and the issues addressed in meetings and staff development activities.

# Professional Community

Conclusions about the level of professional community in Chapter Seven were drawn from team reports and supplemented by use of several items in the teacher survey. The five dimensions of teacher professional community were captured by the following survey items (response alternatives included scales for strongly agree to strongly disagree; frequencies to indicate how often during a week, month, or year; number of hours spent in certain activities; rankings indicating high or low importance).

### Shared Sense of Purpose

1. Most of my colleagues share my beliefs and values about what the central mission of the school should be.
2. Goals and priorities for the school are clear.
3. In this school the teachers and the administration are in close agreement on school discipline policy.

### Collaborative Activity

1. How often since the beginning of the current school year did you receive useful suggestions for curriculum materials from colleagues in your department?
2. How often . . . did you receive useful suggestions for teaching techniques or student activities from colleagues in your department?
3. There is a great deal of cooperative effort among staff members.
4. I make a conscious effort to coordinate the content of my courses with other teachers.
5. In a typical planning period when you meet with other teachers, about how much time is spent on coordinating content, where teachers decide common themes, suggest related materials and activities to guide instruction?
6. Since the beginning of the current school year, about how much time per month have you spent meeting with other teachers on lesson planning, curriculum development, guidance and counseling, evaluation of programs, or other collaborative work related to instruction?

### Collective Focus on Student Learning

1. Importance of higher-level skills (reasoning, problem solving, critical and creative thinking) to your teaching as a goal for your students.

2. Teachers focus on what and how well students are learning rather than how they are teaching.
3. Teachers exhibit a reasonably focused commitment to authentic curriculum and instruction.
4. A focused school vision for student learning is shared by most staff in the school.

*Deprivatized Practice*

1. How often do two or more teaching colleagues regularly observe your students' academic performance, or review their grades or test scores?
2. Except for monitoring student teachers or substitute teachers, how often have you visited another teacher's classroom to observe and discuss their teaching since the beginning of the current school year?
3. Since the beginning of the current school year, how often has another teacher come to your classroom to observe your teaching (exclude visits by student teachers or those required for formal evaluations)?
4. How often since the beginning of the current school year did you receive meaningful feedback on your performance from supervisors or peers?

*Reflective Dialogue*

1. In a typical planning period when you meet with other teachers, about how much time is spent on diagnosing individual students, where teachers discuss problems of specific students and arrange appropriate help?
2. In a typical planning period when you meet with other teachers, about how much time is spent on analyzing teaching, where teachers discuss specific teaching practices and behaviors of team members?
3. How often since the beginning of the current school year did you meet with colleagues to discuss specific teaching behaviors?

## Support for Achievement

Conclusions about the level of support for student achievement described in Chapter Eight were drawn from team reports, supplemented by survey and observation items.

## School

The following items are from the student survey:

How much do you agree with each of the following statements about your current school and teachers? (4-point scale, strongly disagree to strongly agree.)

1. Discipline is fair.
2. Students make friends with students of other racial and ethnic groups.
3. In school I often feel "put down" by other students (reversed).
4. Most of my teachers really listen to what I have to say.
5. Disruptions by other students get in the way of my learning (reversed).
6. My friends and I are treated fairly at this school (reversed).

## Classroom

Two measures were combined to assess support within the classroom. The first measure was the researcher's rating of observed classes on the following item:

*Social Support for Student Achievement*

To what extent is the classroom characterized by an atmosphere of mutual respect and support among teacher and students?

| Negative Social Support | 1...2...3...4...5 | Positive Social Support |
|---|---|---|

Social support can be undermined by teacher or student behavior, comments, and actions that tend to discourage effort, participation, and taking risks to learn or express one's views. For example, teacher or student comments that belittle a student's answer, and efforts by some students to prevent others from taking seriously an assignment serve to undermine support for achievement. Support can also be absent in a class when no overt acts like the above occur, but the overall atmosphere of the class is negative due to previous behavior. Social support is present in classes when the teacher supports students by conveying high expectations for all students: these expectations include that it is necessary to take risks and try hard to master challenging academic work, that all members of the class can learn important knowledge and skills, and that a climate of mutual respect among all members of the class contributes to achievement by all. Mutual respect means that students with less skill or proficiency in a subject are treated in ways that continue to encourage them and make their presence valued. If disagreement or conflict develops in the classroom, the teacher helps students resolve it in a constructive way for all concerned. (Note: token acknowledgments by teacher of student actions or responses do *not* constitute evidence of social support.)

1 = Social support is negative; action/comments by teacher or students result in "put-downs"; classroom atmosphere is negative.

2 = Social support is mixed. Both negative and positive behaviors or comments are observed.

3 = Social support is neutral or mildly positive. Evidence may be mainly in the form of verbal approval from the teacher for student effort and work. However, such support tends to be given to those who are already taking initiative in the class, and it tends not to be given to those who are reluctant participants or less articulate or skilled in the subject.

4 = Social support from the teacher is clearly positive and there is some evidence of social support among students for their peers. Evidence of special efforts by the teacher takes the form of direct expressions that convey high expectations for all; mutual respect; a need to try hard and risk initial failure.

5 = Social support is strong; the class is characterized by high expectations, challenging work, strong effort, mutual respect, and assistance in achievement for all students. Both teacher and students demonstrate a number of these attitudes by soliciting and welcoming contributions from all students, who are expected to put forth their best efforts. Broad participation may be an indication that low-achieving students receive social support for learning.

The second measure was an index from the following items on the student survey:

Do you agree or disagree with the following statements about your social studies/math class: (4-point scale strongly disagree to strongly agree)?

1. If I have trouble with my work, my teacher gives me help.
2. If I have trouble with the work, my friends give me help.
3. The teacher believes I can succeed.
4. Many students don't respect one another (reversed).
5. Many students try to help one another learn.
6. My friends and I help each other with our homework.
7. The teacher expects me to do my best all the time.
8. The teacher gives me extra help when I don't understand something in class.

## Common and Differentiated Approaches to Curriculum and Instruction

Conclusions in Chapter Nine about approaches to equity were based largely on researchers' interpretations of the team reports. Initially they used items on the coding sheet to identify patterns of commonality or differentiation in mathematics and social studies. One such item follows:

> In the target grade for mathematics, which of the following best describes this school (select one answer)?
>
> A. All students have the same curriculum and there are no special classes or programs for any group of students.
> B. Students are exposed to different curricula and/or teaching methods, based on some indication of their prior achievement such as test scores or teacher recommendations.
> C. Students are exposed to different curricula and/or teaching methods, based on students' own interests (which may or may not be related to ability).

## Power Relations

Researchers analyzed team reports to discern different patterns of power relations described in Chapter Ten. Initially they used the following item from the coding work sheet:

> Irrespective of formal decision-making structures, actual power and influence on the most significant issues in this school are (choose the best description):
>
> A. Consolidated in the hands of the principal (or equivalent) and allies.

   B. Consolidated in a small group of staff (whether teachers or
      administrators, or some combination).
   C. Widely shared among teachers.
   D. Widely shared among teachers and administrators.

Information in the team reports was used to discriminate further among the nature of power relations in different schools.

## Influence of External Agencies

For analyses in Chapter Eleven, team reports were coded on the extent to which particular external agents (for example, districts, states, parents, independent developers, universities, professional organizations, foundations, businesses, teacher unions) exerted influence on the schools and also what particular policy tools these agents used. The most frequently used policy tools were professional development programs, funding of staff and school activities, testing and assessment, technical support, and mandates. Less frequent tools were school evaluation, curriculum frameworks, college entrance requirements, waivers, school choice plans, school charters, teacher evaluation, textbooks, and collective bargaining agreements.

# Features of the SRS Schools

## Notes

Year 1 = 1991–92 school year; Year 2 = 1992–93 school year; Year 3 = 1993–94 school year. Urbanicity classification is based on census data and CORS researchers' judgments of the environment in which most students live. School choice = proportion of students/parents who selected the school instead of being assigned by the district. Average SRS achievement and average authentic pedagogy measures are explained in Chapters One and Two.

## Elementary Schools

Ashley Elementary (Year 2)

1. Site-based management and shared decision making; included teachers, parents, and community representatives
2. School of choice: visual and performing arts magnet
3. Teachers in grade-level teams with common planning time
4. Pedagogy emphasized small groups, manipulatives, projects, whole language, integrated curriculum, and heterogeneously grouped classes

| | | | |
|---|---|---|---|
| Geographic region: | South | Student enrollment: | 648 |
| Urbanicity of school: | Urban | | |

*Student body ethnicity*

| | | | |
|---|---|---|---|
| African American: | 34 percent | White: | 66 percent |
| Asian: | 0 percent | Other: | 0 percent |
| Hispanic: | 0 percent | | |
| Free or reduced-fee lunch: | 36 percent | School choice: | Some |
| Staff size: | 53 | | |
| White/Anglo staff: | 75 percent | Female staff: | 94 percent |
| Average SRS achievement: | 6.78 | | |
| Average authentic pedagogy: | 26.17 | | |

## Careen Elementary (Year 3)

1. School of choice for parents and teachers
2. Pedagogy based on Applied Learning; featured projects that promoted inquiry; heterogeneous grouping
3. Student assessment by portfolios; narrative reports
4. Shared decision making and site-based management; included staff, parents, and community representatives
5. Year-round calendar; teachers and students stay together for two years

| | | | |
|---|---|---|---|
| Geographic region: | Southwest | Student enrollment: | 319 |
| Urbanicity of school: | Urban | | |

*Student body ethnicity*

| | | | |
|---|---|---|---|
| African American: | 29 percent | White: | 44 percent |
| Asian: | 5 percent | Other: | 0 percent |
| Hispanic: | 22 percent | | |

| | | | |
|---|---|---|---|
| Free or reduced-fee lunch: | 37 percent | School choice: | All |
| Staff size: | 26 | | |
| White/Anglo staff: | 56 percent | Female staff: | 83 percent |

Average SRS achievement:     6.53
Average authentic pedagogy:  26.63

## Falls River Elementary (Year 3)

1. Full inclusion of all special needs students (special education, bilingual, Chapter I) in regular classrooms
2. Special needs and regular teachers teamed
3. Instruction featured whole language, thematic curriculum, and cross-grade grouping
4. Site-based management and shared decision making by teachers

| | | | |
|---|---|---|---|
| Geographic region: | Southwest | Student enrollment: | 449 |
| Urbanicity of school: | Urban | | |

*Student body ethnicity*

| | | | |
|---|---|---|---|
| African American: | 9 percent | White: | 6 percent |
| Asian: | 0 percent | Other: | 5 percent |
| Hispanic: | 79 percent | | |

| | | | |
|---|---|---|---|
| Free or reduced-fee lunch: | 82 percent | School choice: | Few |
| Staff size: | 52 | | |
| White/Anglo staff: | 29 percent | Female staff: | 82 percent |

Average SRS achievement:     4.72
Average authentic pedagogy:  16.67

## Eldorado Elementary (Year 2)

1. School of choice
2. Two-way bilingual instruction (Spanish/English) for all students
3. Site-based management and shared decision making; included staff, parents, and community representatives
4. Teachers in teams with common planning time

| | | | |
|---|---|---|---|
| Geographic region: | North Central | Student enrollment: | 360 |
| Urbanicity of school: | Urban | | |

*Student body ethnicity*

| | | | |
|---|---|---|---|
| African American: | 22 percent | White: | 15 percent |
| Asian: | 15 percent | Other: | 0 percent |
| Hispanic: | 63 percent | | |

| | | | |
|---|---|---|---|
| Free or reduced-fee lunch: | 71 percent | School choice: | All |

| | | | |
|---|---|---|---|
| Staff size: | 41 | | |
| White/Anglo staff: | 44 percent | Female staff: | 72 percent |

Average SRS achievement:      5.62
Average authentic pedagogy:  22.47

## Humboldt Elementary (Year 1)

1. Site-based management and shared decision making made by whole faculty
2. Heterogeneous grouping of students
3. Most teachers in teams with common planning time
4. Students stay with teacher for two years
5. Member of national school reform organization

| | | | |
|---|---|---|---|
| Geographic region: | Southwest | Student enrollment: | 1,015 |
| Urbanicity of school: | Urban | | |

*Student body ethnicity*

| | | | |
|---|---|---|---|
| African American: | 5 percent | White: | 12 percent |
| Asian: | 5 percent | Other: | 0 percent |
| Hispanic: | 78 percent | | |

| | | | |
|---|---|---|---|
| Free or reduced-fee lunch: | 87 percent | School choice: | None |

| | | | |
|---|---|---|---|
| Staff size: | 63 | | |
| White/Anglo staff: | 76 percent | Female staff: | 94 percent |

Average SRS achievement:      5.66
Average authentic pedagogy:  19.50

## Lamar Elementary (Year 3)

1. School of choice with charter status
2. Site-based management and shared decision making; included staff, parents, and community representatives
3. Heterogeneous, multigrade, team-taught classes
4. Thematic, interdisciplinary, inquiry-based curriculum
5. Strong technology emphasis; long-term involvement with major computer company

| | | | |
|---|---|---|---|
| Geographic region: | West | Student enrollment: | 384 |
| Urbanicity of school: | Urban | | |

*Student body ethnicity*

| | | | |
|---|---|---|---|
| African American: | 25 percent | White: | 40 percent |
| Asian: | 14 percent | Other: | 4 percent |
| Hispanic: | 18 percent | | |

| | | | |
|---|---|---|---|
| Free or reduced-fee lunch: | 26 percent | School choice: | All |

| | | | |
|---|---|---|---|
| Staff size: | 16 | | |
| White/Anglo staff: | 50 percent | Female staff: | 100 percent |

Average SRS achievement:    6.71
Average authentic pedagogy: 24.29

## Sumpter Elementary (Year 1)

1. Shared decision making by whole faculty
2. No principal; administration by elected teacher management team
3. Many special programs served disadvantaged population
4. Inclusion; special education teachers team with regular teachers
5. Participation in state's school restructuring alliance

| | | | |
|---|---|---|---|
| Geographic region: | Southwest | Student enrollment: | 613 |
| Urbanicity of school: | Urban | | |

*Student body ethnicity*

| | | | |
|---|---|---|---|
| African American: | 0 percent | White: | 35 percent |
| Asian: | 0 percent | Other: | 0 percent |
| Hispanic: | 65 percent | | |

| | | | |
|---|---|---|---|
| Free or reduced-fee lunch: | 69 percent | School choice: | None |

| | | | |
|---|---|---|---|
| Staff size: | 49 | | |
| White/Anglo staff: | 56 percent | Female staff: | 89 percent |

Average SRS achievement:    5.38
Average authentic pedagogy: 20.96

Winema Elementary (Year 2)

1. Shared decision making jointly sponsored by union and district
2. Waivers from district to allow teachers to develop their own curriculum
3. Thinking skills curriculum used by some staff
4. Member of national school restructuring organization

| Geographic region: | Southeast | Student enrollment: | 1,271 |
| Urbanicity of school: | Suburban | | |

*Student body ethnicity*

| African American: | 6 percent | White: | 84 percent |
| Asian: | 3 percent | Other: | 0 percent |
| Hispanic: | 7 percent | | |

| Free or reduced-fee lunch: | 11 percent | School choice: | None |

| Staff size: | 88 | | |
| White/Anglo staff: | 88 percent | Female staff: | 92 percent |

| Average SRS achievement: | 6.15 |
| Average authentic pedagogy: | 21.16 |

# Middle Schools

Baldwin Middle (Year 2)

1. Teachers in teams with common planning time
2. School day organized around five seventy-minute periods
3. Daily advisory period to promote personalized relationships between teachers and small groups of students
4. Shared decision making by teachers
5. Participation in state's school restructuring alliance and national school restructuring organization

| Geographic region: | North Central | Student enrollment: | 448 |
| Urbanicity of school: | Suburban | | |

*Student body ethnicity*

| African American: | 0 percent | White: | 100 percent |
| Asian: | 0 percent | Other: | 0 percent |
| Hispanic: | 0 percent | | |

| Free or reduced-fee lunch: | 20 percent | School choice: | None |

| Staff size: | 34 | | |
| White/Anglo staff: | 100 percent | Female staff: | 75 percent |

| Average SRS achievement: | 6.07 |
| Average authentic pedagogy: | 17.30 |

## Copan Middle (Year 3)

1. Teachers in teams with common planning time
2. Programs for special needs students integrated with regular classes (special education, dropout prevention, gifted and talented)
3. Staff development program on site for all teachers
4. Member of national school restructuring organization

| | | | |
|---|---|---|---|
| Geographic region: | Southeast | Student enrollment: | 1,972 |
| Urbanicity of school: | Suburban | | |

*Student body ethnicity*

| | | | |
|---|---|---|---|
| African American: | 7 percent | White: | 91 percent |
| Asian: | 2 percent | Other: | 0 percent |
| Hispanic: | 0 percent | | |

| | | | |
|---|---|---|---|
| Free or reduced-fee lunch: | 15 percent | School choice: | None |

| | | | |
|---|---|---|---|
| Staff size: | 143 | | |
| White/Anglo staff: | 86 percent | Female staff: | 74 percent |

| | |
|---|---|
| Average SRS achievement: | 7.50 |
| Average authentic pedagogy: | 23.75 |

## Morris Middle (Year 1)

1. School of choice
2. Teachers in teams with common planning time and control over class schedules
3. Students in heterogeneous families
4. Shared decision making; included staff, parents, students

| | | | |
|---|---|---|---|
| Geographic region: | West | Student enrollment: | 617 |
| Urbanicity of school: | Urban | | |

*Student body ethnicity*

| | | | |
|---|---|---|---|
| African American: | 10 percent | White: | 19 percent |
| Asian: | 22 percent | Other: | 9 percent |
| Hispanic: | 40 percent | | |

| | | | |
|---|---|---|---|
| Free or reduced-fee lunch: | 39 percent | School choice: | All |

| | | | |
|---|---|---|---|
| Staff size: | 43 | | |
| White/Anglo staff: | 50 percent | Female staff: | 73 percent |

| | |
|---|---|
| Average SRS achievement: | 6.50 |
| Average authentic pedagogy: | 21.67 |

## Okanagon Middle (Year 3)

1. Charter school
2. Shared decision making and site-based management; included staff, parents, and community representatives
3. Teachers in teams with common planning time; students in heterogeneous families
4. Teachers performed some administrative and counseling tasks
5. Pedagogy guided by "Okanagon Standard" for student performance
6. Community resources and social services on site to support disadvantaged students and families
7. Member of national school restructuring organization

| | | | |
|---|---|---|---|
| Geographic region: | West | Student enrollment: | 1,359 |
| Urbanicity of school: | Urban | | |

*Student body ethnicity*

| | | | |
|---|---|---|---|
| African American: | 34 percent | White: | 8 percent |
| Asian: | 41 percent | Other: | 0 percent |
| Hispanic: | 17 percent | | |

| | | | |
|---|---|---|---|
| Free or reduced-fee lunch: | 54 percent | School choice: | Few |
| Staff size: | 205 | | |
| White/Anglo staff: | 89 percent | Female staff: | 75 percent |

Average SRS achievement:    6.17
Average authentic pedagogy: 22.29

## Ottawa Junior High (Year 3)

1. Administrative leadership team of three teachers replaced principal and vice-principal
2. Consolidation of departments into three divisions: arts and humanities, science and technology, life and practical skills
3. Teachers in interdisciplinary teams with common planning time
4. Heterogeneous grouping included students with severe disabilities

| | | | |
|---|---|---|---|
| Geographic region: | Northeast | Student enrollment: | 721 |
| Urbanicity of school: | Rural | | |

*Student body ethnicity*

| | | | |
|---|---|---|---|
| African American: | 0 percent | White: | 100 percent |
| Asian: | 0 percent | Other: | 0 percent |
| Hispanic: | 0 percent | | |

| | | | |
|---|---|---|---|
| Free or reduced-fee lunch: | 21 percent | School choice: | None |
| Staff size: | 116 | | |
| White/Anglo staff: | 100 percent | Female staff: | 54 percent |

Average SRS achievement:    6.10
Average authentic pedagogy: 20.34

## Red Lake Middle (Year 2)

1. School of choice
2. Students select courses from among many options; core "connections" courses required
3. Seventy-minute periods; courses meeting every other day
4. Site-based management and shared decision making; included teachers, parents, and students
5. Community-based learning; service learning
6. Student advisory; teachers and students stay together for three years

| | | | |
|---|---|---|---|
| Geographic region: | West | Student enrollment: | 786 |
| Urbanicity of school: | Urban | | |

*Student body ethnicity*

| | | | |
|---|---|---|---|
| African American: | 2 percent | White: | 93 percent |
| Asian: | 3 percent | Other: | 1 percent |
| Hispanic: | 1 percent | | |

| | | | |
|---|---|---|---|
| Free or reduced-fee lunch: | 14 percent | School choice: | Most |

| | | | |
|---|---|---|---|
| Staff size: | 57 | | |
| White/Anglo staff: | 100 percent | Female staff: | 61 percent |

| | |
|---|---|
| Average SRS achievement: | 7.59 |
| Average authentic pedagogy: | 24.77 |

## Selway Middle (Year 1)

1. School of choice
2. Differentiated staff (part-time principal, four lead teachers, generalist-teachers, interns, educational assistants, clerical staff, teacher aides)
3. Four lead teachers responsible for decision making, curriculum development, and staff hiring and training
4. Site-based management and shared decision making on policy matters; included parents and four lead teachers
5. Pedagogy based on technology and use of community resources (museums, public libraries, internships); assessment by portfolios
6. Heterogeneous multi-age classes for grades 4–8; student choice of courses based on interest and personal growth plan

| | | | |
|---|---|---|---|
| Geographic region: | North Central | Student enrollment: | 283 |
| Urbanicity of school: | Urban | | |

*Student body ethnicity*

| | | | |
|---|---|---|---|
| African American: | 20 percent | White: | 63 percent |
| Asian: | 3 percent | Other: | 3 percent |
| Hispanic: | 11 percent | | |

| | | | |
|---|---|---|---|
| Free or reduced-fee lunch: | 42 percent | School choice: | All |

| | | | |
|---|---|---|---|
| Staff size: | 28 | | |
| White/Anglo staff: | 53 percent | Female staff: | 53 percent |

| | |
|---|---|
| Average SRS achievement: | 6.81 |
| Average authentic pedagogy: | 19.04 |

Shining Rock Middle (Year 2)

1. Teachers in teams with flexible scheduling and common planning time
2. Interdisciplinary curriculum
3. Shared decision making through teams and weekly staff meetings
4. Human services and other community resources coordinated at school to support disadvantaged students

| | | | |
|---|---|---|---|
| Geographic region: | West | Student enrollment: | 428 |
| Urbanicity of school: | Urban | | |

*Student body ethnicity*

| | | | |
|---|---|---|---|
| African American: | 10 percent | White: | 72 percent |
| Asian: | 8 percent | Other: | 5 percent |
| Hispanic: | 4 percent | | |

| | | | |
|---|---|---|---|
| Free or reduced-fee lunch: | 33 percent | School choice: | Few |

| | | | |
|---|---|---|---|
| Staff size: | 39 | | |
| White/Anglo staff: | 92 percent | Female staff: | 76 percent |

Average SRS achievement:  6.83
Average authentic pedagogy: 19.66

# High Schools

Cibola High (Year 3)

1. School of choice for students and staff
2. Organized by divisions: I (grades 7–8), II (grades 9–10), and III (grades 11–12)
3. Interdisciplinary content teams in divisions I and II; classes in two-hour blocks
4. Graduation by exhibition from division III
5. Teacher advisories for small groups of students (12 to 15); teachers and students stay together for two years
6. Site-based management and shared decision making by staff
7. Membership in national school restructuring organization

| | | | |
|---|---|---|---|
| Geographic region: | East | Student enrollment: | 456 |
| Urbanicity of school: | Urban | | |

*Student body ethnicity*

| | | | |
|---|---|---|---|
| African American: | 46 percent | White: | 13 percent |
| Asian: | 2 percent | Other: | 1 percent |
| Hispanic: | 38 percent | | |

| | | | |
|---|---|---|---|
| Free or reduced-fee lunch: | 51 percent | School choice: | All |

| | | | |
|---|---|---|---|
| Staff size: | 52 | | |
| White/Anglo staff: | 52 percent | Female staff: | 62 percent |

Average SRS achievement:  8.04
Average authentic pedagogy: 27.33

## Fremont High (Year 1)

1. Ninth-grade teachers in teams with flexible schedules and planning time; interdisciplinary and thematic curriculum
2. Shared decision making and site-based management that included parents, students, and community representatives
3. Social services and community resources to support at-risk students and families located on site
4. Membership in national school restructuring organization

| | | | |
|---|---|---|---|
| Geographic region: | Upper South | Student enrollment: | 1,016 |
| Urbanicity of school: | Urban | | |

*Student body ethnicity*

| | | | |
|---|---|---|---|
| African American: | 25 percent | White: | 75 percent |
| Asian: | 0 percent | Other: | 0 percent |
| Hispanic: | 0 percent | | |

| | | | |
|---|---|---|---|
| Free or reduced-fee lunch: | 48 percent | School choice: | None |

| | | | |
|---|---|---|---|
| Staff size: | 102 | | |
| White/Anglo staff: | 93 percent | Female staff: | 61 percent |

| | |
|---|---|
| Average SRS achievement: | 6.60 |
| Average authentic pedagogy: | 20.07 |

## Flinders High (Year 2)

1. Four divisions: culture and literature; math, science, and technology; health and physical education; fine arts
2. Students grouped in "houses"
3. College preparatory curriculum for most students
4. Many students in heterogeneous classes
5. Shared decision making; included staff, parents, and students

| | | | |
|---|---|---|---|
| Geographic region: | West | Student enrollment: | 2,286 |
| Urbanicity of school: | Urban | | |

*Student body ethnicity*

| | | | |
|---|---|---|---|
| African American: | 16 percent | White: | 40 percent |
| Asian: | 22 percent | Other: | 10 percent |
| Hispanic: | 13 percent | | |

| | | | |
|---|---|---|---|
| Free or reduced-fee lunch: | 21 percent | School choice: | None |

| | | | |
|---|---|---|---|
| Staff size: | 148 | | |
| White/Anglo staff: | 81 percent | Female staff: | 59 percent |

| | |
|---|---|
| Average SRS achievement: | 7.00 |
| Average authentic pedagogy: | 20.33 |

## Huron High (Year 2)

1. School of choice
2. Site-based management and shared decision making included teachers, students, and parents
3. Tenth-grade core curriculum of U.S. history, science, English/writing; interdisciplinary units, heterogeneous grouping
4. Core teachers in teams with common planning time, block scheduling (150 minutes)
5. Teacher advisory for small groups of students

| | | | |
|---|---|---|---|
| Geographic region: | West | Student enrollment: | 1,472 |
| Urbanicity of school: | Urban | | |

*Student body ethnicity*

| | | | |
|---|---|---|---|
| African American: | 1 percent | White: | 83 percent |
| Asian: | 0 percent | Other: | 1 percent |
| Hispanic: | 15 percent | | |

| | | | |
|---|---|---|---|
| Free or reduced-fee lunch: | 5 percent | School choice: | Most |

| | | | |
|---|---|---|---|
| Staff size: | 129 | | |
| White/Anglo staff: | 95 percent | Female staff: | 70 percent |

| | |
|---|---|
| Average SRS achievement: | 6.91 |
| Average authentic pedagogy: | 19.67 |

## Island High (Year 3)

1. Three administrators form leadership team for decision making; three-school campus (middle, high, and tech-prep magnet)
2. Teacher teams in ninth and tenth grades (no common planning time)
3. Social services and community resources for at-risk students and families on site
4. Membership in national school restructuring organization

| | | | |
|---|---|---|---|
| Geographic region: | Upper South | Student enrollment: | 1,222 |
| Urbanicity of school: | Urban | | |

*Student body ethnicity*

| | | | |
|---|---|---|---|
| African American: | 35 percent | White: | 54 percent |
| Asian: | 9 percent | Other: | 2 percent |
| Hispanic: | 0 percent | | |

| | | | |
|---|---|---|---|
| Free or reduced-fee lunch: | 79 percent | School choice: | Few |

| | | | |
|---|---|---|---|
| Staff size: | 99 | | |
| White/Anglo staff: | 73 percent | Female staff: | 72 percent |

| | |
|---|---|
| Average SRS achievement: | 6.04 |
| Average authentic pedagogy: | 20.67 |

## Marble Canyon High (Year 3)

1. School of choice
2. Twelve-week trimesters; 70-minute periods; internships for all students
3. Schedule coordinated with community college that provided many resources for students
4. Site-based management and shared decision making by staff
5. Assessment by portfolio
6. Peer evaluation by teachers

| | | | |
|---|---|---|---|
| Geographic region: | East | Student enrollment: | 525 |
| Urbanicity of school: | Urban | | |

*Student body ethnicity*

| | | | |
|---|---|---|---|
| African American: | 15 percent | White: | 38 percent |
| Asian: | 4 percent | Other: | 1 percent |
| Hispanic: | 42 percent | | |

| | | | |
|---|---|---|---|
| Free or reduced-fee lunch: | 8 percent | School choice: | All |

| | | | |
|---|---|---|---|
| Staff size: | 32 | | |
| White/Anglo staff: | 78 percent | Female staff: | 64 percent |

Average SRS achievement:  6.22
Average authentic pedagogy: 22.17

## South Glen High (Year 2)

1. Shared decision making by staff
2. Departments reconfigured into teams with lead teachers
3. Ninety-minute classes; eight periods scheduled over two days
4. Outcome-based education and Total Quality Management

| | | | |
|---|---|---|---|
| Geographic region: | Southeast | Student enrollment: | 730 |
| Urbanicity of school: | Urban | | |

*Student body ethnicity*

| | | | |
|---|---|---|---|
| African American: | 38 percent | White: | 61 percent |
| Asian: | 0 percent | Other: | 0 percent |
| Hispanic: | 1 percent | | |

| | | | |
|---|---|---|---|
| Free or reduced-fee lunch: | 19 percent | School choice: | None |

| | | | |
|---|---|---|---|
| Staff size: | 62 | | |
| White/Anglo staff: | 71 percent | Female staff: | 60 percent |

Average SRS achievement:  4.66
Average authentic pedagogy: 17.32

## Wallingford High (Year 1)

1. Ninth- and tenth-grade teachers in interdisciplinary teams meeting two or three times a week
2. Class periods two hours long
3. Heterogeneous grouping
4. School restructuring team involved staff in planning and decision making
5. Member of national school restructuring organization

| | | | |
|---|---|---|---|
| Geographic region: | East | Student enrollment: | 912 |
| Urbanicity of school: | Urban | | |

*Student body ethnicity*

| | | | |
|---|---|---|---|
| African American: | 100 percent | White: | 0 percent |
| Asian: | 0 percent | Other: | 0 percent |
| Hispanic: | 0 percent | | |

| | | | |
|---|---|---|---|
| Free or reduced-fee lunch: | 34 percent | School choice: | None |
| Staff size: | 66 | | |
| White/Anglo staff: | 17 percent | Female staff: | 50 percent |

| | |
|---|---|
| Average SRS achievement: | 4.53 |
| Average authentic pedagogy: | 17.21 |

# SRS Researchers, Support Staff, and National Advisory Panel

## SRS Researchers and Support Staff

Lisa Byrd Adajian
John Balwit
Michael Bennett
Mark Berends
Patricia Berman
Janet Bixby
Amy Cantoni
Rudolfo Careago
David Chawszczewski
Jay Cradle
Rhonda Dix
Kenneth Doane
Eileen Ewing
Mary Fish
Lorene Folgert
Sherian Foster
Adam Gamoran
Kubilay Gok
Dayle Hagland
Emily Hall
Donna Harris

Mary Hartzheim
Mary Jo Heck
Daniel Hoover
Christopher Jacobson
Lois Johnson
Jean Jolin
M. Bruce King
Jean King
Sharon Kruse
James Ladwig
Virginia Long
Karen Seashore Louis
Leon Lynn
Helen Marks
Norma Maynard
Mary Morzinski
Fred Newmann
Jean Norman
Martin Nystrand
Eric Osthoff
Yuksel Ozden

Byong-Jin Park
Kent Peterson
Andrew Porter
Karen Prager
Diane Randall
Mark Rigdon
Sheila Rosenblum
David Scheer
Walter Secada
Laurie See

BetsAnn Smith
Corrine Solsrud
Deborah Stewart
Vera Titunik
Valli Warren
Gary Wehlage
Matthew Weinstein
Stephen Witte
Carol Wright
Jung-Ho Yang

## National Advisory Panel

Richard C. Wallace Jr. (chair)
Professor
University of Pittsburgh
Pittsburgh, Pennsylvania

Ronald J. Areglado
Director
National Principals Academy
National Association
of Elementary School
Principals
Alexandria, Virginia

Jomills Henry Braddock II
Professor
University of Miami
Coral Gables, Florida

Ronald S. Brandt
Executive Editor
*Journal of Educational Leadership*
Association for Supervision
and Curriculum Development
Alexandria, Virginia

Rueben A. Carriedo
Assistant Superintendent
San Diego City Schools
San Diego, California

Larry Cuban
Professor
Stanford University
Palo Alto, California

Sonia Hernandez
Policy Coordinator
California State
Department of Education
Sacramento, California

James W. Keefe
Director of Research
National Association of
Secondary School Principals
Reston, Virginia

Ann Lieberman
Professor
Teachers College,
Columbia University
New York, New York

Milbrey W. McLaughlin
Professor
Stanford University
Palo Alto, California

Yvonne A. Robinson
Gavin Elementary School
Chicago Heights, Illinois

Brian Rowan
Professor
University of Michigan
Ann Arbor, Michigan

Albert Shanker, President
Bella Rosenberg,
Assistant to the President
American Federation
of Teachers
Washington, D.C.

Ron Anson (ex officio),
Liaison
Office of Educational
Research and Improvement
U.S. Department
of Education
Washington, D.C.

# References

Abbott, A. (1991). The order of professionalization: An empirical analysis. *Work and Occupations, 18*(4), 355–384.

Aiming for Higher Standards (1995). *Educational Leadership, 52,* 6.

Alexander, W., & McEwin, C. K. (1989). *Schools in the middle: Status and progress.* Columbus, OH: National Middle School Association.

American Association for the Advancement of Science. (1993). *Benchmarks for science literacy: Project 2061.* New York: Oxford University Press.

American Federation of Teachers. (1994). What college-bound students abroad are expected to know about biology: A special report. *American Educator, 18*(1), 7–30.

Ames, N. L., & Miller, M. (1994). *Changing middle schools: How to make schools work for young adolescents.* San Francisco: Jossey-Bass.

Apple, M. W. (1996). *Cultural politics and education.* New York: Teachers College Press.

Archbald, D., & Newmann, F. M. (1988). *Beyond standardized tests: Assessing authentic academic achievement in the secondary school.* Reston, VA: National Association of Secondary School Principals.

Armstrong, T. (1994). *Multiple intelligences in the classroom.* Alexandria, VA: Association for Supervision and Curriculum Development.

Ball, D. L. (1990). Reflections and deflections of policy: The case of Carol Turner. *Educational Evaluation and Policy Analysis, 12*(3), 263–276.

Ball, S. J. (1987). *The micro-politics of the school: Towards a theory of school organization.* London: Methuen.

Beck, L. G. (1994). Cultivating a caring school community: One principal's story. In J. Murphy & K. S. Louis (Eds.), *Reshaping the principalship: Insights for transformational reform efforts* (pp. 177–202). Thousand Oaks, CA: Corwin.

Berends, M., & King, M. B. (1994). A description of restructuring in nationally nominated schools: Legacy of the iron cage? *Educational Policy, 8*(1), 28–50.

Berlak, H., Newmann, F. M., Adams, E., Archbald, D. A., Burgess, T., Raven, J., & Romberg, T. (1992). *Toward a new science of educational testing and assessment.* Albany, NY: SUNY Press.

Berliner, D. C., & Biddle, B. J. (1995). *The manufactured crisis: Myths, fraud, and the attack on America's public schools.* Reading, MA: Addison-Wesley.

Berman, P., & McLaughlin, M. W. (1978). *Federal programs supporting education change: Vol.2: Implementing and sustaining innovations.* Santa Monica, CA: RAND.

Bimber, B. (1994). *The decentralization mirage: Comparing decision making arrangements in four high schools.* Santa Monica, CA: RAND.

Blase, J. (Ed.). (1991). *The politics of life in schools: Power, conflict, and cooperation.* Newbury Park, CA: Sage.

Boyer, E. L. (1983). *High school.* New York: Harper & Row.

Bracey, G. W. (1991, October). Why can't they be like we were? *Phi Delta Kappan,* pp. 104–117.

Bracey, G. W. (1996). International comparisons and the condition of American education. *Educational Researcher, 25*(1), 5–11.

Britton, E., & Raizen, S. (Eds.). (1996). *Examining the examinations: An international comparison of science and mathematics examinations for college-bound students.* Boston: Kluwer Academic Publishers.

Brookover, W. B., & Lezotte, L. (1981). Education equity: A democratic principle at a crossroads. *Urban Review, 13*(2), 65–71.

Brooks, J. G., & Brooks, M. G. (1993). *In search of understanding: The case for constructivist classrooms.* Alexandria, VA: Association for Supervision and Curriculum Development.

Brough, J. A. (1995). Middle level education: An historical perspective. In M. J. Wavering (Ed.), *Educating young adolescents: Life in the middle.* New York: Garland.

Bruer, J. T. (1993). *Schools for thought: A science of learning in the classroom.* Cambridge, MA: MIT Press.

Bryk, A. S., Easton, J. Q., Kerbow, D., Rollow, S. G., & Sebring, P. A. (1993). *A view from the schools: The state of reform in Chicago.* Chicago: University of Chicago, Consortium on Chicago School Research.

Bryk, A. S., Lee, V. E., & Holland, P. (1993). *Catholic schools and the common good.* Cambridge, MA: Harvard University Press.

Bryk, A. S., Lee, V. E., & Smith, J. L. (1990). High school organization and its effects on teachers and students: An interpretive summary of the research. In W. H. Clune & J. F. Witte (Eds.), *Choice and control in American education: Vol. 2. The practice of choice, decentralization and school restructuring.* Philadelphia: Falmer Press.

Bryk, A. S., & Raudenbusch, S. W. (1992). *Hierarchical linear models: Applications and data analysis methods.* Newbury Park, CA: Sage.

Bryk, A. S., Raudenbush, S. W., & Congdon, R. T. (1994). *Hierarchical linear modeling with the HLM/2L and the HLM/3L programs.* Chicago: Scientific Software International.

Bull, B. L., Fruehling, R. T., & Chattergy, V. (1992). *The ethics of multicultural and bilingual education.* New York: Teachers College Press.

California Department of Education. (1992). *It's elementary: Elementary grades task force report.* Sacramento, CA: Author.

Campbell, P. B., & Klein, S. (1982). Equity issues in education. In H. Mitzel (Ed.), *Encyclopedia of educational research* (5th ed., pp. 581–587). New York: Free Press.

Carnegie Task Force on Teaching as a Profession. (1986). *A nation prepared: Teachers for the 21st century.* Washington, DC: Carnegie Forum on Education and the Economy.

Carpenter, T. P., Fennema, E., Peterson, P. L., Chiang, C., & Loef, M. (1989). Using knowledge of children's mathematics thinking in classroom teaching: An experimental study. *American Educational Research Journal, 26*(4), 499–531.

Cawelti, G. (1994). *High school restructuring: A national study.* Arlington, VA: Educational Research Service.

Chubb, J. 1988. Why the current wave of school reform will fail. *Public Interest, 90,* 28–49.

Coalition of Essential Schools. (1992). *The exhibition collection.* Providence, RI: Brown University, Coalition of Essential Schools.

Cobb, P., Wood, T., Yackel, E., Nicholls, J., Wheatley, G., Trigatti, B., & Perlwitz, M. (1991). Assessment of a problem-centered second-grade mathematics project. *Journal for Research in Mathematics Education, 22*(1), 3–29.

Cohen, D. K. (1990). A revolution in one classroom: The case of Mrs. Oublier. *Educational Evaluation and Policy Analysis, 12*(3), 326–346.

Cohen, D. K. (1995). What standards for national standards? *Phi Delta Kappan, 76*(10), 751–757.

Cohen, E. (1986). On the sociology of the classroom. In J. Hannaway & M. E. Lockheed (Eds.), *The contributions of the social sciences to educational policy and practice: 1965–1985.* Berkeley, CA: McCutchan.

Coleman, J. S. (1975). What is meant by "and equal educational opportunity"? *Oxford Review of Education, 1*(1), 27–29.

Coleman, J. S., & Hoffer, T. (1987). *Public and private high schools: The impact of community.* New York: Basic Books.

Coleman, J. S., Hoffer, T., & Kilgore, S. (1982). *High school achievement: Public, Catholic, and private schools compared.* New York: Basic Books.

Committee for Economic Development. (1985). *Investing in our children.* Washington, DC: Committee for Economic Development.

Conley, D. T. (1993). *Roadmap to restructuring: Policies, practices and the emerging visions of schooling.* Eugene, OR: ERIC Clearinghouse of Educational Management.

Conley, S. (1991). Review of research on teacher participation in school decision making. In G. Grant (Ed.), *Review of Research in Education* (Vol. 17). Washington, DC: American Educational Research Association.

Cotton, J. L., Vollrath, D. A., & Froggatt, K. L. (1988). Employee participation: Diverse forms and different outcomes. *Academy of Management Review, 13,* 8–22.

Cuban, L. (1990). Reforming again, again, and again. *Educational Researcher, 19*(1), 3–13.

Cuban, L. (1993). *How teachers taught: Constancy and change in American classrooms, 1880–1990* (2nd ed.). New York: Teachers College Press.

Darling-Hammond, L. (1988). Policy and professionalism. In A. Lieberman (Ed.), *Building a professional culture in schools.* New York: Teachers College Press.

Darling-Hammond, L., & Goodwin, A. L. (1993). Progress towards professionalism in teaching. In G. Cawelti (Ed.), *Challenges and achievements of American education: The 1993 ASCD yearbook* (pp. 19–52). Alexandria, VA: Association for Supervision and Curriculum Development.

Delpit, L. (1995). *Other people's children: Cultural conflict in the classroom.* New York: New Press.

Eisner, E. W. (1995). Standards for American schools: Help or hindrance? *Phi Delta Kappan, 76*(10), 758–764.

Elmore, R. F. (1995). Structural reform and educational practice. *Educational Researcher, 24*(9), 23–26.

Elmore, R. F., & Associates. (1990). *Restructuring schools: The next generation of educational reform.* San Francisco: Jossey-Bass.

Elmore, R. F., Peterson, P., & McCarthey, S. (1996). *Restructuring in the classroom: Teaching, learning, and school organization.* San Francisco: Jossey-Bass.

Feinberg, L. (1990). Multiple-choice and its critics: Are the alternatives any better? *College Board Review, 157,* 12–17.

Fine, M. (Ed.). (1994). *Chartering urban school reform: Reflections on public high schools in the midst of change.* New York: Teachers College Press.

Firestone, W. A., Herriott, R., & Wilson, B. (1987). *Explaining differences between elementary and secondary schools: Individual, organizational, and institutional perspectives.* Philadelphia: Research for Better Schools.

Fullan, M. G. (1991). *The new meaning of educational change* (2nd ed.). New York: Teachers College Press.

Gamoran, A., Nystrand, M., Berends, M., & LePore, P. C. (1995). An organizational analysis of the effects of ability grouping. *American Educational Research Journal, 32*(4), 687–715.

Gardner, H. (1983). *Frames of mind: The theory of multiple intelligences.* New York: Basic Books.

Gardner, H. (1993). *Multiple intelligences: The theory in practice.* New York: Basic Books.

George, P. S., Stevenson, C., Thomason, J., & Beane, J. (1992). *The middle school—and beyond.* Alexandria, VA: Association for Supervision and Curriculum Development.

Good, T. L., & Brophy, J. E. (1994). *Looking in classrooms* (6th ed.). New York: HarperCollins.

Goodlad, J. I. (1984). *A place called school: Prospects for the future.* New York: McGraw-Hill.

Grissmer, D. W., Kirby, S. N., Berends, M., & Williamson, S. (1994). *Student achievement and the changing American family.* Santa Monica, CA: RAND.

Hallinan, M. T. (1994). Tracking: From theory to practice. *Sociology of Education, 67,* 79–84.

Hannaway, J. (1993). Decentralization in two school districts: Challenging the standard paradigm. In J. Hannaway & M. Carnoy (Eds.), *Decentralization and school improvement.* San Francisco: Jossey-Bass.

Hargreaves, A. (1994). *Changing teachers, changing times: Teachers' work and culture in the postmodern age.* New York: Teachers College Press.

Herman, J. L., Aschbacher, P. R., & Winters, L. (1992). *A practical guide to alternative assessment.* Alexandria, VA: Association for Supervision and Curriculum Development.

Jencks, C. (1972). *Inequality: A reassessment of the effect of family and schooling in America.* New York: HarperCollins.

Johnson, J., & Immerwahr, J. (1994). *First things first: What Americans expect from the public schools.* New York: Public Agenda.

Kearns, D. T., & Doyle, D. P. (1988). *Winning the brain race: A bold plan to make our schools competitive.* San Francisco: Institute for Contemporary Studies Press.

Kliebard, H. M. (1986). *The struggle for the American curriculum: 1893–1958.* Boston, MA: Routledge & Kegan Paul.

Knapp, M. S., Shields, P. M., & Turnbull, B. J. (1992). *Academic challenge for the children of poverty: Summary report.* Washington, DC: Office of Policy and Planning, U.S. Department of Education.

Kozol, J. (1991). *Savage inequalities: Children in America's schools.* New York: Crown.

Kruse, S. D. (1995). *Community as a foundation for professionalism: Case studies of middle school teachers.* Unpublished doctoral dissertation, University of Minnesota.

Kruse, S. D., Louis, K. L., & Bryk, A. S. (1995). An emerging framework for analyzing school-based professional community. In K. S. Louis,

S. D. Kruse, & Associates, *Professionalism and community: Perspectives on reforming urban schools* (pp. 23–44). Thousand Oaks, CA: Corwin.

Kyle, R.M.J. (1993). *Transforming our schools: Lessons from the Jefferson County Public Schools/Gheens Professional Development Academy, 1983–1991.* Louisville, KY: Gheens Foundation.

Kymlicka, W. (1991). *Contemporary political philosophy: An introduction.* Oxford: Clarendon.

Lawler, E. E. III (1991). *High-involvement management.* San Francisco: Jossey-Bass.

Lee, V. E., & Smith, J. B. (1995). Effects of high school restructuring and size on gains in the achievement and engagement for early secondary school students. *Sociology of Education, 68*(4), 241–270.

Lee, V. E., Smith, J. B., & Croninger, R. G. (1995a). *Another look at high school restructuring.* Issues in Restructuring Schools, No. 9. Madison, WI: Center on the Organization and Restructuring of Schools, Wisconsin Center for Education Research, University of Wisconsin.

Lee, V. E., Smith, J. B., & Croninger, R. G. (1995b, June). *Understanding high school restructuring effects on the equitable distribution of learning in mathematics and science.* Madison, WI: Center on Organization and Restructuring of Schools, Wisconsin Center for Education Research, University of Wisconsin.

Leithwood, K., Jantzi, D., & Fernandez, A. (1995). Transformational leadership and teachers' commitment to change. In J. Murphy & K. Louis (Eds.), *Reshaping the principalship: Insights from transformational reform efforts* (pp. 77–98). Thousand Oaks, CA: Corwin Press.

Leithwood, K., & Montgomery, D. (1982). The role of the elementary school principal in program movement: A review. *Review of Educational Research, 52*(3), 309–339.

Levin, M., Newmann, F. M., & Oliver, D. W. (1969). *A law and social science curriculum based on the analysis of public issues: Final report.* Washington, DC: Office of Education, Bureau of Research, U.S. Department of Health, Education, and Welfare.

Lewis, A. C. (1995). An overview of the standards movement. *Phi Delta Kappan, 76*(10), 744–750.

Lieberman, A. (Ed.). (1988). *Building a professional culture in schools.* New York: Teachers College Press.

Lieberman, A. (Ed.). (1995). *The work of restructuring schools: Building from the ground up.* New York: Teachers College Press.

Little, J. W. (1990). The persistence of privacy: Autonomy and initiative in teachers' professional relations. *Teachers College Record, 91,* 509–536.

Little, J. W. (1993). Professional community in comprehensive high schools: The two worlds of academic and vocational teachers. In

J. W. Little & M. McLaughlin (Eds.), *Teachers' work: Individuals, colleagues and contexts* (pp. 137–163). New York: Teachers College Press.

Little, J. W. (1994). Teachers' professional development in a climate of educational reform. *Educational Evaluation and Policy Analysis, 15*(2), 129–151.

Louis, K. S., Kruse, S. D., & Associates (1995). *Professionalism and community: Perspectives on reforming urban schools.* Thousand Oaks, CA: Corwin Press.

Louis, K. S., & Marks, H. (1996) *Does professional community affect the classroom? Teachers' work and student experiences in restructureing schools.* Madison, WI: Center on Organization and Restructuring of Schools, Wisconsin Center for Education Research, University of Wisconsin.

Louis, K. S., Marks, H., & Kruse, S. D. (1996). Teachers' professional community in restructured schools. *American Educational Research Journal, 33* (4).

Louis, K. S., & Miles, M. B. (1990). *Improving the urban high school: What works and why.* New York: Teachers College Press.

Maeroff, G. I. (1988). *The empowerment of teachers: Overcoming the crisis of confidence.* New York: Teachers College Press.

Malen, B., Ogawa, R., & Kranz, J. (1990). What do we know about school-based management? In W. H. Clune & J. F. White (Eds.), *Choice and control in American education* (Vol. 2). New York: Falmer Press.

Marks, H. M. (1995). *Student engagement in the classrooms of restructuring schools.* Madison, WI: Center on Organization and Restructuring of Schools, Wisconsin Center for Education Research, University of Wisconsin.

Marks, H., Gamoran, A., & Newmann, F. M. (1995). *Technical appendix to authentic pedagogy and student performance.* Madison, WI: Center on Organization and Restructuring of Schools, Wisconsin Center for Education Research, University of Wisconsin.

Marks, H. M., & Louis, K. S. (1996). *Does teacher empowerment affect the classroom? The implications of teacher empowerment for teachers' instructional practice and student academic performance.* Madison, WI: Center on Organization and Restructuring of Schools, Wisconsin Center for Education Research, University of Wisconsin.

Marshall, H. H. (Ed.). (1992). *Redefining student learning: Roots of educational change.* Norwood, NJ: Ablex.

Marshall, R., & Tucker, M. (1992). *Thinking for a living: Education and the wealth of nations.* New York: Basic Books.

McCarthey, S. J., & Peterson, P. L. (1993). Creating classroom practice within the context of a restructured professional development school. In D. K. Cohen, M. W. McLaughlin, & J. E. Talbert (Eds.), *Teaching for understanding: Challenges for policy practice* (pp. 130–166). San Francisco: Jossey-Bass.

McLaughlin, M. (1994). Strategic sites for teachers' professional development. In P. O. Grimmett & J. P. Neufeld (Eds.), *The struggle for authenticity: Teacher development in a changing educational context.* New York: Teachers College Press.

McLaughlin, M. W., & Talbert, J. E. (1993). *Contexts that matter for teaching and learning: Strategic opportunities for meeting the nation's educational goals.* Stanford, CA: Stanford University, Center for Research on the Context of Secondary School Teaching.

Meier, D. 1995. *The power of their ideas: Lessons for America from a small school in Harlem.* Boston: Beacon Press.

Metz, M. H. (1986). *Different by design: The context and character of three magnet schools.* New York: Routledge & Kegan Paul.

Muncey, D. E., & McQuillan, P. J. (1993). Preliminary findings from a five-year study of the Coalition of Essential Schools. *Phi Delta Kappan, 74*(6), 486–489.

Murphy, J. (1991). *Restructuring schools: Capturing and assessing the phenomena.* New York: Teachers College Press.

Murphy, J. (1994). Transformational change and the evolving role of the principal: Early empirical evidence. In J. Murphy and K. Louis (Eds.), *Reshaping the principalship: Insights from transformational reform efforts* (pp. 20–56). Thousand Oaks, CA: Corwin.

Murphy, J., & Beck, L. G. (1995). *School-based management as school reform: Taking stock.* Newbury Park, CA: Corwin Press.

National Center for Education Statistics. (1990). *The state of mathematics education.* Washington, DC: U.S. Department of Education.

National Commission on Excellence in Education. (1983). *A nation at risk.* Washington, DC: U.S. Government Printing Office.

National Council of Teachers of Mathematics (1989). *Curriculum and evaluation standards for school mathematics.* Reston, VA: National Council of Teachers of Mathematics.

National Education Goals Panel. (1991). *The National Education Goals report: Building a nation of learners.* Washington, DC: Author.

Natriello, G., McDill, E. L., & Pallas, A. (1990). *Schooling disadvantaged students: Racing against catastrophe.* New York: Teachers College Press.

Newmann, F. M. (1993). Beyond common sense in educational restructuring: The issues of content and linkage. *Educational Researcher, 22*(2), 4–13, 22.

Newmann, F. M., King, M. B., & Rigdon, M. (1996). *Accountability and school performance: Implications from restructuring schools.* Madison, WI: Wisconsin Center for Education Research.

Newmann, F. M., Marks, H. M., & Gamoran, A. (1996). Authentic pedagogy and student performance. *American Journal of Education, 104*(4), 280–312.

Newmann, F. M., Secada, W. G., & Wehlage, G. G. (1995). *A guide to authentic instruction and assessment: Vision, standards, and scoring.* Madison, WI: Center on Organization and Restructuring of Schools, Wisconsin Center for Education Research, University of Wisconsin.

Newmann, F. M., & Wehlage, G. G. (1995). *Successful school restructuring: A report to the public and educators.* Madison, WI: Center on Organization and Restructuring of Schools, Wisconsin Center for Education Research, University of Wisconsin.

Odden, E., & Wohlstetter, P. (1995). Making school-based management work, *Educational Leadership, 52*(5), 32–36.

Peterson, P. L. (1990a). The California Study of Elementary Mathematics. *Educational Evaluation and Policy Analysis, 12*(3), 257–262.

Peterson, P. L. (1990b). Doing more in the same amount of time: Cathy Swift. *Educational Evaluation and Policy Analysis, 12*(3), 277–296.

Peterson, P. L., McCarthey, S. J., & Elmore, R. F. (1996). Learning from school restructuring. *American Educational Research Journal, 33*(1), 119–153.

Popkewitz, T. S., Tabachnick, B. R., & Wehlage, G. G. (1982). *The myth of educational reform: A study of school responses to a program of change.* Madison, WI: University of Wisconsin Press.

Powell, A. G., Farrar, E., & Cohen, D. K. (1985). *The shopping mall high school: Winners and losers in the educational marketplace.* Boston: Houghton Mifflin.

Prawat, R. S. (1992). Teachers' beliefs about teaching and learning: A constructivist perspective. *American Journal of Education, 100*(3), 354–395.

Quality Education for Minorities Project. (1990). *Education that works: An action plan for the education of minorities.* Cambridge, MA: Massachusetts Institute of Technology.

Quigley, C. N., & Bahmueller, C. F. (1991). *Civitas: A framework for civic education.* Calabasas, CA: Center for Civic Education.

Raven, J. (1992). A model of competence, motivation, and behavior, and a paradigm for assessment. In H. Berlak et al., *Toward a new science of educational testing and assessment* (pp. 85–116). Albany, NY: SUNY Press.

Ravitch, D. (1995). *National standards in American education: A citizen's guide.* Washington, DC: The Brookings Institution.

Regnier, P. (1994). The illusion of technique and the intellectual life of schools. *Phi Delta Kappan, 76*(1), 82–83.

Resnick, L. B. (1987a). Learning in school and out. *Educational Researcher, 61*(9), 13–20.

Resnick, L. (1987b). *Education and learning to think.* Washington, DC: National Academy Press.

Resnick, L. B. (Ed.). (1989). *Knowing, learning, and instruction: Essays in honor of Robert Glaser.* Hillsdale, NJ: Lawrence Erlbaum.

Rowan, B. (1994). Comparing teachers' work with other occupations: Notes on the professional status of teaching. *Educational Researcher, 23*, 4–18.

Sandia National Laboratories. (1993). Perspectives on education in America: An annotated briefing. *Journal of Educational Research, 86*(5), 259–310.

Sarason, S. B. (1971). *The culture of the school and the problem of change.* Boston: Allyn & Bacon.

Sarason, S. B. (1982). *The culture of the school and the problem of change* (2nd ed.). Boston: Allyn & Bacon.

Sarason, S. B. (1990). *The predictable failure of educational reform: Can we change course before it's too late?* San Francisco: Jossey-Bass.

Shanker, A. (1990). The end of the traditional model of schooling—and a proposal for using incentives to restructure our public schools. *Phi Delta Kappan, 71*(5), 344–357.

Shedd, J. B., & Bacharach, S. B. (1991). *Tangled hierarchies: Teachers as professionals and the management of schools.* San Francisco: Jossey-Bass.

Silver, E., & Lane, S. (1995). Can instructional reform in urban middle schools help students narrow the mathematics performance gap? *Research in Middle Level Education, 18*(2), 49–70.

Siskin, L. (1991). Departments as different worlds: Subject subcultures in secondary schools. *Educational Administration Quarterly, 27*, 134–160.

Siskin, L. (1994). Is the school the unit of change?: Internal and external contexts of restructuring. In P. P. Grimmett & J. P. Neufeld (Eds.), *The struggle for authenticity: Teacher development in a changing educational context.* New York: Teachers College Press.

Sizer, T. R. (1984). *Horace's compromise: The dilemma of the American high school.* Boston: Houghton Mifflin.

Sizer, T. R. (1992). *Horace's school: Redesigning the American high school.* Boston: Houghton Mifflin.

Slavin, R. E., Madden, N. A., Dolan, L. J., Wasisk, B. A., Ross, S. M., & Smith, L. J. (1994). "Whenever and wherever we choose": The replication of "Success for All." *Phi Delta Kappan, 75*(8), 639–647.

Smith, M. S., & O'Day, J. (1991). Systemic school reform. In S. H. Fuhrman & B. Malen (Eds.), *The politics of curriculum and testing* (pp. 233–267). Philadelphia: Falmer.

Smylie, M. A. (1994). Redesigning teachers' work: Connections to the classroom. In L. Darling-Hammond (Ed.), *Review of Research in Education* (Vol. 20, pp. 129–177). Washington, DC: American Educational Research Association.

Smyth, J. (Ed.). (1993). *A socially critical view of the self-managing school.* Bristol, PA: Falmer Press.

Spindler, G., & Spindler, L. (Eds.). (1987). *Interpretative ethnography of education: At home and abroad*. Hillsdale, NJ: Erlbaum.

Struggling for Standards (1995). *Education Week*, April 12. Special Report.

Talbert, J. E. (1991). *Boundaries of teachers' professional communities in U.S. high schools* (Paper 91–130). Stanford, CA: Stanford University, Center for Research on the Context of Secondary School Teaching.

Talbert, J. (1994). Constructing a school wide professional community: The negotiated order of a performing arts school. In J. W. Little & M. W. McLaughlin (Eds.), *Teachers' work: Individuals, colleagues and contexts* (pp. 164–184). New York: Teachers College Press.

Tharp, R. G. (1982). The effective instruction of comprehension: Results and description of the Kamehameha Early Education Program. *Reading Research Quarterly, 17*(4), 503–527.

Tyack, D., & Cuban, L. (1995). *Tinkering toward utopia: A century of public school reform*. Cambridge, MA: Harvard University Press.

Wagner, T. (1994). *How schools change: Lessons from three communities*. Boston: Beacon Press.

Wasley, P. A. (1994). *Stirring the chalkdust: Tales of teachers changing classroom practice*. New York: Teachers College Press.

Wehlage, G., & Osthoff, E. (1996). *Consensus and conflict: Parent participation in twenty-four restructured schools*. Madison, WI: Wisconsin Center for Education Research.

Wehlage, G. G., Rutter, R. A., Smith, G. A., Lesko, N., & Fernandez, R. R. (1989). *Reducing the risk: Schools as communities of support*. Bristol, PA: Falmer.

Weiler, H. N. (1990). Comparative perspectives on educational decentralization: An exercise in contradiction? *Educational Evaluation and Policy Analysis, 12*(4), 433–448.

Weiss, C. H., Cambone, J., & Wyeth, A. (1992). Trouble in paradise: Teacher conflicts in shared decision making. *Educational Administration Quarterly, 28*(3), 350–367.

Wells, G., & Chang-Wells, G. L. (1992). *Constructing knowledge together: Classrooms as centers of inquiry and literacy*. Portsmouth, NH: Heinemann Educational Books.

Wiemers, N. J. (1990). Transformation and accommodations: A case study of Joe Scott. *Educational Evaluation and Policy Analysis, 12*(3), 297–308.

Wiggins, G. P. (1993). *Assessing student performance*. San Francisco: Jossey-Bass.

Wigginton, E. (1985). *Sometimes a shining moment: The Foxfire experience*. Garden City, NY: Anchor Press, Doubleday.

Wilson, S. M. (1990). A conflict of interests: The case of Mark Black. *Evaluation and Policy Analysis, 12*(3), 309–326.

Wohlstetter, P., Smyer, R., & Mohrman, S. A. (1994). New boundaries for school-based management: The high involvement model. *Educational Evaluation and Policy Analysis, 16*(3), 268–286.

Wolf, D., Bixby, J., Glenn III, J., & Gardner, H. (1991). *To use their minds well: Investigating new forms of student assessment.* Review of Research in Education, 17. Washington, DC: American Educational Research Association, 31–74.

Zeichner, K. M., & Tabachnick, B. R. (1991). Reflections on reflective teaching. In B. R. Tabachnick & K. M. Zeichner (Eds.), *Issues and practices in inquiry oriented teacher education* (pp. 1–21). Wisconsin Series on Teacher Education. London: Falmer Press.

# About the Authors

All authors served as principal investigators or in other central research roles for the Center on Organization and Restructuring of Schools between 1990 and 1995.

**Kenneth B. Doane** is a program coordinator at Partners in School Innovation, an AmeriCorps national service organization working to improve public schools in low-income communities throughout the San Francisco Bay Area. He has served as a consultant to several other school reform initiatives, including the national program evaluation of Library Power, and has taught middle school English and humanities in Berkeley.

**Adam Gamoran** is professor of sociology and educational policy studies at the University of Wisconsin at Madison. His research focuses on inequality in school systems, including studies of ability grouping, instruction, and achievement from first grade through high school. Gamoran has served as a principal investigator in other research centers and will continue his work on school organization, teaching, and learning at newly established national research centers focusing on achievement in mathematics, science, and English.

**M. Bruce King** is a researcher at the Wisconsin Center for Education Research, University of Wisconsin at Madison. He was a classroom teacher for eleven years. His research interests include teacher empowerment, pedagogy and social equality, and citizenship education. His publications appear in *American Educational Research Journal, Teaching and Teacher Education, Theory and Research in Social Education,* and *Educational Policy.* He is currently collaborating with educators, parents, and community members to plan and begin a charter school.

**Sharon D. Kruse** is an assistant professor of educational foundations and leadership at the University of Akron. Her research interests focus on educational reform, the development of community in schools, and issues of organizational learning. She taught for ten years in public schools in elementary and middle school grades. In 1995 she published *Professionalism and Community: Perspectives on Reforming Urban Schools* with Karen Seashore Louis and Associates.

**Karen Seashore Louis** is associate dean for academic affairs and professor of educational policy and administration at the University of Minnesota. Her primary research interests are in school improvement and knowledge utilization in education. Over the past decade, her research has focused primarily on urban schools. Among her recent books are *Professionalism and Community: Perspectives on Reforming Urban Schools* (with Sharon Kruse and Associates, 1995) and *Reshaping the Principalship: Insights from Transformational Reform Efforts* (coedited with Joseph Murphy, 1994). She is currently coprincipal investigator of the National Study of Charter Schools.

**Helen M. Marks** is an assistant professor of educational policy and leadership at the Ohio State University. With experience as a school teacher and administrator, she conducts research on the relationship of school organization, pedagogy, and policy to students' experience of school; service learning; social capital in schools and communities; and aspects of teacher professionalism. Her publications have focused on gender equity, including the relative effectiveness of single-sex and coeducational schooling, comparisons of public and private education, and teacher empowerment.

**Fred M. Newmann,** professor of curriculum and instruction at the University of Wisconsin at Madison, directed the National Center on Effective Secondary Schools and the Center on Organization and Restructuring of Schools. With initial experience as a high school history and social studies teacher, he has thirty years of experience in school reform research, curriculum development, and teacher education. He has contributed new curriculum in the analysis of public controversy and community-based learning and research publications on curriculum for citizenship, higher-order thinking in social studies, education and the building of community, student engagement in secondary schools, authentic instruction and assessment, and school restructuring.

**Eric Osthoff,** a dissertator in educational policy studies at the University of Wisconsin at Madison, has worked on several national studies of school reform conducted by the Center for Policy Research in Education and the Center on Organization and Restructuring of Schools.

**Kent D. Peterson** is professor of educational administration at the University of Wisconsin at Madison and former director of the National Center for Effective Schools Research and Development. Peterson has been studying the work, leadership, and school improvement strategies of principals for the past twenty years. In addition to his research and writing, he has directed and developed leadership academies for school districts, states, and regional laboratories. He is the coauthor (with Terrence Deal) of *The Leadership Paradox: Balancing Logic and Artistry in Schools* (Jossey-Bass, 1994).

**Andrew C. Porter,** professor of educational psychology at the University of Wisconsin at Madison, is director of the Wisconsin Center for Education Research and codirector of the National Institute for Science Education, funded by the National Science Foundation. Previously he was a professor at Michigan State University, where he codirected the Institute for Research on Teaching. At the National Institute of Education in Washington, D.C., he was a visiting scholar and then associate director of Basic Skills Research. Porter's research has led to contributions in the areas of teacher decision making, educational policy, school process indicators (including opportunity to learn), and assessment.

**Walter G. Secada,** professor of curriculum and instruction at the University of Wisconsin at Madison, has been an associate director of the National Center for Research in Mathematical Sciences Education, director of a training and technical assistance resource center for bilingual education, and an associate dean. His scholarly research and teacher development efforts have included equity in education, mathematics education, bilingual education, and reform. Currently he is studying issues in postsecondary science, mathematics, engineering, and technology education; how children negotiate the ages of six to twelve; and Hispanic dropout prevention.

**Gary G. Wehlage,** professor of curriculum and instruction at the University of Wisconsin at Madison, has been associate director of the National Center on Effective Secondary Schools and the Center on Organization and Restructuring of Schools. Formerly a high school history and economics teacher, he has done research on effective schools for at-risk youth. Recent publications include *Reducing the Risk: Schools as Communities of Support and Building New Futures for At-Risk Youth,* an evaluation of the New Futures Initiative, a multicity project aimed at promoting school-community collaboration. His most recent work has addressed the problem of developing social capital in neighborhoods, communities, and schools.

**Matthew G. Weinstein** is director of secondary education at Macalester College. He is an active member of SciMath reform project in Minnesota and program chair of the Committee on the Anthropology of Science, Technology and Computing. His research interests focus on qualitative methodology, the relationship of science to culture, and science education reform based on the anthropology of science.

# Index